Marco Zeschky
EXPLORATION FOR INNOVATION

Marco Zeschky

Exploration for Innovation
Capability-based Search Approaches in Established Firms

Bibliografische Information Der Deutschen Bibliothek
Die Deutsche Bibliothek verzeichnet diese Publikation in der Deutschen Nationalbibliografie; detaillierte bibliografische Daten sind im Internet über http://dnb.ddb.de abrufbar.

Zugl.: Dissertation, Universität St. Gallen, 2009

© HARLAND media, Lichtenberg (Odw.) 2010
www.harland-media.de

Gedruckt auf alterungsbeständigem Papier nach ISO 9706 (säure-, holz- und chlorfrei).

Printed in Germany

ISBN 978-3-938363-65-2

Acknowledgements

The underlying thesis is the result of my time as Research Associate at the Institute of Technology Management at the University of St. Gallen in Switzerland. I would like to express my deep gratitude to Professor Oliver Gassmann for supervising my thesis and for giving me the opportunity and freedom to pursue my academic interests and aspirations. His support during the research process was always inspiring and encouraging. I would also like to thank Professor Fritz Fahrni for co-supervising my thesis and for providing me with valuable advice.

During my time as a Research Associate, I was allowed to conduct some part of my research at the Wharton School of Business in Philadelphia. I am indebted to Professor Ian C. MacMillan for being my faculty sponsor, for inspiring discussions, and for giving me valuable feedback to my research work. My gratitude extends to the Swiss National Science Foundation from which I received financial support during my time at Wharton.

I would also like to thank the many people who contributed directly and indirectly to this work. Representative for all my interview partners, I would like to thank Dr. Thomas Stährfeldt, Wolfgang Hohma, Benedikt Schlichting, Dr. Andreas Bong, Dr. Walter Odoni, and Dr. Diethelm Boese. I would also like to thank my colleagues and friends at the Institute of Technology Management for the many memorable academic and non-academic hours I was allowed to spend with them. Special thanks go to Nicole Ziegler and Dr. Javier Perez-Freije for commenting on the entire manuscript accompanied by valuable discussions.

Finally, I am deeply grateful to my parents for their unconditional love and support, the striving for education, discipline, commitment and reflection throughout my entire life. It is to them I dedicate this work.

St. Gallen, May 2009   Marco Zeschky

Abstract

The ability to continuously develop both incremental and radical innovations is a hallmark of successful companies. Incremental innovations are important to secure the short-term survival of the firm. Radical innovations are important because they enable the firm to stay competitive in the long run. Therefore, maintaining a balance between exploitation of existing capabilities for the development of incremental innovations and exploration for new knowledge for the development of radical innovations is paramount for firm success. However, in contrast to exploitation, returns from exploration are uncertain and remote in time. As a consequence, exploration activities are often crowded-out in favor of exploitative innovation projects. Although much is known about incremental product innovation, there is little insight how firms successfully explore for new knowledge for radical innovation, which is subject to analysis of this thesis.

Due to scarce practical insights into exploration, this thesis applies a qualitative, case-study based research approach. Based on responses from *Ciba, Gore, Hilti,* and *Bühler,* existing literature on exploration is extended by examining the relationship between exploration activities and exploration success. The case study analysis reveals that firms' exploration success depends on three parameters: exploration propensity, efficacy, and efficiency. Exploration propensity largely depends on the firm's overall corporate strategy and product strategies. To reduce uncertainty and ensure efficacy, firms' exploration approach entails stretching existing capabilities stemming from the core business and matching them with requirements of new domains. Finally, exploration efficiency is attained by ensuring dedicated organizational structures and by employing individuals with broad experience and a wide knowledge background.

The results challenge conventional beliefs that radical innovation is a result from searching and combining distant pieces of knowledge. Firms cannot afford to search randomly for new knowledge, but their exploration efforts must ultimately pay off. This research reveals that firms have found ways how to effectively reduce uncertainty during exploration by searching for distant yet related new knowledge.

Zusammenfassung

Die Fähigkeit kontinuierlich sowohl inkrementale und radikale Innovationen zu entwickeln ist ein Gütesiegel erfolgreicher Unternehmen. Während inkrementale Innovationen massgeblich das kurzfristige Überleben sichern, sind radikale Innovationen wichtig um auch langfristig am Markt zu bestehen und wettbewerbsfähig zu bleiben. Daher ist eine Balance zwischen Nutzung bestehender Fähigkeiten für die Entwicklung inkrementaler Innovationen (Exploitation) und der Erforschung neuen Wissens für die Entwicklung radikaler Innovationen (Exploration) entscheidend für den Firmenerfolg. Im Gegensatz zu Exploitation sind Erträge durch Exploration jedoch unsicher und nicht zeitnah. Deshalb werden Explorationsanstrengungen häufig zugunsten von exploitativen Innovationsprojekten verdrängt. Während viel Erfahrung über inkrementale Produktinnovation besteht, gibt es wenig Erkenntnisse darüber, wie Firmen erfolgreich nach neuem Wissen für radikale Innovationen suchen. Letzteres ist Gegenstand der Untersuchung in dieser Arbeit.

Aufgrund der geringen praktischen Erkenntnisse bezüglich Exploration wird in dieser Arbeit ein qualitativer, Fallstudien-basierter Forschungsansatz angewendet. Durch die Untersuchung von Zusammenhängen zwischen Explorationsaktivitäten und -erfolg auf Basis von Erkenntnissen der Firmen *Ciba*, *Gore*, *Hilti* und *Bühler* wird bestehende Literatur über Exploration ergänzt. Die Fallstudienanalyse zeigt, dass der Erfolg von Explorationsaktivitäten von Firmen massgeblich von drei Parametern bestimmt wird: Explorationsneigung, -effektivität und -effizienz. Die Explorationsneigung hängt stark von der Firmen- und Produktstrategie ab. Um Unsicherheit zu reduzieren und Effektivität zu steigern werden bestehende Fähigkeiten, die vom Kerngeschäft herrühren, ausgeweitet und an die Bedürfnisse neuer, zukunftsorientierter Bereiche angepasst. Schliesslich wird die Effizienz durch bestimmte organisationale Strukturen und den gezielten Einsatz von Personen mit breitem Erfahrungshintergrund und grossem Wissensschatz unterstützt.

Die Ergebnisse der Untersuchung relativieren die übliche Annahme, dass radikale Innovationen ihren Ursprung in entferntem Wissen haben. Firmen können es sich nicht leisten ungezielt nach neuem Wissen zu suchen; vielmehr müssen sich Explorationsanstrengungen innerhalb eines bestimmten Zeithorizonts rentieren. Diese Forschungsarbeit zeigt, dass Firmen Wege gefunden haben, Unsicherheiten durch die Suche nach entferntem, aber verwandtem Wissen wirksam zu reduzieren.

Index

Contents .... **XIII**

Figures .... **XVII**

Tables .... **XIX**

Abbreviations .... **XXI**

1. Introduction **1**
   1.1. Motivation and goal 1
   1.2. Terms and definitions 17
   1.3. Research concept 22
   1.4. Thesis structure 27

2. Theoretical key issues in exploration for innovation **31**
   2.1. Tensions and relations between exploration and exploitation 31
   2.2. Organizational learning perspective on exploration 35

3. Practical key issues in exploration for innovation **45**
   3.1. Exploration and exploitation in the light of innovation 45
   3.2. Creativity in exploration and innovation 48
   3.3. Exploration and innovation in established firms 51
   3.4. Reference framework 63

4. Empirical findings on exploration for innovation **67**
   4.1. Case selection 67
   4.2. Case 1: Ciba AG 70
   4.3. Case 2: W. L. Gore & Associates 80
   4.4. Case 3: Hilti AG 92
   4.5. Case 4: Bühler AG 102

5. Conceptualizing firms' exploration approach **113**
   5.1. Single-case summary 113
   5.2. Conceptual framework development 126
   5.3. Cross-case analysis 127
   5.4. Summary of the conceptual model 156

6. Theoretical implications ... 159
- 6.1. Directed exploration in organizational learning ... 159
- 6.2. Theoretical base for exploration for innovation ... 160
- 6.3. Hypotheses on firms' exploration propensity ... 167
- 6.4. Hypotheses on firms' exploration efficacy ... 169
- 6.5. Hypotheses on firms' exploration efficiency ... 172
- 6.6. Summary of hypotheses ... 176

7. Managerial implications ... 177
- 7.1. Design parameters for increased exploration propensity ... 177
- 7.2. Design parameters for increased exploration efficacy ... 180
- 7.3. Design parameters for increased exploration efficiency ... 184
- 7.4. Summary ... 186

8. Conclusion ... 189
- 8.1. Implications for management theory ... 189
- 8.2. Implications for management practice ... 194

References ... 201

Appendix ... 221

Contents

Figures .... **XVII**

Tables .... **XIX**

Abbreviations .... **XXI**

1. Introduction 1
   1.1. Motivation and goal 1
      1.1.1. Relevance of research subject 1
      1.1.2. Deficits in current research 3
      1.1.3. Research objective 16
   1.2. Terms and definitions 17
   1.3. Research concept 22
      1.3.1. Research classification 22
      1.3.2. Research methodology 22
   1.4. Thesis structure 27

2. Theoretical key issues in exploration for innovation 31
   2.1. Tensions and relations between exploration and exploitation 31
      2.1.1. Strategic management 32
      2.1.2. Organization design 33
      2.1.3. Technological innovation 34
   2.2. Organizational learning perspective on exploration 35
      2.2.1. Characteristics of exploration and exploitation 36
      2.2.2. Search motivation and search behavior 38
      2.2.3. Cognitive and experiential search 39
      2.2.4. Exploitation: problemistic and local search 40
      2.2.5. Exploration: slack and distant search 42

3. Practical key issues in exploration for innovation 45
   3.1. Exploration and exploitation in the light of innovation 45
      3.1.1. Developing exploitative innovation 46
      3.1.2. Developing exploratory innovation 47
   3.2. Creativity in exploration and innovation 48
      3.2.1. Recombinant search 49

	3.2.2.	Analogical search	50
3.3.		Exploration and innovation in established firms	51
	3.3.1.	Framework for innovation in established firms	52
	3.3.2.	Opportunity identification	55
	3.3.3.	Facilitating opportunity identification	60
3.4.		Reference framework	63

4. Empirical findings on exploration for innovation 67

4.1.		Case selection	67
4.2.		Case 1: Ciba AG	70
	4.2.1.	Company profile	70
	4.2.2.	R&D organization and resources	70
	4.2.3.	Exploration strategy and procedure	72
	4.2.4.	Environmental aspects conducive to exploration	78
	4.2.5.	Summary	78
4.3.		Case 2: W. L. Gore & Associates	80
	4.3.1.	Company profile	80
	4.3.2.	R&D organization and resources	81
	4.3.3.	Exploration: strategy and procedure	84
	4.3.4.	Environmental aspects conducive to exploration	89
	4.3.5.	Summary	91
4.4.		Case 3: Hilti AG	92
	4.4.1.	Company profile	92
	4.4.2.	R&D organization and resources	93
	4.4.3.	Exploration: strategy and procedure	95
	4.4.4.	Environmental aspects conducive to exploration	100
	4.4.5.	Summary	101
4.5.		Case 4: Bühler AG	102
	4.5.1.	Company profile	102
	4.5.2.	R&D organization and resources	103
	4.5.3.	Exploration: strategy and procedure	105
	4.5.4.	Environmental aspects conducive to exploration	109
	4.5.5.	Summary	110

5. Conceptualizing firms' exploration approach 113

5.1.		Single-case summary	113
	5.1.1.	Strategic and procedural approaches	114

	5.1.2. Organizational set up	118
	5.1.3. Influence on R&D performance	123
5.2.	Conceptual framework development	126
5.3.	Cross-case analysis	127
	5.3.1. Elements impacting exploration propensity	129
	5.3.2. Elements impacting exploration efficacy	134
	5.3.3. Elements impacting exploration efficiency	149
5.4.	Summary of the conceptual model	156

6. Theoretical implications 159
6.1. Directed exploration in organizational learning 159
6.2. Theoretical base for exploration for innovation 160
    6.2.1. The absorptive capacity of firms 161
    6.2.2. Firms' exploration approach and absorptive capacity 165
6.3. Hypotheses on firms' exploration propensity 167
6.4. Hypotheses on firms' exploration efficacy 169
6.5. Hypotheses on firms' exploration efficiency 172
6.6. Summary of hypotheses 176

7. Managerial implications 177
7.1. Design parameters for increased exploration propensity 177
    7.1.1. Living firm values 177
    7.1.2. Defining a challenging product strategy 178
7.2. Design parameters for increased exploration efficacy 180
    7.2.1. Stretching existing capabilities 180
    7.2.2. Focusing on applications, effects, and outcomes 181
    7.2.3. Exploring along the value chain 182
7.3. Design parameters for increased exploration efficiency 184
    7.3.1. Designing an exploration organization 184
    7.3.2. Fostering broad and deep knowledge structures 186
7.4. Summary 186

8. Conclusion 189
8.1. Implications for management theory 189
    8.1.1. Summary and contributions to research 189
    8.1.2. Directions for further research 193
8.2. Implications for management practice 194

	8.2.1.	Central statements and recommendations	194
	8.2.2.	Future directions and trends	198

References **201**

Appendix **221**

Figures

Figure 1: Literature streams related to exploration for innovation 10
Figure 2: Exploration and exploitation as two ends of the same continuum 20
Figure 3: Approach to conducting the research project 26
Figure 4: Structure of the thesis 29
Figure 5: Reference framework 64
Figure 6: Core and beyond core business at Ciba 73
Figure 7: Innovation project categorization at Ciba 74
Figure 8: Ciba's exploration process 77
Figure 9: Scope of technology-market engagement at Gore 83
Figure 10: Gore's exploration strategy 85
Figure 11: Project risk matrix at Gore 88
Figure 12: Hilti organization 94
Figure 13: Hilti business model 96
Figure 14: Time-To-Market process at Hilti 98
Figure 15: Bühler Organization 103
Figure 16: Core business and value chain at Bühler 106
Figure 17: Search fields at Bühler 107
Figure 18: Conceptual framework of exploration for innovation 127
Figure 19: Relationship between product core concepts and core components 138
Figure 20: Concept of technological competence leveraging 143
Figure 21: Capability stretching and matching within exploration 147
Figure 22: Concept of abstraction and analogy in exploration 154
Figure 23: Summary of the conceptual model 157
Figure 24: Potential and realized absorptive capacity 163
Figure 25: Relationship between firms' absorptive capacity and exploration 166
Figure 26: Horizontal and vertical exploration within the value chain 183
Figure 27: Summary of managerial implications 188

Tables

Table 1: Research interests in entrepreneurship 5
Table 2: Overview of knowledge distribution in problem situations 13
Table 3: Overview of empirical dataset 25
Table 4: Management fields concerned with exploration and exploitation 35
Table 5: Types and characteristics of corporate entrepreneurship 54
Table 6: Sample companies for in-depth case studies 68
Table 7: Comparison of exploration strategy across sample companies 118
Table 8: Comparison of exploration facilitators across sample companies 123
Table 9: R&D effectiveness measure of sample companies 125
Table 10: Comparison of exploration scope across sample companies 133
Table 11: Overview of sample firms' leverage potential 145
Table 12: Locus of knowledge exploration in sample firms 152
Table 13: Overview of hypotheses 176
Table 14: Implications of focusing on applications, effects, and outcomes 182

Abbreviations

CE	Corporate Entrepreneurship
CTO	Chief Technology Officer
CIO	Chief Innovation Officer
CR&T	Corporate Research & Technology
e.g.	for example, for instance (Latin: *exempli gratia*)
ePTFE	Extended Polytetrafluorethylen
et al.	and others (Latin: *et alii/alia*)
FFE	Fuzzy front-end
i.e.	that is to say, in other words (Latin: *id est*)
NASA	National Aeronautics and Space Administration
NGP	New Growth Platform
NPD	New Product Development
PTFE	Polytetrafluorethylen
R&D	Research and development
USD	United States Dollar

1. Introduction

1.1. Motivation and goal

1.1.1. Relevance of research subject

In order to be successful over time, firms must exploit existing competencies to meet current market demands and at the same time explore new possibilities and technologies to secure the long-term survival of the firm (March 1991; Levinthal and March 1993). Few firms can independently develop and nourish the wide range of knowledge, technologies, and skills needed to compete in constantly changing environments (D'Aveni 1994). Therefore, although a firm's internal research efforts play a critical role in overall innovation, firms must consider the external innovation potential to be competitive (Cohen and Levinthal 1990; Almeida, Phene et al. 2003). However, exploration for new know-how and technologies poses a major challenge for large, and established firms, as exploration is typically associated with uncertainty while exploitation is associated with safe and prompt returns. As a consequence, established firms hesitate to engage in exploration, and subsequently risk missing vital technological developments and innovations, which may threaten the competitiveness of the firm.

Technological change has a tremendous impact on economic growth, the development of entire industries, and on the single firm (Solow 1957). Fundamental technological changes affect the rise and fall of established firms both within and across interdependent industries. Furthermore, major technological shifts have competence-destroying or competence-enhancing effects. "Competence-destroying discontinuities are so fundamentally different from previously dominant technologies that the skills and knowledge base required to operate the core technology shift", and "competence-enhancing discontinuities are order-of-magnitude improvements in price/performance that build on existing know-how within a product class" (Tushman and Anderson 1986).

Researchers have argued that established firms are in the best position to initiate and exploit new possibilities which are enabled by technological change if it builds on competencies that they already possess (Ahuja and Lampert 2001). Therefore, competence-enhancing breakthroughs are mostly initiated by existing, successful firms, while competence-destroying breakthroughs mostly have their locus in new firms that enter an established industry. On the other hand, established firms have major problems when the technological change is of competence-destroying kind, as skills that have been successful in the past are rendered obsolete, and as they face tremendous hurdles to overcome this change and build new competencies (Tushman and Anderson 1986).

Changing technological environments have a big impact on firms' exploration behavior. Firms which are able to first recognize and take advantage of technological opportunities enjoy earlier learning effects than competitors and benefit from early mover advantages. Exploration is particularly important for firms who act in technology-based industries (Leonard-Barton 1992) and who strive to be technology leader, as by investing in R&D and technological innovation they are able to shape environmental conditions in their favor (Tushman and Anderson 1986). On the other hand, firms that do not engage in exploration activities to create technological variation may lose their ability to absorb and benefit from technological evolution. However, merely introducing incremental innovations is not sufficient; pioneering firms must identify new business opportunities which involve new technologies, new markets, and new business models. Therefore, pioneering search behavior involves a conscious effort to move away from current organizational routines and knowledge bases (March 1991; Miner, Bassoff et al. 2001).

Market-leading firms that aspire to be pioneers in the use of new knowledge and in the exploitation of new business opportunities are naturally urged to explore new knowledge domains (Conant, Mokwa et al. 1990; Sidhu, Volberda et al. 2004). Indeed, prospector firms are considered to engage strongly in exploration activities and information acquisition (Miles and Snow 1978), which contrasts defender, analyzer, and reactor types of organizations who are much less inclined to engage in exploratory activities (Sidhu, Volberda et al. 2004). Even more, such firms might be urged to find problems which might not have explicitly been expressed by markets or customers but which – if they are introduced to the market – will ultimately lead to competitive advantage.

However, as exploration typically aims at learning new knowledge and technologies it is associated with high uncertainty (March 1991). This uncertainty arises for several reasons: first, high levels of exploration increase knowledge integration costs as the proportion of new knowledge to be integrated into a new firm's knowledge base evokes technological and organizational challenges (Katila and Ahuja 2002). Second, an excessive increase in the breadth of exploration can hurt product output through decreasing reliability, which is the firm's ability to respond to new information correctly. In general, researchers have found that search efforts for innovation which include a high amount of new knowledge are less likely to succeed than innovation projects that search closely related knowledge (Cyert and March 1992).

Therefore, established firms must find ways how to deal with this uncertainty inherent in exploration and thus find ways how to effectively engage in exploration. Literature lacks empirical investigations and understanding about the specific process of exploration and insights about how firms actually successfully explore despite the uncertainty and risk accompanying it (Argote 1999; Katila and Ahuja 2002). Although extant literature unanimously advocates that exploration is vital for the long-term survival and performance of the firm (March 1991; Tushman and O'Reilly III 1996; Gavetti and Levinthal 2000; He and Wong 2004; Gupta, Smith et al. 2006; Greve 2007), there is very limited empirical insight in how established firms actually explore.

This study investigates how established firms engage in exploration pertaining to the identification of new technologies, markets, and business opportunities. This work goes beyond conventional discussions about exploration, which tend to interpret exploration as the firm's experimenting with random pieces of knowledge, and assumes that successful firms have actually found ways how to effectively engage in exploration and deal with its inherent uncertainty. This study aims at developing a sound scientific model as well as developing managerial guidelines for how to explore for new knowledge and business opportunities. Thus, this study moves beyond existing literature by focusing on the actual process of exploration in contrast to merely treating it as an empirical phenomenon.

1.1.2. Deficits in current research

Issues on exploration and exploitation are a recurring and underlying theme in studies pertaining to several management fields such as strategic management (Burgelman

1991; Floyd and Lane 2000; McGrath 2001), organizational learning (March 1991; Levinthal and March 1993; Crossan and Bedrow 2003; Holmqvist 2004), organization design (Volberda 1996; Rivkin and Siggelkow 2003), technological innovation (Duncan 1976; Tushman and O'Reilly III 1996; Benner and Tushman 2002; Benner and Tushman 2003; Nerkar 2003), and knowledge literature (e.g. Kogut and Zander 1992; Grant and Baden-Fuller 2004). These studies have particularly investigated the tension between exploration and exploitation and how a balance between the two can be achieved within the organizational boundaries of the firm. Although these studies have produced many valuable insights, research has not investigated how exploration is actually conducted within the firm. In particular, research has assumed that exploration is typically crowded out in favor of exploitative activities because of the uncertainty inherent in exploration. However, researchers and managers alike still lack insights in how exploration in established firms is actually conducted. As a consequence, most discussions about exploration and exploitation are fairly abstract and lack empirical evidence.

For the purpose of this study, literature pertaining to corporate entrepreneurship, organizational learning, and new product development is considered. Literature on corporate entrepreneurship illustrates how new business opportunities are identified and developed in large and established firms. Organizational learning literature provides valuable insights into the motivation and behavior of organizations when searching for new knowledge, how firms learn and appraise new knowledge, and how organizations implement new knowledge. Finally, literature on new product development illustrates the challenges in managing innovation and particularly the very early phases of the innovation process, the so called 'fuzzy front-end'. In the following, these three literature streams are briefly described to show their relations and shortcomings with respect to exploration for innovation.

Corporate entrepreneurship
Literature on general entrepreneurship is vast and stems from many different disciplines such as economics, sociology, or psychology, and consequently leads to diverse definitions and terms as to what entrepreneurship is and what it exactly entails. The plethora of studies on entrepreneurship can be divided in three main categories: *what* happens when entrepreneurs act, *why* they act, and *how* they act (Stevenson and Jarillo 1990). Research on the first question is concerned with the results of the actions of the entrepreneur and not with the entrepreneur or his actions per se. This perspective is

usually taken by economists such as Schumpeter (1934). The second question is concerned with the entrepreneur as an individual considering its background, environment, goals, values, and motivations. In this current, the causes of individual entrepreneurial action constitute the primary interest of the researcher. Finally, the 'how' question considers entrepreneurial management and how entrepreneurs are able to achieve their aims, irrespective of personal reasons or environmental inducements. Table 1 summarizes the different lines of inquiry in entrepreneurship literature.

	Causes	*Behavior*	*Effects*
Main question	▪ Why	▪ How	▪ What
Basic discipline	▪ Psychology, sociology	▪ Management	▪ Economics
Contributions	▪ Importance of individual ▪ Environmental variables are relevant		▪ Entrepreneurship is the function by which growth is achieved ▪ Distinction between entrepreneur and manager

Source: Stevenson and Jarillo (1990)

Table 1: Research interests in entrepreneurship

Corporate entrepreneurship (CE) focuses explicitly on entrepreneurship within large and established organizations. CE has since long been recognized as one essential driver of new businesses and sustaining corporate competitiveness (e.g. Covin and Miles 1999; Dess, Ireland et al. 2003; Ireland and Webb 2007). CE manifests as actions of strategic renewal, new product development, and other forms of innovation (Guth and Ginsberg 1990). The avenues for achieving innovation are manifold and include internal innovations, joint ventures or acquisitions, strategic renewal (Dess, Ireland et al. 2003), product, process, and administrative innovations (Covin and Miles 1999), diversification (Burgelman 1991), and processes by which individuals contribute to renewal or innovation within the firm.

Covin and Miles (1999) define corporate entrepreneurship as being engaged in increasing competitiveness through efforts aimed at the rejuvenation, renewal, and redefinition of organizations, their markets, or industries. They furthermore describe CE to involve product or process innovation, a propensity to risk-taking by the firm's key

decision makers, a pioneering behavior regarding new product-market offers, and the early adoption of new administrative techniques or process technologies. They describe three common phenomena which are most often viewed as examples of corporate entrepreneurship:
- An established organization enters a new business
- An individual champions a new product idea within a corporate context
- An entrepreneurial philosophy permeates an entire organization's outlook and operations

Other authors have argued that, in general, entrepreneurship focuses on newness and novelty such as new products, new processes, and new markets as means for innovation and wealth creation (Lumpkin and Dess 1996; Daily, McDougall et al. 2002). Lumpkin and Dess (1996) consider a firm as entrepreneurial when it shows signs of autonomy, innovativeness, risk-taking, proactiveness, and competitive aggressiveness. Morris and Kuratko (2002) consider corporate entrepreneurship as entrepreneurial behavior inside established mid-sized and large organizations. Other definitions see CE as 'a formal or informal activity aimed at creating new business in established firms through product and process innovations and market developments' (Zahra 1991).

Despite the numerous different definitions of corporate entrepreneurship, a common underlying theme is that they are all linked to an overall innovative behavior of the established firm. Thus, corporate entrepreneurship can be considered all kinds of activities which aim at innovating existing or entering new product-market combinations or internal processes. However, to spark innovation, organizations need innovative ideas and need to identify opportunities in the first place before they can be exploited to generate innovation. In this respect, Hitt, Ireland et al. (2001) define entrepreneurship as 'the identification and exploitation of previously unexploited opportunities', and literature is univocal in agreeing that opportunity recognition is at the heart of entrepreneurship (McCline, Bhat et al. 2000; Shane 2000). Thus, the entrepreneurial process can be characterized as entailing two distinct phases, where the first phase entails the identification of an opportunity, and where the second phase entails the exploitation of this opportunity.

Although literature on corporate entrepreneurship offers many insights on different types of entrepreneurship and its relationship to firm performance, there are limited insights in how established firms explore new opportunities and search for new ideas to arrive at renewal and innovation (Ahuja and Lampert 2001). In particular, there is limited insight into how opportunities are actually recognized within the first part of the entrepreneurial process.

Organizational learning

Literature on organizational learning is vast and has been elaborated in many different disciplines and literatures such as psychology, social learning theory, strategic management, knowledge management, and others. Argyris (1999) divides literature on organizational learning in the two main categories 'practice-oriented' (which he also denotes 'learning organization') and 'academic-oriented' (which he denotes 'organizational learning') to point out the different interests of both audiences and thus the differing language and foci. Accordingly, the practice-oriented literature entails notions of 'organizational adaptability, flexibility, avoidance of stability traps, propensity to experiment, readiness to rethink means and ends, inquiry orientation, realization of human potential for learning in the service of organizational purposes, and creation of organizational settings as contexts for human development' (Argyris 1999). In particular, the process of learning knowledge has been described as a process entailing knowledge acquisition, information distribution, and information interpretation (Huber 1991). In contrast, the scholarly literature of organizational learning focuses on questions such as what kind of organizational learning is desirable. Furthermore, discussions extend to the question what is treated as an organization, and thus what level of aggregation, i.e. individual, interpersonal, group, intergroup, or whole-organization, an organization entails. Organizational learning is also viewed by some scholars as potentially detrimental, if learning occurs in a way that fosters existing routines, thus hindering organizational change and reform (Fiol and Lyles 1985; Levitt and March 1988).

Another common distinction in organizational learning pertaining to how organizations actually learn entails the two categories *behavioral learning* and *cognitive learning*. In behavioral learning, classic assumptions entail that firms are goal-oriented and routine-based systems. Thus, firms respond to experience by repeating behaviors that have proved to be successful in the past (Cyert and March 1992). This learning approach describes the acquisition, distribution, and storage of information and knowledge in a firm (Levitt and March 1988; Huber 1991). The main focus of this approach is the adaptive learning concept, where trial-and-error learning leads to routines and processes that subsequently leads to selective advantage of the firm (Herriott, Levinthal et al.

1985). In contrast to trial-and-error learning in behavioral learning, in cognitive learning the focus is on the content of learning and on processes that improve the creation of knowledge in a firm, on the utilization of knowledge to improve creativity, quality of interaction, and other types of performance (Lumpkin and Lichtenstein 2005). In this context, organizational learning entails the process of exploiting externally-stored knowledge or transforming internally stored knowledge to increase the strategic assets of the firm, where assets are knowledge or 'thought-process' assets. Thus, cognitive learning is closely connected to the question what knowledge is relevant to the firm and where and how such knowledge can be found and learned. However, where and how such knowledge can be found has not been discussed to date in literature from a firm perspective.

Although literature on organizational learning has discussed and developed several concepts of learning processes, and how learning occurs, literature is rather normative and descriptive and lacks insights in how organizations at the level of the firm actually search for new knowledge, and thus how and what they actually learn. Furthermore, because organizational learning entails a critical link to strategy, there is a need for insights on processes at the entire organization level (Crossan and Bedrow 2003).

New product development
In general, new product development is *the* central activity for the competitive advantage for many firms (Brown and Eisenhardt 1995). New product development is assumed as a means to lead to organizational diversification, adaptation, and reinvention to match evolving markets and technical conditions (Schoonhoven, Eisenhardt et al. 1990).

Pertaining to the exploration of new knowledge for new product development (NPD), past research has investigated how ideas are generated in the fuzzy front-end (FFE) of the innovation process. The FFE is considered the time when an opportunity is first considered worthy of further ideation, exploration, and assessment and ends when a firm decides to invest in the idea and ultimately launch the project (Khurana and Rosenthal 1997; Kim and Wilemon 2002). Thus, the FFE can be defined as the period between when an opportunity is first considered and when an idea is judged ready for development.

The effective management of front-end activities can contribute directly to the success of a new product (McGuinness and Conway 1989; Cooper, Edgett et al. 1998) or shorten the innovation process (Smith and Reinertsen 1998). Moenert, De Meyer et al. (1995) note that during the FFE, an organization formulates a product concept and determines whether it should invest resources to develop that idea. Thus, the front-end focuses on organizing activities that precede the actual development phase and attempt to seek information regarding market relevance and technical feasibility as early as possible to reduce uncertainties. In other words, effective management of search activities prior to any physical development activities may reduce uncertainty and thus the risk of investing in non-profitable projects. Therefore, management needs to establish approaches through which the search for new knowledge for subsequent innovation is effectively facilitated.

Despite vast literature on the management and the success factors of the FFE and the new product development process, there is limited insight into how ideas within the FFE are sourced in the first place (Kim and Wilemon 2002). Although FFE actions are associated with seeking knowledge, learning, creativity, and experimenting, it is unclear how idea sourcing is conducted, and how knowledge is actually accessed, channeled, and used (Leonard 1995).

In summary, there is extensive literature on corporate entrepreneurship, organizational learning, and new product development. These literature streams entail innovation as an underlying theme and consider the question how innovation can be spurred within the firm, what the motivation and behavior of firms are regarding the search for new knowledge, and how the innovation process can be managed effectively for successful innovation. In particular, these literature streams entail notions about how and why firms search for new knowledge which might be beneficially applied for innovation (see figure 1). Therefore, the next sessions discuss the intersections of these literature streams with respect to the search, identification, and generation of knowledge and innovative ideas to illustrate respective research shortcomings in greater detail.

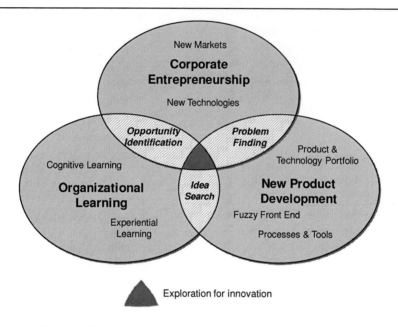

Figure 1: Literature streams related to exploration for innovation

Opportunity identification

Opportunities must first be identified before they can be exploited. Eckhardt and Shane (2003) define *opportunity identification* as 'situations in which new goods, services, raw materials, markets and organizing methods can be introduced through the formation of new means, ends, or mean-ends relationships'. Similarly, Lumpkin and Liechtenstein (2005) define *opportunity recognition* as 'the ability to identify a good idea and transform it into a business concept that adds value and generates revenues'. Opportunity identification or opportunity recognition are passive approaches where the identification of an opportunity is often described as happening by accident (Shane 2000). Recognition is based on prior knowledge without which an individual could not draw any associations in the currently experienced situation. Therefore, technological change does not generate obvious entrepreneurial opportunities, which allow anyone to identify any given entrepreneurial opportunity which results from that change. In this sense, cognitive limits and the specialization of knowledge allow entrepreneurs to identify only a limited set of all possibly existing opportunities in a given technology. Moreover, opportunity identification can be driven solely by recognition of knowledge already possessed rather than by deliberate search for knowledge needed (Kirzner 1997).

Only recently have researchers started to focus on the process of opportunity identification. With respect to the sources of opportunities as an initial input of the opportunity identification process, Schumpeter (1934) has argued that opportunities emerge from changes in a variety of parts of the value chain, that is, opportunities stemming from
- the creation of new products or services,
- the discovery of new geographical markets,
- the creation or discovery of new raw materials,
- the emergence of new methods of production, and
- the generation of new ways of organizing.

Apart from the objective existence of opportunities in the way described by Schumpeter, opportunities must still be identified by an individual or a group of people. Therefore, Eckhardt and Shane (2003) argue that opportunities also result from information asymmetries between market participants and from exogenous shocks of new information. Furthermore, exogenous shocks are considered to lead to equal challenges for all competitors in a market, indicating that the identification of opportunities is grounded in different perceptions – or information asymmetries – by the single firms.

The identification of opportunities is inherently connected to learning and utilizing new information. Organizational learning literature considers learning as an integral part of exploration endeavors that organizations engage in (Cyert and March 1992). As exploration is associated with increasing internal knowledge variety (McGrath 2001) and with the development of innovations that will sustain the competitive advantage of the firm, exploration is also concerned with the identification of new business opportunities. However, notions from organizational learning considers exploration as mainly increasing organizational knowledge variety without being specific on what type of knowledge might be beneficial for the organization. In contrast, opportunity identification from an entrepreneurial perspective is concerned with learning knowledge which yields more immediate returns regarding the development of innovation. Therefore, exploration and opportunity identification from an entrepreneurial perspective is more concerned with 'controlled' exploration, while exploration from an organizational learning perspective is more concerned with the aspect of learning in general.

In summary, literature on entrepreneurship and knowledge identification almost exclusively focuses on opportunity exploitation and its subsequent stages, with notable exceptions by Shane (2000) and Lumpkin and Lichtenstein (2005). However, literature on knowledge exploration and opportunity identification is scarce. Even more, opportunity identification is treated from a rather normative perspective, i.e. researchers have attempted to classify the different sources of opportunities, but lack providing insights in how the exploration of those opportunities is actually performed. The same is true for organizational learning literature. Although exploration is considered vital for sustainable firm success, there are scarce insights into the relationship between exploration and the identification of new business opportunities. Therefore, the question how firms explore within the context of identifying new business opportunities merits further investigation.

Problem finding
The presence or absence of a specific problem has major implications for the search of new ideas and solutions and the search direction of an individual or the organization. While the space for ideas or solutions to a specific problem is considered to be in the vicinity of existing solutions, the space for ideas which are not problem induced can be quite large. For this reason, effective problem finding and the subsequent solving of these problems is critical for firms which aspire to be innovation leaders in their markets.

The search for problems to be solved can be considered *problem search* or *problem finding* (Rickards and Puccio 1992). Problem finding involves the way problems are formulated when a gap or deficiency in knowledge is detected (Lumpkin and Lichtenstein 2005). From a creativity perspective, problem finding refers to those activities, processes, and events which precede the solving of a clearly posed problem (Dillon 1992). This implies that leading firms also face the challenge to create pictures of how the future could look like, and by that finding corresponding problems and ultimately solutions. Thus, 'asking the right questions' and finding problems that will lead to commercially viable innovations is a major challenge that firms in such circumstances face. Also, this implies the need for approaches toward a more directed type of exploration. Thus, in comparison to problem induced ideas, pioneering firms are confronted with strategic questions with respect to the direction of technology development, market entries, and ultimately with the question in which direction the firm as a whole develops in the future. Research has to date not investigated how firms engage in such type of exploratory activity.

How effective the search and finding of problems is depends on the situation in which the problem is embedded. Problem situations can be distinguished regarding how much of the problem is clearly given at the start, how much of the method for reaching a solution is already at hand, and how extensive the agreement is as to what constitutes a good idea (Getzels 1992). At the extreme and at the most general level, problem situations may be distinguished in 'presented problem situations' and 'discovered problem situations'. The former has a known formulation, a known method of solution, and a known solution. In the latter case, the problem situation is not yet formulated, there is no known method of solution, and no known solution (Getzels 1992). These two problem situations resemble two extreme ends of a continuum, which implies that several combinations cover the spectrum in between (see table 2).

Problem Situation	*Problem*		*Method*		*Solution*	
Type-Case	Others	Individual	Others	Individual	Others	Individual
1	+	+	+	+	+	+
2	+	+	+	-	+	-
3	-	-	-	-	-	-

Source: Getzels (1992)

Table 2: Overview of knowledge distribution in problem situations

In type-case one, the problem is known and clearly formulated to all, the method with which the problem is to be solved is also known, and the problem also has one unique solution, as would be the case with a math problem that a teacher poses to his class. However, in type-case three, none of the attributes are known to anyone, which is why a problem would first need to be found and formulated, and to which methods for solving the problem would have to be invented before the problem can finally be solved. This case might be exemplified by a teacher asking his math class e.g. how many questions can possibly be asked about a rectangle (Getzels 1992).

The distinction between problem finding and problem solving is important for innovating firms because both situations require different approaches (Dillon 1992). Problems are characterized by an existential and psychological aspect, where the first aspect refers to the status of a problem in its physical appearance in the world of events, and where the psychological aspect concerns the relationship between a problem and an observer. Thus, problems might exist for one individual or organization but not to another because of different cognitive abilities and perceptions of what constitutes a problem or not (Dillon 1992; Shane 2000; Eckhardt and Shane 2003). For this reason, pioneering firms which are exploring new domains and which look for new business opportunities need to find ways how 'the right' problems can be effectively searched for.

In summary, although problem finding is an important task for innovative and entrepreneurial firms, there is little practical insight into how firms actually search for problems. In fact, most research has historically focused on problem solving and ignored the fact the problems need to be found and defined first before they can be solved (Dillon 1992; Getzels 1992; Shane 2000).

Idea search
The search for new ideas is closely related to problem solving and refers to the stage in the creative problem solving process where new ideas are searched to solve a given problem (Dillon 1992; Geschka 1992). Therefore, idea search is distinct from problem finding, because the problem is already given. By the same token, idea search is rather related to problem solving as both approaches require creativity of the individual or a group of individuals to come up with new ideas. The search for new ideas or 'idea-generation' is a common activity in the fuzzy front-end of the new product development process (Khurana and Rosenthal 1997; Cooper 1999). Although idea search is often used simultaneously with opportunity identification, there are two main distinctions between the two constructs:
- First, as has been pointed out earlier, opportunity identification often happens in an instant, indicating that there may have been no clearly formulated problem. Idea search, in contrast, is often a planned activity based on a rather clearly formulated problem situation.
- Second, idea search has been implicitly treated in literature on new product development and therefore has been discussed with respect to new product and services. Opportunity identification, in contrast, has mostly been discussed with respect to new business opportunities, entering new markets, new business models, and new product-market combinations. Therefore, opportunity identification is more concerned with 'strategic' moves at the level of the firm.

1.1 Motivation and goal

Creativity is an important precursor for successful idea search. Creativity is considered as a function of knowledge, imagination, and evaluation (De Bono 1990; Parnes 1992), which involves 'the ability to leave structured paths and modes of thinking and merge previously unconnected pieces of knowledge and experience' (Geschka 1992). Existing knowledge plays a vital role in creativity, as for new ideas to be productive there needs to be a link between existing and new knowledge (Finke 1995). Then, creativity relies on imagination and manipulation of knowledge as knowledge per se is only valuable if it is applied and adapted to new circumstances. Furthermore, productive creativity depends on the synthesis, evaluation and development of ideas into usable ideas which have, towards the background of this thesis, a commercially viable impact. Creativity can be spurred by creativity techniques by which individuals or groups can systematically increase the quantity and quality of new ideas. Geschka (1992; 1996) has classified creativity techniques according to their underlying working principle and according to their idea triggering principle. With respect to the working principle, ideas can be generated by stimulating the intuition of the persons involved (i.e. methods fostering intuitive thinking) or by systematically attacking the problem (i.e. systematic idea generation methods). With respect to the triggering principle, ideas can result from the variation and further development of other ideas or concepts or from the confrontation with impressions unconnected with the problem at hand.

The effective generation of ideas for new product development is crucial for all product and service developing companies. Firms which are able to introduce a constant stream of innovations enjoy higher market shares and are better able to sustain competitive advantage. For this reason, the interest in creativity has gone beyond the fields of education and cognitive psychology (Rickards and Puccio 1992) and today is a core subject in the management of innovation (Drucker 2007) and in complex problem-solving (Rickards 1991). Therefore, firms must implement approaches and strategies which spur the creativity of the entire organization, and which are conducive to the overall exploration success.

Conclusion
Although several literature streams have elaborated on the importance of exploration for the short and long-term viability of the firm, most discussions have rather been abstract and lack detailed insights on how exploration is conducted in practice. Furthermore, there is vast literature on new product development which focuses on detailed illustrations of the single phases of the innovation process (e.g. Cooper 1990;

Kleinschmidt and Cooper 1991), the tools which are used within those stages (e.g. von Hippel 1986; Eversheim, Bochtler et al. 1997; Khurana and Rosenthal 1997; Linde, Hall et al. 1999; Weiss 2004), and the overall success factors for new product development (e.g. Montoya-Weiss and Calantone 1994; Cooper 1999). Thus, there is much evidence on how *exploitative* activities for innovation are conducted in the firm, however, evidence on *exploratory* activities is lacking. What is more, discussions have mostly focused on the exploitation of an opportunity that has already been identified (Fiet 1996). In particular, literature has neglected the act of searching and identifying new knowledge for innovation and new business opportunities. Technological change builds the basis for the creation of new processes, new products, new markets, and entrepreneurial activities are central to this process (Schumpeter 1934). However, as Shane (2000) points out, 'before technological change results in this process of entrepreneurial exploitation, entrepreneurs must discover opportunities in which to use the new technology'. As opportunities typically differ from one to another and rarely share predetermined characteristics, the process of opportunity identification is not trivial (Venkataraman 1997).

Apparently, the intersections of the literature streams share similar characteristics in that their underlying theme is the search and identification of new knowledge, business opportunities, and ideas for new product development. However, there is scarce insight into how this is conducted in practice, and to the best of knowledge, these aspects have not been investigated from an integrated perspective. Therefore, this thesis aims at filling this gap by providing in-depth illustrations how exploration activities are conducted within the firm.

1.1.3. Research objective

This research is inspired by the practical need for systematic approaches to and by the lack of empirical insights of exploration. In this respect, it has been argued that firms may be able to exploit new knowledge serendipitously, but that the presence of search routines provides the firm structural, systematic, and procedural mechanisms that allow them to sustain the exploitation of knowledge over extended periods of time (Zahra andGeorge 2002). The main objective of this study is the development of a practical concept that helps established firms and managers in their search efforts for new knowledge pertaining to new technologies, markets and business opportunities for subsequent innovation. Thus, this research aims at answering the following question:

> How do established firms conduct exploration?

To guide the conceptual and empirical part of the research, several sub-questions are formulated. Literature on exploration, entrepreneurship, and diversification has found that innovation activities which are based on existing competencies yield the highest chance of success (Afuah 2002; Miller 2003). Furthermore, existing knowledge is vital for creativity and thus the search for new problems and ideas to be productive. Therefore, firms' exploration approaches may be influenced by existing competencies and knowledge. Thus, the first sub-research question is:

- What criteria determine where exploration is conducted?

Regarding organizational factors, most studies in the literature suggest that organizational factors have a direct impact on exploration and/or exploitation activities (Rivkin and Siggelkow 2003; Gibson and Birkinshaw 2004; Jansen, Van Den Bosch et al. 2006). In line with these studies, the second sub-research question is formulated:

- What are the organizational determinants most conducive to exploration?

To provide answers to these questions, this research develops results pertaining to how to design exploration approaches at the level of the firm. Thus, this research contributes to existing theory and literature on exploration by developing a conceptual model which serves as the basis for the development of hypotheses on the topic. Furthermore, this research aims at translating theoretical insights from the conceptual model into managerially relevant practices by providing guidelines as to what strategies and organizational structures are used.

1.2. Terms and definitions

Exploration and exploitation

Although *exploration* and *exploitation* are frequently cited terms in several management literatures, they commonly refer to an organizational learning perspective imposed by James March (March 1991). March defines exploration to include 'things captured by terms such as search, variation, risk taking, experimentation, play, flexibility, discovery, innovation', and exploitation to include 'such things as refinement, choice, production, efficiency, selection, implementation, execution'. As such, exploration emphasizes improving practices and expanding into new arenas by creating new knowledge, building new understandings, and detecting and correcting misalignments (Lumpkin and Lichtenstein 2005).

The essence of exploration from an organizational learning perspective is creating variety in experience (Levinthal and March 1993; McGrath 2001; Holmqvist 2004). Exploration is a search activity that leads to the variation of internal know-how and organizational routines, structures and systems, new approaches to technologies, business, processes, or products (Zollo and Winter 2002; Crossan and Bedrow 2003), and entails developing new knowledge (Levinthal and March 1993). Exploration typically entails the acquisition of new knowledge that spans either existing technological or organizational boundaries, or both (Rosenkopf and Nerkar 2001; Katila and Ahuja 2002; Subramaniam and Youndt 2005). Exploitation, on the other hand, is about creating reliability in experience (Levinthal and March 1993; Holmqvist 2004) and entails activities such as applying, improving, and extending existing competencies, organizational routines, technologies and processes as well as using and refining existing knowledge (Levinthal and March 1993). Exploitation entails broadening existing knowledge and skills, improving established designs and expanding existing products and services (Benner and Tushman 2003). It thus builds on existing knowledge and reinforces existing skills (Abernathy and Clark 1985).

Exploratory and exploitative innovation
Both exploration and exploitation entail – to different degrees – the search for new knowledge for the purpose of innovation. Benner and Tushman (2002) distinguish between *exploitative innovations*, i.e. innovations which involve 'improvements in existing components and architectures and which build on the existing technological trajectory', and *exploratory innovations*, i.e. innovations which involve 'a shift to a different technological trajectory'. In this sense, *exploitative innovations* are associated with local search, that is, the search strategy of the firm is to scan close and familiar areas, both technologically and geographically, whereas *exploratory innovations* are associated with distant, exploratory search that advances into unknown and unfamiliar areas (Abernathy and Clark 1985; Lewin, Long et al. 1999). In a similar light, other studies on innovation link the concepts of exploration and exploitation to the concepts of radical and incremental innovations (Rosenkopf and Nerkar 2001; Benner and Tushman 2003; Gupta, Smith et al. 2006). These studies illustrate that *radical innovations* originate from exploration activities such as distant search for knowledge,

developing new knowledge, and increasing variety of the firm's knowledge base, whereas *incremental innovations* draw upon exploitation activities such as local search for knowledge, refining and using existing knowledge, and deepening the firm's knowledge base. Exploitative and exploratory innovations as well as incremental and radical innovations are terms which represent the result of prior innovation activities. With respect to search, in this research prior search activities for new knowledge are therefore labeled *exploitative* and *exploratory search*. Therefore, while exploitative search is considered a precursor of exploitative innovation, exploratory search is considered to contribute to the development of exploratory innovations.

Others have adopted a customer and market perspective of innovation. He and Wong (2004) refer to an *explorative innovation strategy* to denote 'technological innovation activities aimed at entering new product-market domains', whereas they refer to an *exploitative innovation strategy* to denote 'technological innovation activities aimed at improving existing product-market positions'. Others have applied the concepts of exploration and exploitation to the innovation process by distinguishing two successive stages. For example, Cheng and Van De Ven (1996) and Duncan (1976) illustrate that the first stage is characterized by exploration activities such as risk taking, searching for alternatives, and discovery, whereas the second stage is characterized by exploitation activities such as testing, refining and implementing the innovation.

The assessment if a search activity is exploratory or exploitative is inherently dependent on the amount of learned new knowledge during the search process rather than the presence or absence of learning (Gupta, Smith et al. 2006; Greve 2007). Furthermore, both exploitative and exploratory search activities can ultimately lead to exploitative (incremental) or exploratory (radical) innovation, and even modest changes in technical innovations can cause strong competitive consequences for the firm (Henderson and Clark 1990). Therefore, exploration and exploitation are argued to be two extreme ends of the same continuum (Gupta, Smith et al. 2006) (see figure 2).

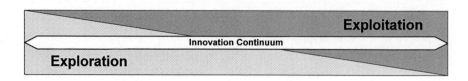

Figure 2: Exploration and exploitation as two ends of the same continuum

Thus, what might seem an exploratory innovation to one firm might be considered a mere exploitative innovation to another firm. As a consequence, the extent of exploration in an innovation launch can be defined as its technological and market novelty for the focal firm (Greve 2007). Therefore, in this thesis, exploration or search is defined as the identification of new knowledge and business opportunities. Although not the focus of this study, this definition includes subsequent experimentation with the new knowledge for the aim of product innovation and new business development.

Competencies and capabilities

Firms require resources and competencies to achieve the fundamental goals the firm has set out to. Resources resemble tangible and intangible firm assets which are permanently tied to the firm (Wernerfelt 1984). Examples are brand names, knowledge and technology, machinery, capital, or skilled people. However, resources are not valuable per se, but they must be coordinated in an efficient way to arrive at desirable outcomes. Prahalad and Hamel (1990) define competencies as "the collective learning in the organization, especially how to coordinate diverse production skills and integrate multiple streams of technologies." From a more knowledge and tacit point of view, Baden-Fuller and Volberda (1997) define competencies as involving shared knowledge among a large group of units within the complex firm. Thus, a competence draws on several routines which have been refined, stored, and codified, or socialized. As a consequence, competencies are not bound to a specific single product, but are transferable to other products or applications (Wernerfelt 1984; Prahalad and Hamel 1990; Danneels 2002).

Capabilities are quite similar to competencies, but the term is used more frequently in organizational learning literature. In this research, the terms capability and competence are used interchangeably to denote a capacity to integrate, combine, and deploy tangible and intangible resources through distinctive organizational processes in order to achieve desirable objectives. Capabilities consist of routines, which are persistent patterns of organizational procedures (Nelson and Winter 1982). These routines serve as the nervous system (Winter 2000) or building blocks (Dosi, Nelson et al. 2000) of capabilities. By definition, routines constitute more atomistic units of behavior than capabilities (Lavie 2006). The configuration of a capability therefore pertains to the composition of the constituting routines, the attributes of these routines, and the interdependencies across these routines.

Established firms
Although entrepreneurship can happen through a single actor outside of an organization, the focus of this research is how large and established firms explore for new knowledge and business opportunities, and thus how innovation emerges in established firms. Many large firms have difficulties in developing really new products in a sustainable manner (Henderson and Clark 1990; Ahuja and Lampert 2001; Colarelli O'Connor and Mark 2001). This is often due to institutionalized practices and bureaucratic routinization and control to support high volume production of standard products (Dougherty and Heller 1994). Established firms are typically organized to achieve maximum efficiency in their processes and to develop a constant stream of incremental innovations. Therefore, researchers have argued that the development of more radical innovations imposes many challenges on the established firm, because such type of innovations do not fit established structures (Henderson and Clark 1990), which ultimately requires organizational adaptation. Large and established firms compete in mature markets, which are characterized by intense competition and a fairly large amount of players (Smith and Cooper 1988).

In this thesis, established firms refers to firms which emerge as leaders in or survivors in an industry (Ahuja and Lampert 2001). As such, they are characterized by satisfying some market needs or demands. Furthermore, in a competitive environment, they must attempt to develop competitive advantages over other firms which offer the products to the same market. Finally, such firms need to establish processes which ensure that the above named output criteria and competitive advantage demands are met. Thus, in this thesis, established firms are denoted as such firms which meet the above outlined conditions at least in a minimal fashion.

1.3. Research concept

1.3.1. Research classification

Exploration as a firm challenge and management is an important issue in different literature streams as well as management practice. However, despite being such an important underlying theme in diverse literatures, it has not been sufficiently addressed by empirical research to date. This thesis aims to bridge this gap. Therefore, this research is based on inductive field research aiming at contributing to existing literature by constructing representations of observable elements and their interrelations, and by generating questions and presenting propositions relevant to explaining typical phenomena (Eisenhardt 1989; Kromrey 1995). New findings are derived from both existing literature on the topic at question and the insights that originate directly from the analysis of the data of the field research. Subsequently, theory building occurs through connecting and disconnecting data and existing literature throughout the whole research process (Mintzberg 2005), so that sufficient depth is provided to achieve an understanding of these interrelations and dynamics (D'Iribarne 1996).

As a result of this process, research hypotheses are developed that extend existing or represent new theory on the subject of firms' exploration approaches. This result differs strongly from the outcomes that occur after testing preliminarily formulated hypotheses, which can be accepted or rejected on a broad scale to generalize the findings (Eisenhardt 1989).

1.3.2. Research methodology

Due to the fact that there is limited insight in how firms proceed with exploratory search activities, and thus because of the novelty and the importance for management practice of the research object, this study applies an exploratory, qualitative research design. In a qualitative research project, the analytical process is an iterative one, involving constant alternations between data collection and analysis. In this research, data analysis will be guided by Eisenhardt's (1989) approach to building theory from case study research.

The main criteria in qualitative empirical research are reliability and validity of results. Usually, three types of validity can be differentiated: construct validity, internal validity, and external validity. According to Yin (2003), construct validity can be increased by using multiple sources of evidence, establishing a chain of evidence between the question asked, data collected and conclusion drawn, and having key informants review the draft case study report and agree upon it. Internal validity of causal relationships requires a reliable process of analyzing data and comparing emerging concepts and theories with previous literature for generalization and theory building from cases. It can be enhanced by pattern matching, explanation building and time-series analyses. In addition, the concept of triangulation is central with respect to internal validity (Yin 2003). External validity confirms that the findings can be generalized. Lastly, reliability is to ensure that another researcher could conduct the same research with the same procedure at later times (Eisenhardt 1989). Validity and reliability is ensured during the proposed research by combining the semi-structured data with the results of thoroughly conducted desk research, internal documentation, as well as presentations by managers and R&D personnel. The interpretations are then confirmed in follow-up interviews.

Sample Selection
The empirical research was carried out between 2006 and 2008 and consisted of two phases. The first phase attempted to gain general insights into firms' exploration behavior, activities and challenges on a broad scale. This led to case studies that contained strategic, operational, and organizational approaches to exploration from 14 companies. Eleven of them - Alcan, BMW, Ciba, Hilti, Lonza, Reichle & DeMassari, SIG allCap, Schindler, Sevex, W.L. Gore & Associates, ZF Friedrichshafen participated in contracted research projects. These companies attempt to develop a constant stream of innovation and have been adopting new approaches to develop more radical innovations in a sustainable fashion. Furthermore, many of these companies are global leaders in their respective markets. All companies are based in Germany, Switzerland, or Liechtenstein, act in different industries, range from medium-sized enterprises to large multinationals, and represent all categories pertaining to the technology intensity and technology life-cycle from high-tech, medium-high-tech, medium-low-tech, and low-tech industries (OECD 2005). Thus, the sample maximizes the heterogeneity of exploration approaches.

In phase two, an in-depth analysis of companies with advanced and new exploration approaches was conducted. Based on the case firms investigated in phase one, those were selected that have the highest potential for learning new insights with respect to their exploration approach as the firms have been market and technology leaders for many decades and still continue to be. Thus, sampling has been conducted according to theoretical rather than random sampling (Eisenhardt 1989). While random sampling is typically found in theory testing on a broad scale, theoretical sampling is the preferred sampling strategy when new or existing theory is developed or advanced (Eisenhardt 1989; Yin 2003). Furthermore, although there is no ideal number of case studies within qualitative research, between four and ten cases is usually sufficient to meet minimum criteria for developing new insights. Therefore, this research presents in-depth case studies of four firms which show very distinct exploration patterns which are transparently observable.

The four in-depth case firms have been chosen because they offer highest learning potential. In addition, the case firms are characterized by a distinct proactive behavior towards innovation. Proactiveness refers to 'processes aimed at anticipating and acting on future needs by seeking new opportunities which may or may not be related to the present line of operations, introductions of new products and brands ahead of competition' (Lumpkin and Dess 1996). Despite operating in a low-speed cycled industry, *Ciba* has adopted an exploration strategy that has led to high-impact innovation. *W.L. Gore & Associates* is known for producing a constant stream of innovations in a wide range of applications, which are based on a unique exploration strategy. *Hilti* has been a global market and innovation leader for decades and excels at adopting and exploiting new exploration approaches on a regular basis. Finally, *Bühler*, which is the only case firms which did not participate in the contracted research in phase one, has managed to explore and incorporate entirely new technologies in their existing product portfolio and has managed to exploit them successfully for innovation. Table 3 illustrates the companies involved in this research.

Research Phase		Number of Interviews	Companies
Phase I	Literature review and explorative interviews about exploration on a broad scale	41	ABB, Alcan, Bühler, BMW, Ciba, Georg Fischer, Fischer, Hilti, Leica Geosystems, Schindler, Sevex, SIG allCap, Reichle & DeMassari, W. L. Gore & Associates, ZF Friedrichshafen
Phase II	In-depth case studies of global market leading firms	31	Ciba, W.L. Gore & Associates, Hilti, Bühler
Total		72	15

Table 3: Overview of empirical dataset

Data collection

In all phases, data has been collected through personal face-to-face or telephone semi-structured interviews of 60-90 minutes length. The main interview partners were typically chief technology officers (CTOs), R&D directors, R&D line managers, as well as managers and engineers from new business development. All interview partners were identified by 'snowball sampling' and additionally such that all relevant hierarchical levels involved in exploration were addressed. Thus, for specific cases, respondents were asked to name those people in the company who were directly involved in the project at question. These were in all case firms subsequently interviewed. Some of the respondents have been interviewed more than once for follow up questions and approval of earlier data. To ensure consistency, one and the same semi-structured interview guide has been used throughout all interviews. Whenever possible, this interview guide has been sent to the interviewee in advance. Questions addressed the firms' strategic attitude towards exploration, its subsequent exploration activities and the organizational settings corresponding to these activities. All interview data is complemented by written company information such as internal memos, presentations, and publicly available information to increase validity. Site visits and workshops enabled complementary personal observations as well. Also, follow-up interviews have been conducted to confirm the case study interpretations from the interview data. This triangulation through combining multiple sources of evidence contributes to confirm the validity and reliability of the research data (Voss, Tsikriktsis et al. 2002; Yin 2003).

Furthermore, Van de Ven's (2007) model of 'Engaged Scholarship' is adopted to ensure that essential steps in the research project are addressed and supported in terms of relevance, validity, reliability, impact, and coherence. The model captures the major processes entailed in conducting the research project (see figure 3).

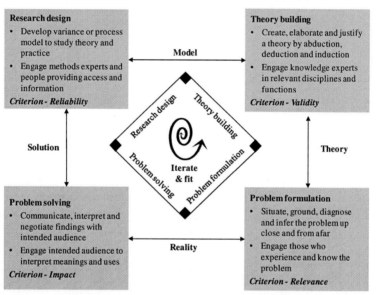

Source: Van de Ven (2007)

Figure 3: Approach to conducting the research project

Data analysis and theory building
Due to the fact that there are limited insights in how firms engage in exploratory search activities, and thus because of the novelty of the research object, this research applies an exploratory qualitative research design. In qualitative research, the analytical process is an iterative one, involving constant alternations between data collection and analysis. In this research, data analysis will be guided by Eisenhardt's (1989) approach to building theory from case study research. This research contributes to existing theory by constructing representations of observable elements and their interrelations, and by generating questions and presenting propositions relevant to explaining typical phenomena (Kromrey 1995). Theory building occurs through connecting and

disconnecting data and existing theory throughout the whole research process, which provides sufficient depth to achieve an understanding of these interrelations and dynamics (D'Iribarne 1996).

First, a reference framework will be constructed that underlies the exploration of the phenomenon under investigation (Eisenhardt 1989; Miles and Hubermann 2005). This framework selects and explains the main aspects to be studied within the case studies (Voss, Tsikriktsis et al. 2002). The framework will be developed from literature streams and theoretical insights relevant for exploratory search activities. This ensures that subsequent collection of qualitative data is based on a sound theoretical approach. The resulting reference framework will enable a focus on the subsequent case data collection, such that the determining elements of search activities can be acquired and analyzed. From the four basic types of design for case studies, this research follows a multiple-case design with the firm's exploration activities as the unit of analysis (Yin 2003). Additionally, mini-cases and narratives will be used to illustrate theoretical concepts and approaches for coping with different innovation challenges. Therefore, several cases are studied in detail to gain an in-depth understanding of their natural setting, complexity, and context (Punch 2005).

1.4. Thesis structure

This thesis is structured as follows (see figure 4):
- Chapter 2 illustrates the theoretical foundation of this research. As exploration is a critical mechanism by which organizations learn new knowledge and identify new business opportunities, the topic of exploration is presented from an organizational learning perspective. Furthermore, as exploration is a recurring and underlying theme in diverse management literature streams and as the construct has seen many different interpretations, this chapter illustrates the theoretical foundations of exploration as an organizational phenomenon. Therefore, it is separated from practical key issues on exploration, which is the topic of chapter 3.
- In chapter 3, key issues from a practical point of view are illustrated. Exploration is illustrated as a central underlying theme in the development of innovation and in research on entrepreneurship. The detailed review of literature on general innovation management and entrepreneurship serves as the basis for the

development of the reference framework and for subsequent investigation why and how firms engage in exploration activities.
- Based on insights gained from applying the reference framework in practice, chapter 4 illustrates in-depth case studies pertaining to exploration activities in selected firms.
- Chapter 5 analyzes insights gained from the case studies and illustrates common characteristics as well as differences across the cases. This analysis is conducted based on referring back to the literature in chapter two. Furthermore, tentative design recommendations for exploration are conceptualized.
- In chapter 6, insights gained from the cross-case analysis are embedded into existing literature on exploration. The theory of absorptive capacity is used to explain why and how firms engage in exploration activities. Subsequently, research hypotheses are derived to extend existing literature and theory pertaining to exploration.
- Chapter 7 derives implications for managerial practice as to how to approach exploration activities in the organization. Also, an overview on how to implement these implications in practice is provided.
- In chapter 8, finally, the research results as well as implications for management theory and practice are summarized.

1.4 Thesis structure

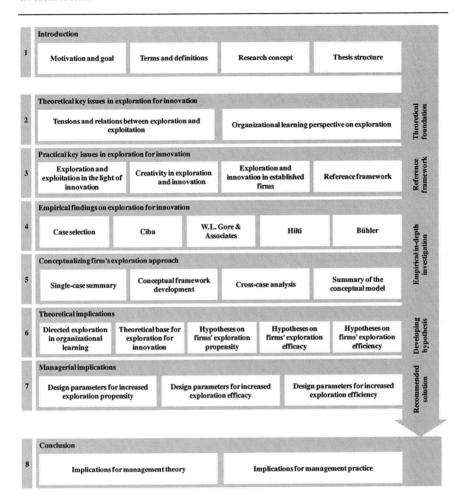

Figure 4: Structure of the thesis

2. Theoretical key issues in exploration for innovation

The exploration for new knowledge and new business opportunities is a vital precondition for firms' long-term competitiveness. However, exploration is associated with activities which are fairly different from daily business and routines which are prevalent in established organizations. As a consequence, exploration activities are difficult to combine with exploitation activities, and both are argued to compete for the same scarce resources. Therefore, there are tensions between exploration and exploitation in the organization, and management needs to find ways how to efficiently combine the two activities. In chapter 2.1, these tensions are illustrated from different management perspectives to point out the challenges inherent in the two activities, and to point out that both activities are not exclusive to each other but represent two ends of the same continuum. Furthermore, although notions of exploration and exploitation is a recurring theme in diverse management fields, discussions and explanatory approaches mostly rest on discussions in organizational learning. Therefore, chapter 2.2 illustrates the organizational learning perspective on exploration and which provides fundamental insights in firms' approach and behavior towards engaging in exploration activities.

2.1. Tensions and relations between exploration and exploitation

Distinctions between exploration and exploitation can be found in studies pertaining to various management fields. Most of these studies implicitly or explicitly make the argument that it is beneficial for firms to combine, somehow, exploration and exploitation (March 1991). Many studies furthermore point to the fact that the business environment has major implications on the firm's innovation behavior. Thus, in rather stable environments, firms tend to focus on short-term profitability, use and refine their existing knowledge (Levinthal and March 1993), leverage competencies (Sanchez, Heene et al. 1996), pursue incremental innovations (Tushman and O'Reilly III 1996), and aim at improving organizational efficiency (Volberda 1996). On the other hand, firms in turbulent environments face growing forces towards change, respectively leading to the pursuit of new knowledge, build competencies, pursue radical innovations and flexibility.

In the following sections, these tensions are further illustrated from the perspective of different management fields. The following sections aim to provide a profound background to the ongoing discussions in research and the broad spectrum where exploration and exploitation are discussed. The discussion of these different perspectives provides useful insights as exploration and exploitation cannot be clearly distinguished and are often overlapping, thus representing two ends of the same continuum (Gupta, Smith et al. 2006).

2.1.1. Strategic management

The topic of exploration and exploitation is a central theme in strategic management literature. Firms need both diversity and order in their strategic activities to maintain their short and long-term viability (Burgelman 1983). Burgelman argues that diversity results primarily from autonomous strategic activities, whereas order results from an induced concept of strategy. In this sense, autonomous strategic activities are related to the concept of exploration, as 'autonomous strategy exploits initiatives that emerge through exploration outside of the scope of the current strategy and that provide the basis for entering into new product-market environments' (Burgelman 2002). In contrast, induced strategic activities are related to the concept of exploitation as they are 'within the scope of a company's current strategy and (…) extend it further in its current product-market environment'. Others have argued that the strategic renewal of the firm requires exploratory activities whose proper implementation will lead to developing new competencies while simultaneously exploiting existing ones (Crossan and Bedrow 2003). As a consequence, there is a tension between when strategic renewal is targeted but organizational learning processes are not in place to allow for such a renewing process.

Similar distinctions between exploration and exploitation have been made in competence based strategic management. There, distinctions are made regarding competence building and competence leveraging (Sanchez, Heene et al. 1996). Both the building of new competencies and the leveraging of current competencies are assumed to determine whether the firm will gain competitive advantage or not (Hamel and Heene 1994). The argument is that competence building is associated with 'qualitative changes in (…) existing stocks of assets and capabilities, including new abilities to co-ordinate and deploy new or existing assets and capabilities in ways that help a firm achieve its goals' (Sanchez, Heene et al. 1996). The building of new competencies aims at changing the status quo to enable the firm to cope with environmental changes by creating new strategic options for future action. In contrast, competence leveraging aims at applying existing assets and capabilities to current or new markets. To achieve this, the firm may require quantitative changes in assets to those the firm already uses. Furthermore, competence leveraging aims at preserving the status quo to deal with current competitive forces (Sanchez and Thomas 1996).

Others have considered the firm as an information processing entity, where the firm has to manage a trade-off between two efficiency oriented search processes in strategic management, i.e. dynamic efficiency and static efficiency (Ghemawat and Costa 1993). Here, dynamic efficiency entails the continuous reconsideration of initial conditions geared towards the development of new products, processes or capabilities, whereas static efficiency entails the continuous search for improvements within a fixed set of initial conditions aimed at refining existing products, processes, or capabilities.

2.1.2. Organization design

Studies on organization design have made distinctions by identifying elements which are conducive to exploration related activities and processes, and design elements which are conducive to exploitation related activities and processes. This is reflected by firms that have implemented either mechanistic or organic management forms (Burns and Stalker 2001). According to them, the mechanistic form is characterized by high levels of differentiation of functional tasks and a hierarchical structure of control, authority and communication, and is appropriate in stable environmental conditions. The organic form is characterized by high levels of integration of individuals' specialized knowledge and a network structure of control, authority and communication, and is appropriate in changing environmental conditions.

Studies on organizational design have investigated how specific organizational design elements stimulate or hinder the simultaneous pursuit of exploration and exploitation (Volberda 1996; Rivkin and Siggelkow 2003; Gibson and Birkinshaw 2004). Gibson and Birkinshaw (2004), for instance, illustrate that an organization design, characterized by a combination of 'hard' (discipline and stretch) and 'soft' (support and trust) design elements fosters both high levels of exploitation oriented actions, i.e. geared toward alignment, and exploration oriented actions, i.e. geared toward adaptability. Rivkin and Siggelkow (2003) investigate interdependencies among organizational design elements and illustrate how they may be combined to encourage both broad search and stability within the organization. Similarly, Sheremata (2000) identifies organizational elements which stimulate creative action by increasing the quantity and quality of ideas, knowledge, and information, that an organization can access, which he calls 'centrifugal forces'. Also, he identifies organizational elements which stimulate collective action by integrating dispersed ideas, knowledge, and information, called 'centripetal forces'.

2.1.3. Technological innovation

Exploration and exploitation is also found in studies pertaining to technological and product innovation. Innovations have been classified in terms of exploratory innovations and exploitative innovations. Exploitative innovations involve improvements in existing components and architectures and build on the existing technological trajectory (Benner and Tushman 2002; Jansen, Van Den Bosch et al. 2005). Exploratory innovations, on the other hand, entail innovations which involve a shift to a different technological trajectory. These arguments are very close to the concepts of radical and incremental innovations. Here, studies illustrate that radical innovations are typically based on exploration activities such as distant search for knowledge, developing new knowledge, and increasing variety of the firm's knowledge base, whereas incremental innovations draw upon exploitation activities such as local search for knowledge, refining and using existing knowledge, and deepening the firm's knowledge base (Rosenkopf and Nerkar 2001; Katila and Ahuja 2002; Subramaniam and Youndt 2005). Ultimately, researchers have distinguished exploratory and exploitative activities to take place in two different stages of the innovation process (Duncan 1976; Cheng and van de Ven 1996). There, the first stage is characterized by exploration activities such as risk taking, searching for new alternatives, and discovery, while the second stage is characterized by exploitation activities such as testing, refining, and implementing the innovation.

A tension between both types of innovations emerge because in contrast to exploitative innovations, exploratory innovations are associated with high uncertainty and returns remote in time. Therefore, firms tend to invest more resources in the development of exploitative innovations than in exploratory innovations. The same argument is valid when considering a customer or market dimension (Abernathy and Clark 1985; Danneels 2002). For instance, He and Wong (2004) refer to an 'exploitative innovation strategy to denote technological innovation activities aimed at entering new product market domains', whereas they refer to an exploitative innovation strategy to denote 'technological innovation activities aimed at improving existing product-market positions'.

Table 4 provides an oversight of the different management fields illustrated in this research where exploration and exploitation and their respective tensions are discussed.

	Strategic management	*Organization design*	*Technological innovation*
Research interest	- Why are some firms more competitive than others? - How do firms balance flexibility and efficiency?	- How do firms organize for flexibility and efficiency?	- Why are some firms more able to develop radical innovations than others?
Unit of analysis	- Firm level	- Firm level	- Firm level - Individual level

Table 4: Management fields concerned with exploration and exploitation

2.2. Organizational learning perspective on exploration

In the following chapters, the concept of exploration and exploitation is illustrated and substantiated from an organizational learning perspective, thus providing a deeper understanding of why and how firms engage in exploration activities. The exploration of new knowledge, of new domains such as new markets and technologies, and ultimately of new organizational capabilities is inevitably connected to the concept of learning. In fact, next to all management fields illustrated throughout this thesis have some of their explanations rooted in literature on organizational learning. In particular, the concept of exploration and exploitation always rests on concepts of organizational learning.

While the first section describes why firms engage in exploration and how they typically behave with respect to exploration, the subsequent sections are concerned with specific types of search. There, distinctions are made which illustrate that search on the individual level may to some extent depend on cognitive aspects which may facilitate search processes. Furthermore, distinctions are made which illustrate firms' search behavior when solving given problems ('problemistic search') which is associated with exploitative (local) search, and when searching for new problems ('slack search') which is associated with exploratory (distant) search.

2.2.1. Characteristics of exploration and exploitation

Organizational learning literature has also discussed that tensions exist between exploration and exploitation in that it is difficult to engage in either one of the activities without detrimental effects on the other activity (Levinthal and March 1993; Floyd and Lane 2000; Benner and Tushman 2003). By trying to do both the firm risks to be mediocre at both (March 1991). Moreover, exploitation activities are associated with quickly attainable goals which have a high probability of success, whereas exploration is associated with considerable risks and costs which may never be offset by appropriate benefits. The two activities entail incompatible structures, systems, or processes that compete with each other inside the firm for scarce attention, while each resource unit can only be allocated to either exploration or exploitation (Garcia and Calantone 2002; Benner and Tushman 2003). Thus, the experience of success from exploitation activities can make firms fall victim to a 'success trap', so that exploratory activities are 'crowded out' over time by triggering a reduction in investments in experimentation (Levinthal and March 1993; Burgelman 1994; Christensen 1997). Furthermore, past successes of exploitative tasks create path dependencies, because search choices vie for scarce resources and entail path dependencies on account of prior investments (Sidhu, Commandeur et al. 2007). Thus, such path dependencies that built on previous resource allocation patterns create 'innovation traps' that restrict the commitment of resources in future periods. As a consequence, the selection of innovations becomes biased towards exploitative innovations, and exploratory innovations are crowded out (Benner and Tushman 2002). Finally, the impetus for innovation and the subsequent allocation of resources is usually shaped by the demands of existing customers in existing markets. Therefore, resource allocation processes have the tendency to nourish sustaining innovations that address current customers' needs (Christensen and Bower 1996). Due to these problems, the simultaneous pursuit of exploration and exploitation within the same organizational unit is considered to be difficult (Tushman and O'Reilly III 1996; O'Reilly III and Tushman 2004).

Furthermore, exploration implies a search process to identify new knowledge, technological competencies, and business opportunities. This search is typically associated with a large search scope, large search breadth, or both (Katila and Ahuja 2002). In fact, Rosenkopf and Nerkar (2001) show that those innovations with more impact on a broader set of technological areas have been created by exploratory search in distant technological domains. However, such search processes that advance broadly into distant domains imply considerable complexity, search cost, and risk: discontinuous or radical innovations associated with exploration activities imply fundamental changes to the current technology and thus transcend current organizational knowledge (Ahuja and Lampert 2001). Thus, any search that deviates too much from the firm's existing knowledge base will hurt product performance (Martin and Mitchell 1998). By the same token, innovations that serve different customer sets or rely on new and unknown technologies are associated with high uncertainty and are difficult to measure (Henderson, Del Alamo et al. 1998). While the benefits of exploitation are certain, positive, and close in time, the returns of exploratory activities, if any, are distant and uncertain (March 1991; Levinthal and March 1993). The probability of finding valuable new knowledge elements is small and, even if a firm succeeds in doing so, it is possible that the same product idea has already been discovered (Katila and Ahuja 2002). Finally, even if exploratory search yields useable knowledge, acquisition cost and integration difficulties may outstrip the benefits of this knowledge (Sidhu, Commandeur et al. 2007).

Because of the tensions outlined above, some authors have described the relation between exploration and exploitation as a trade-off (Christensen and Bower 1996; Benner and Tushman 2003). Thus, they argue that exploration and exploitation cannot be combined at the same time or in the same place. As a consequence, the assumption is that, for instance, an increase of exploitation in a specific organizational unit is associated with a decrease of exploration, and vice versa. A second relation between the two activities is seen in the time dimension, arguing that exploration and exploitation engender and/or follow each other over time (Cheng and van de Ven 1996; Winter and Szulanski 2001; Garcia and Calantone 2002). They consider the relationship between exploration and exploitation as oscillating. Again others have argued that both activities can be combined within time and space. This view implies that an increase in exploration may go with an increase in exploitation, or the other way around (Nerkar 2003; Rivkin and Siggelkow 2003; Gibson and Birkinshaw 2004).

2.2.2. Search motivation and search behavior

Search motivation

Organizational goals change as individuals of the organization change, that is, enter or leave the organization, and are furthermore induced by problems. Problems are recognized when aspiration levels differ from organizational aspirations (Cyert and March 1992), and when negative performance feedback provokes problemistic search (Hoang and Ener 2007), which is the search stimulated by a rather specific problem. Thus, exploration is initiated when the firm deviates from its aspiration levels or when there is an attainment discrepancy which results from a mismatch between aspirations and actual performance. As a result, firms are more willing to conduct exploratory search when overall performance decreases compared with, for example, past performance results or competitors. As to organizational expectations with respect to search and in addition to attainment discrepancy, Cyert and March (1992) linked the intensity and success of search to organizational slack. They argued that, depending on available organizational resources, search efforts are intensified both in breadth and depth when the organization deviates from its goals.

Scholars have discussed how performance feedback motivates risk-taking and organizational change as a result of learning from experience (Greve 2003). Such models are based on the assumption that managers continuously interpret how firms have performed with respect to the firm's previous performance record and the performance of a reference group (Cyert and March 1992). Thus, firms are likely to change their behavior and engage in more exploration or exploitation if they experience a performance gain or shortfall relative to either of the benchmarks. As managers observe and learn about what works and what does not, they can continue investing in demonstrated strengths or respond by undertaking organizational changes to improve performance.

Search behavior

In different studies, Cyert and March (1992) have found that organizations avoid uncertainty with respect to two main aspects. First, organizations focus on short-term efficiency rather than focusing on events that lie in the future and do not have immediate impact. They do so by applying standard decision rules which are applicable in situations with known variables. Furthermore, organizations try to limit uncertainty by arranging a negotiated environment, that is, they try to achieve a reasonable and manageable situation by contracting with relevant participants of the environment to reduce uncertainty and bring it within the reach of controllability. Second, organizations solve problems when they occur, and do not engage in activities to anticipate the rise of problems. Thus, organizations engage in search only when a problem arises in terms of a mismatch between current performance and aspiration. Furthermore, it is argued that organizations learn and adapt to new situations. Because of this, the assumption is that also search rules are subject for adaptation. Cyert and March (1992) put this assumption in this way: "when an organization discovers a solution to a problem by searching in a particular way, it will be more likely to search in that way in future problems of the same type; when an organization fails to find a solution by searching in a particular way, it will be less likely to search in that way in future problems of the same type" (Cyert and March 1992). Thus, the consideration of search routines will likely change with success or failure of alternatives to a problem.

2.2.3. Cognitive and experiential search

Cognitive and experiential search are considered the two main categories by which organizations or individuals search for new knowledge (Gavetti and Levinthal 2000). Cognitive search represents a search mechanism where prior experience is used for future search activities. In contrast, experiential search is defined as trying out specific pieces of knowledge, implying that the value of new knowledge needs in fact to be experienced. Cognitive and experiential search are distinguished based on three aspects, that is

- the mode of evaluation of alternatives,
- the extensiveness of alternatives considered, and
- the location of these alternatives relative to current behavior (Gavetti and Levinthal 2000).

Pertaining to the evaluation of alternatives, the cognition approach allows the individual to assess the alternative without actually having to 'test' it under real-life conditions, i.e., the assessment happens based on his understanding of the world and the probable consequences of engaging in the proposed behavior. In contrast, an experiential approach to assessment involves some type of implementation in order to assess its efficacy. Thus, specific search approaches are tried out and altered or adapted according to its outcome (Levitt and March 1988). Furthermore, the extensiveness of alternatives considered tend to be much smaller in the case of cognitive approaches. This is because in the case of experiential approaches, only one alternative at a time can be explored in a sequential manner. Also, pertaining to the degree to which the alternatives differ from the organization's current behavior and to each other, cognitive approaches differ from experiential approaches. Often, experimentation with alternatives that are very different from current behavior are directly connected to the way possible alternatives are evaluated. Therefore, cognitive approaches have a higher likelihood of considering alternatives which are farther away from current behavior without being assessed overly negative.

Literature has shown that cognitive representations are a critical determinant of managerial choice and action (Tversky and Kahneman 1986; Huff 1990; Fiol and Huff 1992; Walsh 1995). In particular, a firm's choice of strategy is often the result of actors' representation of their problem space (Simon 1991). Gavetti and Levinthal (2000) describe cognition as a forward-looking form of intelligence that is premised on an actor's beliefs about the linkage between the choice of actions and the subsequent impact of those actions on outcomes. The beliefs an individual forms result from his mental model of the world. On the other hand, experiential knowledge is the result of positive or negative reinforcement of prior choices (Levitt and March 1988). Thus, firms will engage again in actions that have earlier led to positive outcomes, while actions that have led to negative outcomes are typically avoided.

2.2.4. Exploitation: problemistic and local search

Problemistic search is the process through which decision-makers deal with attainment discrepancy, which arises when organizational performance falls below aspirations. Aspirations embody the type and the magnitude of performance that should be reached by the organization in order to satisfy managers (Hoang and Ener 2007). Problemistic search is typically stimulated by a specific type of problem and directed toward finding a solution to that problem (Cyert and March 1992). Problemistic search thus differs from undirected search and the search for understanding as it has a goal and is performed only to the point where understanding leads to more control. In this regard, problemistic search is engineering rather than pure science (Cyert and March 1992). In a similar light and from a technological innovation perspective, Katila and Ahuja (2002) argue that organization's problem-solving activities involve the creation and recombination of technological ideas. Thus, they view firms primarily as problem-solvers, and describe product development as problem solving (Dougherty and Hardy 1996).

2.2 Organizational learning perspective on exploration

Organizational learning literature argues that R&D is path dependent, which means that R&D will typically repeat behaviors which have been successful in the past when engaging in research and development activities. For the same reason, it is argued that organizations search for novel technologies in areas that enable them to build on their established technology base (Stuart and Podolny 1996). Therefore, path-dependency implies that organizations will stick to what is familiar, and to activities which have been successful in the past. Furthermore, the impact of familiarity because of past actions or existing technologies is that firms tend to search in the vicinity of existing solutions to solve new problems. Reasons for this local search can be found in individual and organizational level processes as well as in the firm's overall innovative capabilities. At the individual level, bounded rationality has implications as the firm's previous development activities form a guideline for future search activities. This is particularly true for environments with high uncertainty where the impact of innovation decisions and competitive behavior is difficult to anticipate. As a consequence, the results of past searches become natural starting points for initiating new searches (Nelson and Winter 1982). At the organizational level, local search is a consequence of established organizational routines (Cyert and March 1992). These routines have been established as responses to the repeated encounter of similar situations and thus represent a source of continuity (Stuart and Podolny 1996). Furthermore, prior successful technology development and prior experience with that makes it more likely that the organization will engage in local search in that area again. Therefore, also R&D as an organizational routine is prone to be path dependent on past search activities, and it is natural to expect that R&D will produce superior results when it is based on the firm's established competencies (Stuart and Podolny 1996).

Research has also discussed local search within incumbent firms. Incumbent firms have been found to have more difficulties with adjusting their technology strategy to environmental changes (Abernathy and Clark 1985; Tushman and Anderson 1986; Henderson and Clark 1990). Particularly in the case of radical innovations which is argued to alter the basis for competition in an industry, incumbents face diminishing value of their existing competencies. In this circumstance, established firms have been found to show a strong path-dependency regarding existing technologies and a slow response to technological change. Furthermore, local search leads incumbents to introduce designs that are similar to those incorporated in their existing products (Martin and Mitchell 1998).

Local search is considered to lead to incremental innovations and is argued to lead to more expertise in the firm's current domain (Rosenkopf and Nerkar 2001). This is because the search for new solutions in areas close to what is already known to the organization is probably fairly similar to existing solutions. As a consequence, new solutions which result from local search efforts may represent incremental innovations from the view of existing solutions. Because this type of innovation may be based on established technologies and based on established search routines, He and Wong (2004) call this 'exploitative innovations'.

2.2.5. Exploration: slack and distant search

Slack is a term used to describe a stock of excess resources which are available to an organization during a given planning cycle (Nohria and Gulati 1996), and which can be a result of organizational performance in prior periods, as a planned buffer, or as a result of poor planning (Voss, Sirdeshmukh et al. 2008). Slack resources are argued to be an important determinant of innovations (Jelinek and Schoonhoven 1990; Schoonhoven, Eisenhardt et al. 1990), as they facilitate 'slack search', that is, experimentation and learning (Levinthal and March 1981), and in that they condition information search, experimentation, and risk-taking (Sidhu, Volberda et al. 2004). They are argued to divert attention away from 'fire fighting' to focus instead on expansive thinking and risky, innovative ventures with potentially high payoffs (Nohria and Gulati 1996). In other words, slack resources are used for search for innovations that would not be approved in the face of scarcity (Cyert and March 1992). Slack resources in the form of monetary resources imply a larger environment-monitoring budget and are therefore argued to facilitate exploration. Thus, firms with fewer monetary resources are argued to focus more likely on monitoring the direct environment rather than getting involved in uncertain, experimental projects (Sidhu, Volberda et al. 2004). In contrast, large and cash-rich companies are more inclined to afford certain kinds of experimental ventures (Ahuja and Lampert 2001).

Unlike problemistic search, slack search is not initiated by existing problems but guided mainly by the interests of the individuals and groups engaged in search (Greve 2007). Organizations with slack resources have greater opportunities for experimentation and less rigid performance monitoring, both of which are needed to create exploratory innovations (Hrebiniak and Joyce 1985; Lounamaa and March 1987). Therefore, slack resources tend to support distant search in terms of searching completely unknown

2.2 Organizational learning perspective on exploration

knowledge domains. On the other hand, the lack of slack resources tend to lead to investments in local search as this is associated with less uncertainty. Some scholars even argue that the identification and subsequent exploitation of entrepreneurial opportunities is not possible without slack resources (Ahuja and Lampert 2001; Ireland, Hitt et al. 2003).

In contrast to local search or exploitation, distant search or exploration occurs in the opposite situation, when organizations try completely new components or combinations which were previously unknown (Fleming 2001). In this regard, boundary-spanning exploration implies the acquisition of knowledge which resides outside of the organization and technological domains (Rosenkopf and Nerkar 2001). Others have conceptualized distant search as the search scope along the supply-, demand- and spatial-side (Sidhu, Volberda et al. 2004). Search in the supply-side of competition entails considerations of e.g. external technologies, production facilities and products. Search on the demand-side entails considerations of customer needs, customer groups while spatial search entails the consideration of different geographic regions or markets.

In summary, although organizational learning literature has extensively discussed the importance, motivation, and types of exploration, there is a lack of insights into the strategy and operational process of exploration. Therefore, there is a need to investigate how firms actually learn, and thus engage in exploration activities for innovation.

3. Practical key issues in exploration for innovation

Exploration for new knowledge and for new business opportunities is vital for firms to stay competitive. This is particularly true if with exploration more radical or disruptive innovations are associated, and if with exploitation constant improvements of existing products and technologies are associated. Therefore, chapter 3.1 illustrates the meaning and importance of exploration for the development of more radical innovations, and points to the empirical shortcomings pertaining to exploration research. As exploration is inherently connected with creativity as an important premise for exploration to be successful, chapter 3.2 illustrates the role of creativity in two common search processes, that is, recombinant and analogical search. Chapter 3.3, finally, illustrates the importance of exploration for the identification of new business opportunities and how opportunity identification can be facilitated. Chapter 3.4 concludes the practical discussions pertaining to exploration by developing a reference framework based on the literature review.

3.1. Exploration and exploitation in the light of innovation

Literature on exploration has pointed to the fact that more radical innovation is often the result of prior exploration activities (Jansen, Van Den Bosch et al. 2006). Jansen, Van Den Bosch et al. (2006) have shown that radical innovations are more often developed when organizations search in more remote knowledge domains. While incremental innovation is the product of learning how to better exploit existing capabilities, radical innovations are derived from exploration activities such as identifying and appropriating entrepreneurial opportunities (Lant and Mezias 1990). Incremental innovations improve existing product-market architectures and help the firm derive maximum value from the firm's current capabilities. As such, they typically entail simple, incremental engineering improvements (Christensen, Johnson et al. 2002) and merely lead to small changes (Tushman and O'Reilly III 1996). Radical innovations often lead to the creation of new markets and new business models and represent, essentially, new ways of playing the competitive game (Ireland, Hitt et al. 2003). In the following, exploration and exploitation are briefly discussed in the light of the development of exploitative (incremental) and exploratory (radical) innovations.

3.1.1. Developing exploitative innovation

The development of exploitative or incremental innovations is considered to be the daily business in product and service offering organizations, and considerable research has been made on various aspects of the incremental new product development (NPD) process. Research has elaborated on new product innovation processes itself (Cooper and Kleinschmidt 1987), on the steps that must be carried out (Cooper 1990; Cooper 1999), on the impact of each step on project and product outcome (Cooper and Kleinschmidt 1986; Cooper 1990), and on the role of models in supporting and improving the NPD process (Mahajan and Wind 1992). In this regard, many innovation models involve a linear process, such that product development involves a predictable or certain process which can be planned as a series of discrete steps (Cooper 1990; Brown and Eisenhardt 1995). In particular, many leading and established firms have implemented a systematic stage-gate process which entails single steps and milestones to be delivered from idea generation to product launch. Each stage entails specific activities or tasks to be solved and are followed by a gate where a go/no-go decision with respect to the continuation of the project is made. Such linear processes, which originate from phased reviewed processes developed by the National Aeronautics and Space Administration (NASA), represent a measurement and control methodology which are designed to ensure that the project proceeds as planned and that every activity within the process is completed in time (Cooper 1994). As a difference to the phased review process developed by NASA, which merely considers technical tasks such as the physical design and the development of the product, the stage-gate process considers marketing and manufacturing as integral parts of the product development process (Cooper 1994). Often, following such a procedure results in product improvements, upgrades, and line extensions (Veryzer Jr 1998).

Although considerable research effort has been made to better understand the managerial processes associated with new product development, most works have implicitly focused on product development as an incremental, evolutionary nature (Veryzer Jr 1998). In contrast to incremental innovations, radical innovations are difficult to integrate in the conventional innovation process because of their high uncertainty. Uncertainty causes the course of projects to become fairly unpredictable and projects to involve many iterations and unforeseen additional activities and resources (Stringer 2000). Because of the different characteristics of incremental from radical innovation projects, literature on new product development has discussed how radical innovation processes are distinct from incremental innovation ones. For example, Veryzer found in an in-depth study of eight cases that radical innovation processes are much more exploratory and less customer driven then the typical incremental NPD process (Veryzer Jr 1998).

3.1.2. Developing exploratory innovation

Exploratory or radical innovations involve the application of significant new technologies or significant new combinations of technologies to new market opportunities (Tushman and Nadler 1986). Radical innovations take its form in new product classes, product substitution, or fundamental product improvements (Rice, Kelley et al. 2001), and often involve dramatic leaps in terms of customer familiarity (Veryzer Jr 1998). Engaging in the development of radical innovation is paramount to maintain a competitive position, however, radical innovation is a risky, costly, and lengthy process that threatens and disrupts existing organizational structures (Utterback 1994). This is particularly true for established firms which are deemed to have difficulties to adapting to external technological change and adapting their internal processes accordingly (Christensen 1997; Hill and Rothaermel 2003).

Discussions pertaining to the development of radical innovations have mostly focused on the antecedents that facilitate or inhibit the development of that type of innovation (e.g. Ettlie, Bridges et al. 1984; Chandy and Tellis 1998; Stringer 2000; Leifer, O'Connor et al. 2001; Stevens and Burley 2003; O'Connor and Ayers 2005; Herrmann, Gassmann et al. 2007). Within these discussions, a particular focus has been laid on the fuzzy front-end of the NPD process, where idea development, idea assessment as well as facilitating organizational structures are crucial aspects for the development of radical innovations.

However, research has largely ignored the questions where radical ideas come from, how they can be found, and what approaches might facilitate the identification of such ideas. c From a psychology literature perspective, radical innovations are more likely created when combining remote pieces of knowledge (Ward 1994; Holyoak and

Thagard 1995). Despite these insights, there is scarce insight into how exploration is performed to facilitate the development of radical or exploratory innovations.

3.2. Creativity in exploration and innovation

The development of both exploitative and exploratory innovations as well as any other kind of innovation requires some creativity on part of the individual or a group of individuals. Because the essence of innovation is newness, innovation always involves that new information and knowledge is applied to arrive at an outcome that is different from the status quo. In this sense, the distinction between invention and innovation is important. While invention refers to the development of new ideas or an act of creation, innovation refers to the commercialization of the invention (Ahuja and Lampert 2001). Therefore, creativity is essential for the development of new ideas disregarding their impact along the incremental-radical innovation continuum. The successful exploration for new knowledge relies on creativity as well, as without it, individuals would not be able to make sense of the new information they encounter, and they would not be able to link existing and new knowledge to form new ideas (Finke 1995; Shane 2000). Creativity as a cognitive capability plays a critical role in the process of exploration because it enables the individual to absorb new information and put it in a business context to form new ideas for subsequent innovation.

From a psychological perspective, creativity represents 'the entire system by which processes operate on structures to produce outcomes that are novel but nevertheless rooted in existing knowledge' (Ward, Smith et al. 1997). Creativity is an outcome of several processes such as conceptual combination, conceptual expansion, metaphor, analogy, mental model construction, and other processes. In all these processes, prior knowledge plays a critical role in any creative endeavor, as without a meaningful link to what has come before, novel ideas are unlikely to be of much use (Finke 1995). For the same reason, novel ideas are unlikely to be deemed creative if the idea shows no features that would fit the situation to which the idea has been created. Therefore, creativity and the development of new ideas strongly depend on the prior knowledge of the individual.

From a management perspective, scholars have argued that most innovations are recombinations of existing knowledge (Schumpeter 1942; Nelson and Winter 1982;

Fleming and Sorenson 2004), and that the ability to produce more radical innovations are found in the knowledge about a product's architecture (Henderson and Clark 1990). The ability to efficiently recombine is argued to depend on the computational power and/or the cognitive abilities of the individual (e.g. Gick and Holyoak 1983; Vosniadou and Ortony 1989). Thus, innovation and the underlying ideas that lead to it is the result from creatively combining two or more previously unrelated pieces of knowledge. In general, the ability to combine such pieces of knowledge depends on the individual's breadth of knowledge, implying that the broader the knowledge the more likely is the individual to be creative from 'bisociation' (Ireland, Hitt et al. 2003) where bisociation is the combination of two or more previously unrelated matrices or skills or information (Smith and Di Gregorio 2002). The ability to combine different pieces of knowledge for innovation has also been termed 'combinative capability' (Kogut and Zander 1992). Combinative capability is considered to be vital for the identification of entrepreneurial opportunities (Ireland, Hitt et al. 2003). Therefore, combinative abilities and thus creativity can contribute to the development of innovations that in turn produce competitive advantage, which is why combinative abilities and creativity are important components of entrepreneurship.

In the following sections, two search methods are illustrated which rely to different degrees on creativity. Recombinant search resembles a representative search approach as viewed from a management perspective and corresponds to experiential search as described in chapter 2.2.3. Analogical search, in contrast, resembles a representative search approach as discussed in psychology literature and as such represents a cognitive search approach. While recombinant search relies more on computational power, analogical search takes strongly advantage of creativity as a cognitive ability. Although search theory discusses search with respect to decision-making under uncertainty (e.g. Reinganum 1982), the following two search approaches represent search approaches which are an underlying theme in entrepreneurship and management literature.

3.2.1. Recombinant search

Research on technology has argued that invention is a process of recombination, where invention is a result of combining technological components in a new manner (Nelson and Winter 1982; Fleming and Sorenson 2004). The possible combinations of components for the purpose of innovation seem infinite, however, as the agents in a process of recombination are people, the scope of recombinations is assumed to be limited by the cognitive abilities of the individual. Social construction and previous association play an important role in an assessment if certain technologies or components belong together (Fleming 2001). This is in line with the arguments of bounded rationality and local search, where localness corresponds to inventors' familiarity with their recombinant search space. Local search or exploitation occurs when an inventor recombines from a familiar set of technology components or refines a previously used combination. Distant search or exploration occurs in the opposite situation, when inventors try completely new components or combinations' (Fleming 2001). Furthermore, it is argued that local search and local recombination is more certain and on average more successful, too (Benner and Tushman 2003). Also, local search is associated with a higher chance of successful technology development since search is rooted in areas in which the firm has prior experiences. Local exploration builds on similar technology that reside within the firm.

However, local search also decreases the potential to develop radically different inventions of much greater impact. On the other hand, organizations that seek technological breakthroughs should experiment with new combinations, possibly with old components, even though this might lead to an increased number of failures.

3.2.2. Analogical search

The role and importance of analogies in innovation has mostly been limited to product design and psychology literature (Dahl and Moreau 2002). Analogical thinking is a mechanism underlying creative tasks, in which people transfer information from a familiar setting and use it for the development of ideas in a new setting (Gentner and Rattermann 1993; Dahl and Moreau 2002). It happens if a familiar problem is used to solve a novel problem of the same type (Reeves and Weisberg 1994). Analogies can be drawn in different settings and directions. In some cases, a solution is found in one industry and applied to solve a problem in another industry. In other instances, the analogy was drawn from a solution looking for a problem (Gavetti, Levinthal et al. 2005). In all cases, the search for a solution is stimulated by a rather specific problem. Within this problemistic search (Cyert and March 1992), analogies to settings quite similar to the place of origin can be drawn, potentially providing a solution. Similar to research on technological innovation, researchers in cognitive psychology commonly agree that innovation entails reassembling elements from existing knowledge bases in a novel fashion (Gagne and Shoben 1997; Hampton 1998). The combination of two or more previously unrelated matrices or skills or information takes place when individuals combine information to identify an opportunity (Ireland, Hitt et al. 2003).

Cognitive scientists have argued that similarity of concepts (e.g. problems or situations) at any level of abstraction contributes to the ability of analogical thinking (Keane 1987; Ross 1989; Reeves and Weisberg 1994; Holyoak and Thagard 1997). Thus, similarity of some basic elements between the source where the problem origins (i.e. the problem source) and the source where the analogy is found (i.e. the solution source) is a vital precondition for analogies to be identified. Similarity has also been described in a continuum from near or surface analogies to far analogies (Dahl and Moreau 2002). Near analogies are much easier identified than far analogies, as near analogies often entail obvious surface similarities while far analogies typically entail similarities in the structure of source and target attributes. However, if successfully implemented, far analogies serve as the base for 'mental leaps' and can lead to radical innovation (Holyoak and Thagard 1995). The logic behind this is that if source and target share the same superficial qualities, they often come from the same or close conceptual domain (Ward 1994), which would lead to incremental innovation. Far analogies in contrast combine non-obvious knowledge, thus potentially leading to radical new solutions, or, in terms of this thesis, to exploratory innovations.

In summary, creativity is an essential part of exploration in terms of a cognitive process. Without creativity, exploration would resemble an inefficient and random mathematical recombination process as information is not immediately interpreted. However, exploration is based on the individuals cognitive abilities including prior knowledge to which new pieces of information can be related. Thus, exploration requires creativity to lead to new ideas and the discovery of new business opportunities.

3.3. Exploration and innovation in established firms

The development of radical innovations in established firms is argued to be difficult because they are organized for efficiency in their processes (Dougherty and Heller 1994; Ahuja and Lampert 2001; Hill and Rothaermel 2003). As radical innovation differ from the development of incremental innovations, they do not fit existing structures and impose challenges on the established organization (Ettlie, Bridges et al. 1984; Veryzer Jr 1998). The investigation of these challenges and of how innovation can be developed in established firms is *the* central theme in literature on entrepreneurship. Therefore, this literature stream provides an insightful framework for discussing exploration for innovation. Entrepreneurship literature is, however, not concerned with the development of incremental innovations and thus does not, for example, focus on new product development processes, but is concerned with the question how innovations are generated pertaining to new product-market offerings.

Entrepreneurship is considered as an essential driver for firm growth and firm performance. By means of entrepreneurship, firms are associated with creating wealth by building economies of scale as well as market power (Ireland, Hitt et al. 2003). In turn, these outcomes contribute to additional resources and to achieving competitive advantage and stimulate further growth. Entrepreneurship pertaining to the development of new products involves the identification and exploitation of opportunities in the external environment. Underlying this goal lie entrepreneurial actions which involve the creation of new resources or the combination of existing resources in new ways to develop and commercialize new products, move into new markets, and/or service new customers (Ireland, Hitt et al. 2001).

Research has mostly focused on the antecedents of successful entrepreneurship (e.g. Shane and Venkataraman 2000; Ahuja and Lampert 2001; Hitt, Ireland et al. 2001; Ireland and Webb 2007), and has tried to classify the different types of entrepreneurship that occur in business reality. Despite valuable insights on different aspects of entrepreneurship, research has largely neglected the question how and where new business opportunities are found. Only recently have scholars started to discuss the importance of the identification of new business opportunities, however, a systematic analysis of how this search is performed is missing.

3.3.1. Framework for innovation in established firms

Corporate entrepreneurship (CE) as a distinct stream within the entrepreneurship literature is concerned with the question how innovation and new business opportunities are identified and exploited in large and established firms. CE is considered a 'driver of new businesses within on-going enterprises as achieved through innovation, joint ventures or acquisitions, strategic renewal, product, process, and administrative innovations, and processes through which individuals' ideas are transformed into collective actions through the management of uncertainties' (Dess, Ireland et al. 2003).

Sharma and Chrisman (1999) define corporate entrepreneurship as the 'process by which an individual or a group of individuals, in association with an existing organization, creates a new organization, or instigates renewal or innovation within that organization'. Despite the vast amount of definitions of corporate entrepreneurship, all definitions have in common some type of innovation as the single underlying theme that spans all types of entrepreneurship (Stopford and Baden-Fuller 1994; Covin and Miles 1999). Furthermore, literature commonly agrees that corporate entrepreneurship is characterized by three main aspects (Lumpkin and Dess 1996; Covin and Miles 1999):

- the existence of product or process innovation,
- a risk-taking propensity by the firm's key decision makers, and
- evidence of proactiveness with respect to product-market introductions or the early adoption of new administrative techniques or process technologies.

Covin and Miles (1999) have conceptualized four types of corporate entrepreneurship which aim at establishing innovation, and in which exploration for new knowledge takes place (Dess, Ireland et al. 2003). These four types are labeled *sustained regeneration*, *organizational rejuvenation*, *strategic renewal*, and *domain redefinition*. This categorization allows to subordinate any type of innovation in one of these categories and represents an arch typology of innovation in established firms. Since entrepreneurship is inherently based on the identification and exploitation of new and valuable knowledge, exploration in terms of the identification process happens within a corporate entrepreneurial process, and thus can lead to these types of entrepreneurship.

- *Sustained regeneration* entails the firm's engagement in developing cultures, processes, and structures to support and encourage a continuous stream of new product introductions in its current markets as well as entries with existing products into new markets. The strategy is to explore under-exploited market opportunities based on the firm's existing competencies. Therefore, this type of entrepreneurship is based on exploratory activities with respect to the identification of new markets.
- *Organizational rejuvenation* is referred to as the firm's efforts to improve its competitive position by altering internal processes, structures, and/or capabilities. This strategy often takes form in changes to value chain activities. Therefore, exploration efforts are aimed at improving internal processes and administrative aspects rather than introducing new product-market offerings.

- *Strategic renewal* entails the firm's strategy to alter the way of how the industry currently competes. As such, firms focus on the environmental context and particularly on the strategy that mediates the organization-environment context. Strategic renewal often involves the firm's reposition in a way that allows the simultaneous exploitation of current competitive advantages and exploration for advantages that will lead to future success.
- *Domain redefinition* entails the firm's efforts to proactively create a new product-market arena that others have not recognized or actively sought to exploit. The focus of this approach is exploring what is possible rather than exploiting what is currently available. By this, the firm hopes to be the first mover and thus hopes to create sustainable competitive advantage in an existing industry.

Table 5 summarizes key characteristics of these four types of corporate entrepreneurship.

	Focus of corporate entrepreneurship	*Typical basis for competitive advantage*	*Typical frequency of new entrepreneurial acts*
Sustained regeneration	New products or new markets	Differentiation	High frequency
Organizational rejuvenation	The organization	Cost leadership	Moderate frequency
Strategic renewal	Business strategy	Varies with specific form manifestation	Less frequent
Domain redefinition	Creation and exploitation of product-market arenas	Quick response	Infrequent

Source: Covin and Miles (1999)

Table 5: Types and characteristics of corporate entrepreneurship

Research has argued that the development of internal innovations in established firms often fails because large organizations present hostile environments for creative ideas (Burgelman 1983; Sharma and Chrisman 1999). For example, innovative ideas are often defeated by financial control systems and other formalities which are typical for large organizations and/or bureaucracies (Dess, Ireland et al. 2003). However, notwithstanding insights regarding organizational factors which inhibit the effective development of innovations in mature organizations, ideas must first be developed to enter the process of assessment. Therefore, the source of new ideas is a critical aspect within the entrepreneurial process, putting the identification of opportunities at the center of entrepreneurship. As opportunity identification in mature firms is closely related to the concept of exploration for new knowledge and business opportunities, the next section focuses on this aspect.

3.3.2. Opportunity identification

The sources of opportunities

Shane (2003) defines an entrepreneurial opportunity 'as a situation in which a person can create a new means-ends framework for recombining resources that the entrepreneur believes will yield a profit'. In this regard, an entrepreneurial opportunity is distinct from other approaches by the fact that the creation of a new means-end framework is required rather than just the optimization within an old framework. While Shane discusses the creation of opportunities, other literature has discussed the presence of business opportunities mainly from *Schumpeterian* and *Kirznerian* perspectives:

- The *Schumpeterian* perspective argues that new information such as changes in technologies or new political regulations is the cause of new opportunities to emerge
- The *Kirznerian* perspective argues that opportunities exist even in the absence of new information entailing that people form different beliefs about the efficient use of resources.

In the Schumpeterian perspective, it is assumed that new information is used by entrepreneurs to recombine resources in more valuable ways. Thus, changes in technology, political forces, regulations, or social trends represent new information which the entrepreneur perceives and subsequently exploits by creating more efficient resourced combinations (Schumpeter 1934). This perspective rests on the assumption that information is available to all market agents which only needs to be accessed and exploited. Thus, exploration for new knowledge and new business opportunities in this sense would entail the firm's search for new information in its external environment.

In contrast, Kirzner (1997) argues that opportunities even exist when there is no new information that would lead to a new environmental setting. This is because people form individual beliefs in response to the information they obtain. Consequently, market actors make mistakes in their decisions, creating shortages and surpluses of resources. Thus, "entrepreneurial opportunities exist because of information asymmetries through which different actors develop different beliefs regarding the relative value of resources as well as the potential future value of those resources following their transformation from inputs to outputs" (Ireland, Hitt et al. 2003). Furthermore, prior knowledge plays an important role in which opportunities can be identified. As Venkataraman (1997) points out, each person's idiosyncratic prior knowledge creates a 'knowledge corridor' that allows him/her to recognize certain opportunities, but not others. Prior knowledge, whether developed from work experience, education, or other means, influences the entrepreneur's ability to comprehend, extrapolate, interpret, and apply new information in ways that those lacking that prior knowledge cannot replicate (Shane 2000). In particular, Shane considers three major dimensions of prior knowledge to be important to the process of entrepreneurial discovery: prior knowledge of markets, prior knowledge of ways to serve markets, and prior knowledge of customer problems. As a consequence of this perspective, firms would have to focus their exploration efforts on new markets and the markets' architecture. In addition, successful exploration would require some prior knowledge about the direction and object of exploratory efforts.

Despite the differences between both perspective, researchers have begun to argue that both perspectives actually co-exist simultaneously in an economy (Shane and Venkataraman 2000), and that entrepreneurial firms consider both perspectives. In fact, the Schumpeterian perspective requires that new knowledge be created, while the Kirznerian perspective assumes that differences in the perception of existing knowledge is sufficient for entrepreneurial activities to take place (Lumpkin and Dess 1996; Sidhu, Volberda et al. 2004).

The discovery of opportunities
Shane (2003) has argued that the discovery of new and valuable knowledge and new business opportunities requires the formulation of a new means-ends framework. Thus, new information must not only be gathered but also interpreted and put into a meaningful context within the business environment. Therefore, the process of opportunity discovery is cognitive and cannot be a collective act, implying that individuals and not groups or firms discover entrepreneurial opportunities. Shane argues that people discover opportunities that others do not identify for two reasons: first, they have better access to information about the existence of the opportunity, and second, they are better able than others to recognize opportunities, provided the same amount of information about it, because they have superior cognitive abilities.

Within the opportunity discovery process, literature has made distinctions between the access to information and the recognition of opportunities. Thus, it is argued that information must first be accessed and gained, before new opportunities based on that new information can actually be recognized. As for information access, literature has provided empirical evidence that the exploration and access to valuable knowledge is facilitated by prior life experience, social network structures, and the active search of information.

- *Prior life experience.* In particular, people's job function influence the likelihood if valuable knowledge and opportunities will be discovered or not. For example, people working in a research and development unit are more likely to have access to information about opportunities than historians (Shane 2003). Also, the higher the variation in life experience of an individual, the more likely he has better access to information that helps discover opportunities. This is because people with a wide range of employment or living experience have access to more diverse information (Casson 1995). In fact, research has shown that people with a greater variation in employment experience are more likely to discover entrepreneurial opportunities.
- *Social network structures.* The value of networks for gaining information is widely known. Thus, the structure of a person's social network influences what information they receive, and in what quality, quantity, and speed this information is received (Shane 2003). In fact, it is likely that much of the information for discovering opportunities is spread across a variety of people, including information about potential markets, employees, or ways to organize. Furthermore, the more diverse the social ties within a person's network are, the more likely it is that information is obtained which is heterogeneous, which also contributes to opportunity discovery.
- *Information search.* The active exploration of new information also promises to enhance the likelihood to discover entrepreneurial opportunities. It is argued that people are more likely to find information that is useful through deliberate search than through random behavior. Furthermore, it is argued that the deliberate search in areas where others presumably do not look increases the chance to discover valuable information.

Alongside the importance of information access to the discovery of opportunities, researchers have argued that people are more likely to discover opportunities if they have a better ability than others to recognize opportunities (Shane 2003). The exploration for new knowledge is based on the same concept, as valuable knowledge can only be put in a viable context by the individual's personal abilities. On the one hand, these abilities are facilitated by prior knowledge about for example markets, technologies, and production processes. On the other hand, cognitive abilities of the individual allow to formulate new means-ends frameworks in response to information that they receive. Furthermore, research has discussed how personal traits of the individual such as an entrepreneurial alertness (McGrath and MacMillan 2000) or an entrepreneurial orientation (Lumpkin and Dess 1996; Sidhu, Volberda et al. 2004) contribute to the recognition of entrepreneurial opportunities. These aspects are illustrated in the following subsections.

Prior knowledge
Prior knowledge contributes to opportunity identification, because existing knowledge can be interpreted in new and different ways, and because existing knowledge can be used to solve new problems (Shane 2000). As a consequence, knowledge about an unmet market need or technical problems triggers the individual's ability to formulate solutions (Venkataraman 1997). In particular, research has investigated the impact of prior knowledge about markets and prior knowledge about how to serve markets (Shane 2003). In the first case, demand conditions are easier recognized, while in the latter case, it might be easier for an individual to determine what services or products could be introduced, how these products or services could be distributed best, or what new materials could work best.

Cognitive abilities
Differences in cognitive abilities have been discussed by researchers to lead to differences in the ability to recognize opportunities (Kirzner 1997). It has been argued that some people are better than others at understanding causal links, categorizing information, seeing relationships and patterns in information, understanding how processes work, and evaluating information accurately (Gaglio and Katz 2001). This is because different people interpret information differently and thus perceive different values of the same piece of information. McGrath and MacMillan (2000) consider this to be a personal trait and call this an 'entrepreneurial mindset', which is a specific way of thinking about business that focuses and captures the benefits of uncertainty. In general, organizations that are successful at dealing with uncertainty in their business environment tend to outperform those unable to do so. From an individual perspective, an entrepreneurially minded can identify and exploit new opportunities because he

possesses cognitive abilities that enable him to perceive a different meaning to ambiguous situations (Alvarez and Barney 2002). People with such a mindset are argued to search for opportunities in uncertain business environments and subsequently determine the capabilities needed to successfully exploit them (McGrath and MacMillan 2000; Covin and Slevin 2002).

Shane (2003) discusses how intelligence, perceptive ability, creativity, and 'not seeing risks' also influences the ability to recognize opportunities. Thus, differences in intellectual capacity is argued to increase opportunity identification because of an increased processing power pertaining to gathering and processing information. Differences in perceptive abilities allow one individual to perceive different outcomes of certain activities than other individuals, which implies a better foresight capacity about future outcomes. As has been illustrated earlier, creativity is a central part of the opportunity identification process, as new means-ends frameworks must be created, which always involves the individual's creativity. Finally, people tend to have different perceptions with respect to an opportunity, that is, while some might link more risk to a certain piece of information, others might link it to an opportunity.

Entrepreneurial alertness
Entrepreneurial alertness is closely related to the concept of an entrepreneurial mindset and is also based to some extent on the individual's cognitive abilities. It describes the ability to identify when new goods or services become feasible or when existing goods or services suddenly become valuable to consumers (Ireland, Hitt et al. 2003). It has been described as 'flashes of superior insight' (Alvarez and Barney 2002) and is considered to stimulate the development of an entrepreneurial culture and entrepreneurial leadership in a firm. Furthermore, the search for new markets is influenced by the entrepreneur's insights which can be applied through new goods or services in that market. McGrath and MacMillan (2000) characterize people with entrepreneurial alertness to passionately pursue entrepreneurial opportunities, and to constantly seek new ways to profit from disruptions to the current way of business. They pursue the most promising opportunities in a very disciplined manner and maintain an inventory of entrepreneurial opportunities and pursue them only when they can be matched with competitive advantage. Furthermore, they are considered to have a strong focus on execution, meaning that they carefully analyze opportunities but move quickly to develop competitive advantages to exploit them rather than overanalyzing individual opportunities. Finally, people with an entrepreneurial alertness are

considered to have a commitment to engage everyone in identifying and pursuing entrepreneurial opportunities.

Entrepreneurial alertness is supported when firms engage in an overall entrepreneurial process within the firm. This entails activities such as setting goals, establishing an opportunity register, and determining the timing strategy required to exploit an opportunity (Ireland, Hitt et al. 2003). As the exploitation of entrepreneurial opportunities is considered a wealth-creating activity, pursued goals are more than incremental in nature.

In summary, exploring new knowledge and new business opportunities strongly depends on the individual's prior experience and knowledge, and on its ability to search for information and make sense of that information. New business opportunities are created when a new means-ends framework is created, which, in addition, involves the individual's creativity.

3.3.3. Facilitating opportunity identification

Although the exploration of valuable new knowledge and identification of opportunities strongly depends on the individual, literature has also discussed how conditions pertaining to a supportive firm environment may facilitate the identification of opportunities. Many scholars argue that for entrepreneurship within a firm to be successful, it must be strategically managed (McGrath and MacMillan 2000; Meyer and Heppard 2000). Both entrepreneurship and strategic management are concerned with the question how firms adapt to environmental changes and how they exploit opportunities created by uncertainties and discontinuities (Hitt, Ireland et al. 2001). Ireland, Hitt et al. (2003) argue that firms that are able to identify opportunities but incapable of exploiting them do not realize their potential wealth creation. By the same token, firms with current competitive advantages but without new opportunities identified to pursue and exploit with these advantages may diminish the rate of wealth creation or even reduce previously created wealth.

Managing entrepreneurship

Literature has argued that firms will gain increased competitive advantage and create wealth if they are able to exploit entrepreneurial opportunities. However, such opportunities can only be exploited when the necessary resources are available, which requires the strategic management of these resources. Grant (1991) defines resources as inputs into the production process, which include for example financial capital, skills of individual employees, patens, brand names, and other items. He argues, however, that only few resources are productive by themselves. Instead, firms need the capacity to coordinate bundles of resources to make them productive, which Grant (1991) defines to constitute a firm's capabilities. Therefore, resources are the source of a firm's capabilities, but capabilities are the main source for competitive advantage. Strategic management of resources entails bundling resources "to form capabilities and leverage those capabilities flowing from their financial, human, and social capital to simultaneously enact " (Ireland, Hitt et al. 2003). As resources are usually scarce, strategic management of the firm needs to make choices among competing alternatives about how to spend existing resources (Stopford 2001).

Ireland, Hitt et al. (2003) consider three resources to be critical for allowing for exploratory activities in the firm and thus for allowing entrepreneurship to happen, namely *financial*, *human*, and *social capital*.

- *Financial capital* provides the means to develop and implement strategies. Firms with strong financial resources are more likely and able to engage in exploration activities and identify and exploit entrepreneurial opportunities.
- *Human capital* has been recognized to be one of the most strategic assets a firm possesses (Hitt, Biermant et al. 2001). As such, human capital is considered the knowledge of skills of the firm's entire workforce (Covin and Slevin 2002). Dess, Ireland et al. (2003) have defined it as the "individual capabilities, knowledge, skill, and experience of the company's employees and managers, as they are relevant to the task at hand, as well as the capacity to add to this reservoir of knowledge, skills, and experience through individual learning." As most of the firm's knowledge and skills reside in its human capital, both explicit and tacit knowledge are essential fundamentals for strategic entrepreneurship. While explicit knowledge can be easily codified and transferred across firm boundaries, tacit knowledge, in particular, is considered to be a strategic asset and represents much of what the firm knows with respect to how to compete in the industry, to innovate, and to identify and exploit entrepreneurial opportunities. McGrath and MacMillan (2000) argue that tacit knowledge is particularly important in the identification of entrepreneurial opportunities and in evaluating their potential exploitation. Tacit knowledge is typically embedded in applications, can only be acquired through practice (Grant 1996), and is

increasingly considered as a determinant of different firm performance (Ireland, Hitt et al. 2001).

- *Social capital* entails the set of relationships between individuals and between individuals and organizations that facilitate action between them (Ireland, Hitt et al. 2003). Because of these internal and external relationships, social capital helps to gain access to resources and to absorb new knowledge (Dess, Ireland et al. 2003). These relationships can facilitate exploratory activities.

Establishing an entrepreneurial culture

Organizational culture is a system of shared values and beliefs that shape the firm's structural arrangements and its member's actions to produce behavioral norms (Schein 1991). As a guide, culture influences the cognitive framework that affects how organizational members perceive issues as well as how they view their competitive landscape (Ireland, Hitt et al. 2003). Here, "ideas and creativity are expected, risk taking is encouraged, failure is tolerated, learning is promoted, product, process, and administrative innovations are championed, and continuous change is viewed as a conveyor of opportunities" (Ireland, Hitt et al. 2003). Therefore, an entrepreneurial culture fosters and encourages the continuous search for entrepreneurial opportunities (McGrath and MacMillan 2000). Such a culture develops in organizations where the leaders employ an entrepreneurial mindset.

An organizational culture conducive to the exploration of new knowledge and to the facilitation of entrepreneurship is argued to be supported by people who show 'entrepreneurial leadership'. Entrepreneurial leadership as a specific type of leadership is defined as the ability to influence others to manage resources strategically (Covin and Slevin 2002). Covin and Slevin have argued that entrepreneurial leadership is characterized by six imperatives. First, such leaders foster an entrepreneurial capability where the importance of strategic entrepreneurship is emphasized and where there is a commitment to develop human capital in order to facilitate individual's efforts to develop entrepreneurial capabilities such as agility, creativity, and skills to manage resources strategically (Alvarez and Barney 2002). Second, entrepreneurial leaders openly communicate with others and describe the benefits that they can extract from innovative threat to their own business and by that not only reduce perceived threat but also emphasize potential advantages. Third, entrepreneurial leaders are able to convince people of the value of opportunities and how exploiting them contributes to the firm's overall goals as well as to individual's goals. Fourth, they are said to systematically an frequently question the dominant logic of doing business. They evaluate permanently if the firm is still successfully positioned to be able to identify entrepreneurial opportunities. Fifth, entrepreneurial leaders examine the viability of the markets in which the firm competes, the company's purpose, and how the firm defines success. Changing answers to these aspects influences what the firm identifies as opportunities and how it manages its resources to exploit these opportunities. Sixth and last, effective leaders try to establish a culture in which resources are managed strategically as to support a continued identification and exploitation of entrepreneurial opportunities.

In summary, the development of innovation is the central theme in literature on entrepreneurship. However, most research has focused on the premises and impact of entrepreneurial behavior, while ignoring that opportunities must be identified first before they can be subsequently exploited. Only recently have researchers started to investigate the process of opportunity identification. In this regard, exploration for new knowledge shares many common patterns with opportunity identification, as both are about the search and identification of valuable new knowledge for subsequent innovation.

Exploration and opportunity identification in established firms largely depend on the framework the firms provide for exploration to happen in the first place. Furthermore, research has pointed out that individual aspects such as cognitive abilities and an entrepreneurial alertness play critical roles in if and how new knowledge and new business opportunities can be searched and identified. In summary, literature on entrepreneurship provides valuable insights to the question how firms actually engage in exploration.

3.4. Reference framework

This research aims at contributing to literature and theory on exploration and, more specifically, on the management of exploration. As such, it tries to answer the question how firms actually engage in exploration, which includes the consideration of strategic, organizational, and operational aspects. In order to arrive at sound findings and hypotheses as well as to facilitate and guide data collection and analysis, a reference framework is constructed (Miles and Hubermann 2005). The framework facilitates and guides the process of data collection and facilitates a greater understanding and broader evaluation of the relevant aspects within the case studies. Therefore, the framework is based on insights from a broad literature review and thus builds the foundation for data collection.

The reference framework is based on literature pertaining to insights from several management fields such as strategic management, entrepreneurship, and technological innovation (see figure 5). A particular focus is laid on insights on exploration from the entrepreneurship literature, as this stream rests on the identification of new knowledge and new business opportunities for innovation as its central underlying theme. Literature on entrepreneurship implies that exploration for new knowledge and new business opportunities must be strategically managed, that is, management must establish an environment conducive to exploratory activities. Also, literature on entrepreneurship and product innovation implies that creativity plays a fundamental role in the identification of new opportunities and the development of new ideas.

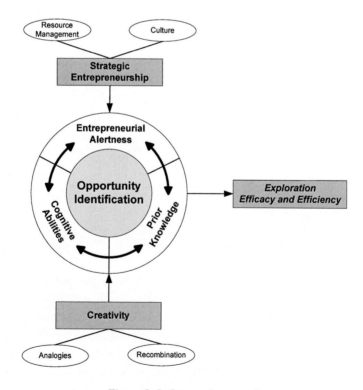

Figure 5: Reference framework

3.4 Reference framework

Furthermore, the reference framework represents a practical model for how firms engage in exploration, and for what is otherwise treated quite abstractly in – in particular – organizational learning literature. Using this model as a guideline for the subsequent case study investigation yields the potential to lead to concrete results, and therefore to moderate and extend notions from organizational learning literature.

The reference framework serves as the basis for conducting the empirical investigation in the case firms and serves as a guideline to ensure that all topics relevant for exploration within the firm are covered. As the investigation process of this type of research is fairly iterative, this research framework is adapted according to new insights which stem from the analysis of the case data. Thus, the framework is subject to re-adaptation with the goal to increasingly better reflect reality, and ultimately to serve as a sound base for the development of hypotheses to extend existing theory and literature on exploration.

4. Empirical findings on exploration for innovation

In this chapter, four case studies pertaining to the exploration in globally leading manufacturing firms are presented. The case studies are the result of the empirical, in-depth investigation phase of this research. The presentation of the cases are based on the theoretical framework depicted in the previous chapter and provides an empirical basis for the subsequent cross-case analysis and theory building. Furthermore, these insights provide the empirical basis for the derivation of managerial recommendations.

4.1. Case selection

The case studies presented in this chapter are all manufacturing companies and global leaders in their respective markets. Despite they act in different industries and serve different customers, they have proactive and distinct exploration activities in common. All companies strive to strengthen their good market positions by employing a market pioneer strategy and by introducing new technologies and innovations first in the market. However, foremost is their characteristic of taking active exploration measures, and the identified similarities in this approach suggest a relationship between this exploration practice and overall innovation effectiveness as can be seen from their historic extraordinary performance. Furthermore, as described in chapter 1.3.2, the cases with the highest identified learning potential were selected due to their successful approach to conducting exploration (Eisenhardt 1989).

Furthermore, the case firms are comparable in size, revenues, R&D structure, and innovation culture. They have realized that future competitiveness can only be secured through better exploration approaches, which is also reflected in their respective innovation strategies. As a consequence of focusing on established and successful firms, and as is typical for such firms, they have established processes and structures pertaining to exploration activities which might not be the case with small and medium sized enterprises. Most importantly, the case firms have been selected due to their long-lasting leading global positions by constantly introducing successful innovations to the market. Thus, their specific approach to exploration has enabled and strengthened them to reach a globally leading position. Table 6 lists the firms which are subsequently presented in in-depth case studies.

Company Name	No. of Employees	Revenues (in billion USD)	Headquarter	Core Business
Ciba	13.000	6.5	Basel, Switzerland	Development and manufacturing of specialty chemicals for a large variety of industries
W.L. Gore & Associates	8.000	2.4	Newark/DE, USA	Development and provision of fluorploymer-products for a large variety of applications and industries
Hilti	20.000	4.2	Schaan, Principality of Liechtenstein	Development and manufacturing of high-end construction tools
Bühler	6.900	1.8	Uzwil, Switzerland	Development and manufacturing of food, chemistry, and die casting processing plants

Table 6: Sample companies for in-depth case studies

The in-depth case studies are structured and presented according to the reference framework developed in chapter 3.4. However, to provide consistent and comparable case studies and to avoid repetition, the case study descriptions follow the firm-specific characteristics instead of rigidly following the framework. To provide a guiding structure, the case presentations follow the following structure:

- *Company profile.* In this section, a brief introduction to the firm's background, environment, key figures, products, markets, and organizational structure is provided to illustrate the firm's framework for exploration activities.
- *R&D organization and strategic management of resources.* This section describes the R&D organization and how exploration is anchored within this structure.
- *Exploration: strategy and procedure.* This section illustrates how the firm engages in exploration from a strategic point of view. Also, the concrete procedural approach is described

- *Entrepreneurial mindset and culture.* In this section, the firm's exploration behavior and the firm culture in which this is embedded are described.
- *Summary.* This last section summarizes the findings by briefly illustrating the most distinct factors for the firm's successful exploration activities.

4.2. Case 1: Ciba AG

4.2.1. Company profile

Ciba is a Swiss based company whose roots date back to 1758 when J.R. Geigy Ltd, the oldest chemicals company in Basel, began trading chemicals and dyes. More than 200 years later in 1971, Geigy merged with *Ciba*, a chemicals company founded in 1884 and located in Basel as well, to form *Ciba*-Geigy Ltd. In 1996 *Ciba*-Geigy and Sandoz merged to form Novartis, one of the world's largest life sciences groups. In 1997, as a result of this merger, the specialty chemicals division was spun out to form *Ciba* Specialty Chemicals and ultimately adopted the name *Ciba* Inc. in 2007. Over the course of more than 250 years, *Ciba* has developed countless innovations and made contributions to the entire chemical industry. Some of the most famous innovations include solvent and weather resistant pigments for paint and plastics, plastic additives to make plastics workable, triclosan antimicrobials or light stabilizer systems for automotive coatings. Today, *Ciba* is a global leader in the development and manufacturing of specialty chemicals which add to the performance, protection, color and strength of plastics, paper, automobiles, buildings, home and personal care products, among other. With more than 13.000 people worldwide, *Ciba* generated revenues of 6.5 billion Swiss Francs in 2007.

4.2.2. R&D organization and resources

R&D organization

Ciba is structured in the three divisions 'Plastic Additives', 'Coating Effects', and 'Water & Paper Treatment'. These divisions research and develop chemical compounds that lead to diverse effects which are used in numerous applications and industries. *Ciba's* research and development competencies are deployed in six 'centers of excellence' which are focused on strengthening and expanding *Ciba's* existing core competencies. Their task is to support today's business based on applications, market impact and science, and to constantly develop new competencies with respect to these aspects. Thus, these centers focus on research for new products and technologies by which new opportunities for existing and new customers are created. Then, several application centers are dedicated to turning these competencies into marketable applications in customer products. These centers typically have an industry focus and thus focus on developing new applications for existing and new products. Then, three 'process innovation & development' centers are devoted to improving production and development processes. Their target is to secure short and long term cost competitiveness of core products or product families through continuous process innovation and improvements. These centers are also in charge of supporting new product development and of driving radical new process innovation. Eventually, *Ciba* maintains regional technical centers to support products near major customer bases.

Accompanying this organizational structure is corporate R&D which supports all research and development activities in the entire group as a central function. In parallel to corporate R&D, *Ciba* maintains a unit named New Growth Platform (NGP) which directly reports to the chief innovation officer (CIO). NGP serves as an incubator for highly explorative projects whose task is to engage in activities that are outside of *Ciba's* core business and thus outside of day-to-day business. Thus, NGP explores new knowledge in industries and technologies where *Ciba* has not operated previously, and which are aimed at generating an overall benefit for the entire *Ciba* group. NGP is further divided in three 'emerging competency' centers, which focus on the topic of security, electronic & energy, and biosciences. In these centers, NGP is engaged in developing the next generation of technological competencies and in identifying and cultivating the right technologies to sustain *Ciba's* future development. NGP projects typically last several years before they are either integrated into existing business lines, continued in entirely new organizations, or even stopped. Furthermore, NGP maintains the front end of the group's innovation process, i.e. the very early phase of any innovation activities where typically technologies are scouted and ideas developed.

Because of its strategic importance, NGP is supervised and reviewed by the management board. For example, exploratory projects initiated in the business lines which are beyond the business line's industry scope are taken out of their project portfolio and integrated in the NGP portfolio. The management board then decides during the course of the development of all exploration projects which projects are further pursued and which ones are stopped.

R&D resources
In 2007, *Ciba* invested 262 million Swiss Francs in research and development activities, which equals 4% of annual sales. On average, 25% of the R&D budget is spent on the pursuit of exploration activities bundled in the New Growth Platform. 20%

of overall R&D people work full-time in NGP. In addition to that, about ten people from the marketing organization are employed by NGP full-time as well to integrate the market perspective of exploration. Finally, NGP draws on additional resources from the single business lines. Through this approach, *Ciba* ensures that no ideas are overlooked which might emerge anywhere in the group. In parallel, if deemed reasonable, the divisions and business lines spend money for exploratory activities as well. If exploratory activities origin in the business line and the unit is able to finance these activities by itself and if these activities furthermore conform with line strategy, these projects stay in the business line. However, NGP takes over exploration activities which might have been initiated in e.g. a business line when the line unit does not have the sufficient resources to pursue the project itself.

4.2.3. Exploration strategy and procedure

In 2007, *Ciba* started an innovation initiative to spur even more profitable growth. This initiative targets several strategically important areas of the entire group and is therefore supervised by the management board. Main targets of the initiative included

- Acceleration of growth and value generation through market and customer focused innovation
- Leveraging of existing competencies and platforms across the organization
- Definition of strategic direction and development of new technology platforms
- Simplification of the organization and simplification of interfaces between entities
- Over-proportional focus of resources on high potential and high rewarding areas

This innovation initiative accompanies *Ciba's* general exploration approach and to this end serves as a guideline for exploration activities. *Ciba's* overall innovation strategy is initiated both bottom-up and top-down and is aligned according to its markets. Thus, from bottom-up, the markets define the innovation strategy for the single business lines. The single business line strategies are then merged to form the *Ciba* group innovation strategy. Furthermore, *Ciba* defines itself as specialty chemicals company, implying that the majority of turnover is generated by small amounts rather than bulk or mass products. Therefore, and more top-down, corporate strategy entails some general fields of action within which the business lines operate. Corporate strategy is furthermore built around *Ciba's* six core competencies, which aim at serving *Ciba's* core business (see figure 6).

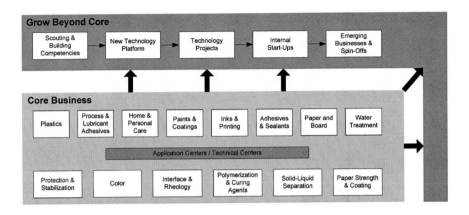

Figure 6: Core and beyond core business at Ciba

Strategic parameters distinguish the activities in NGP from the rest of the group's R&D efforts. While it is the explicit divisional and business line strategy to engage in innovation activities within the group's core business and core strategy, NGP operates almost exclusively outside of this scope. Thus, the business lines have defined which industries they compete in and which competencies are required to meet the demands of those industries. As a consequence, business lines mainly engage in exploitation activities while exploration activities are limited in its scope to their respective industries (e.g. exploring additional functionalities of color pigments), and which aim at developing new products. Furthermore, the business lines typically do not have the necessary resources to engage in activities with highly uncertain outcome. Thus, while business lines mainly engage in exploitative activities to develop product innovations, NGP engages in exploration to develop new business opportunities.

Exploration strategy

In general, *Ciba* categorizes its innovations projects according to their intended goal in maintain, grow, expand, and build projects (see figure 7).

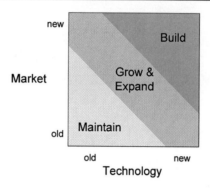

Figure 7: Innovation project categorization at Ciba

Maintaining existing business entails new effects for the current franchise area with a typically high cannibalization of existing product sales. Growing existing business means that new effects are developed for current franchise areas with low cannibalization of existing product sales, while expanding existing business also includes new effects for existing markets but with no cannibalization of existing product sales but rather generating only new sales. Building new business and technologies, then, entails the development of new effects for new franchise areas, where only new sales are generated and existing business is not cannibalized. Based on this categorization, NGP exclusively engages in build projects which are typically of purely explorative nature, and which go beyond today's current business. For this reason, build projects are internally called 'growing beyond the core' which implies entering or developing new business areas. While maintain, grow, and expand projects are based on the calculation of a net present value, internal rate of return, and the anticipated payback time, build projects follow a rating scheme where the cumulated net sales after five years are projected, and where project costs and the link of existing capabilities to future business are the most important assessment criteria.

Ciba's exploration strategy pertaining to build projects is based on existing competencies and the firm-wide core strategy pertaining to innovation. Thus, *Ciba* explores both technologies and markets which are adjacent to its current core business with respect to technology platforms and markets. *Ciba* defines its core based on the main businesses in which they are involved, that is, business such as e.g. plastics, process and lubricant adhesives, home and personal care, coatings, ink and printing etc (see figure 6). Furthermore, *Ciba* tries to match its current core competencies with demands in emerging markets, which is also considered an adjacent move. For example, *Ciba* regularly selects interesting trends stemming from hypes which occur in society and analyzes how its existing competencies can be adapted to these emerging trends. If the adaptation to these trends promises to lead to competitive advantage, and if *Ciba* does not own the technological competencies to complete this move by itself, the missing competencies are acquired by e.g. acquisitions.

Exploration activities at *Ciba* are furthermore constrained by the corporate vision, which entails that all activities must meet fundamental demands such as being ethically and morally defensible, and that they must fit into the overall corporate strategy. Corporate vision entails envisioning what *Ciba's* core business could potentially look like in a period of ten or more years from now. The guiding question to defining this future core is what *Ciba* is able to do as an organization and to ponder on what is possibly achievable based on today's competencies. This is in contrast to *Ciba's* former approach, where the guiding question was how *Ciba* can best adapt to existing structures and boundaries. Based on the new vision about what is possible, *Ciba* then explores into adjacencies from its current core competencies 'Protection & Stabilization', 'Color', 'Interface & Rheology', 'Polymerization & Curing Agents', 'Solid-Liquid Separation', and 'Paper Strength & Coating'. *Ciba* aims at developing the core by repositioning the firm according to its corporate vision with respect to the development of respective technological and other competencies. Through this procedure, *Ciba* expands the core subsequently into new technology and market arenas. The corporate vision is translated into more specific strategies and finally broken down by segments and business lines in yearly reviews to define strategic fields for the next years.

Through this approach of adjacent moves, *Ciba* tries to limit the risk of failure by avoiding the exploration of new areas which are too far away from today's core business. Past experience has shown that the chances of success decrease exponentially the farther away *Ciba* has explored from the core, which is why *Ciba* has adapted its current exploration strategy.

As a consequence of this exploration strategy, technologies which might have business potential but which require *Ciba* to build entirely new competencies are not internally pursued. In this case, the acquisition of firms with the respective competencies is a common approach to fill the competence gap.

Conducting exploration at Ciba

In general, the *Ciba* exploration process is initiated by scouting activities which are based on two initiatives, one originating directly in NGP, the other originating in the division or in the business line. In a first step, scouting is performed within the boundaries imposed by *Ciba's* exploration strategy which entails the scanning of promising technologies and overall trends in areas where *Ciba* has no prior experience. These scouting activities are typically conducted by people from marketing and R&D.

Technologies scouted in this process are put in the context of *Ciba's* current business, which entails the assessment if there might be potential for application in any of *Ciba's* business lines. In contrast, exploratory activities conducted outside of NGP (i.e. in the divisions and business lines) are typically closer to the core business and try to answer more specific questions. Scouting activities within NGP are conducted both by 'NGP-employed' people and by people who come from a business line and who then are employed by NGP (between 30-50% of their capacity) exclusively for this task. Thus, NGP draws on resources from the business line case by case. This procedure is usually supported by the head of a business line who needs to agree on 'lending out' one of his people when a specific question is pursued which could also help advance his own business line. In addition to exploratory activities at NGP, exploration with the aim of product innovation is conducted within the daily work of all R&D people, who explore new ideas and technologies within their 'free' time which amounts to about 10% of their regular working time. In general, scouting is a very individual process where *Ciba* has not set up any specific procedural rules.

Ideas resulting from the scouting process regarding a new technology are further worked out into a comprehensive concept which entails scenarios or a business model pertaining to a new technology platform for example. This concept furthermore considers forecasts regarding market potential, technological feasibility, and thus also the question whether *Ciba* is able to pursue the project with its existing competencies or if there is a competence gap that still would need to be overcome. Within the frame of such works and as is the case with any concept that is worked out, *Ciba* obtains deep knowledge and insights about specific technologies or applications. This serves subsequently as the basis for assessing whether the technology bears potential benefits for *Ciba*. The concept is subsequently presented to a committee consisting of top management executives including the chief innovation officer and several board members which evaluates the projects on a regular basis and decides if the exploration direction fits the corporate strategy. If the committee deems the results interesting or if a business potential has been outlined, the idea further undergoes a filter process where the most promising ideas are selected. After the concept has been worked out and approved by the committee, the idea is presented to all business lines and research centers which assess the idea potential for their own business. If deemed interesting by one or several business lines or the research centers, they start investing own resources and continue to finance the further development of the technology. Typically, there is always at least one business line interested in the new technology platform, indicating that most ideas are further pursued and not stopped. The business line and/or NGP then start a technology development project, where the new technology is further detailed, and where any remaining uncertainties are resolved. This phase usually lasts several years, and when the new technology is mature enough to sustain itself, internal start-ups are built which try to commercialize the new technology (see figure 8).

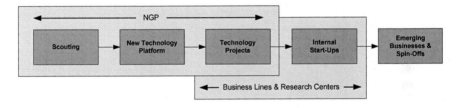

Figure 8: Ciba's exploration process

Usually, there is a high conformity between the result of initial exploratory activities and later technology development as *Ciba* tries to ensure already during the scouting process that the potential technology has some link to *Ciba's* existing business. However, in case that no business line is interested in a specific idea or technology, NGP can still take over the idea and further pursue it as NGP has the necessary budget to pursue uncertain ideas. NGP has implemented a process which ensures the efficient evaluation and filtering of all exploration activities. In the case that a business line is interested in the new technology, that technology is integrated in the current business of the line or its division. If the technology cannot be integrated in an existing business, an entirely new business might be created which is internally maintained or spun out. However, reintegration or spin-outs are only done when the new business is self-sustaining, that is, when it is clear that it can maintain its own business and generate respective revenues.

4.2.4. Environmental aspects conducive to exploration

Because of its complex organizational structure, it is difficult for *Ciba* to maintain identical approaches and the same innovation culture across all organizational levels and units. In general, however, *Ciba* is open-minded to failure and 'dry runs', as such activities are considered helpful for learning new insights. This is particularly true for the New Growth Platform, where it is explicitly accepted that exploratory activities might have no commercially viable outcome. For example, scouting activities are not forced to undergo revisions and are only subject for a first proper assessment when a concept has been developed which is presented to the committee.

As the New Growth Platform is set up by executive management to help *Ciba* explore new technologies, and as 25% of the overall R&D budget are granted to this unit, there is strong upper management support for these kind of activities. Furthermore, the CIO continuously communicates NGP activities and the overall need for innovation in every part of the entire organization. Although every segment is autonomous regarding how much time is invested into exploratory activities, there are business lines that encourage their people to engage in exploratory activities. Thus, there are business lines which grant their people up to 15-25% of working time on the pursuit of exploration activities.

People who engage in exploratory scouting activities within NGP are typically open-minded and are characterized by their ability and willingness to connect to other people in the organization and to building an internal network. Furthermore, these people are characterized by having a will to advance things and to leave a footprint in the group. *Ciba* actively tries to involve such people in exploration activities to ensure a maximum outcome and communication about any new technologies within the entire group. These people are of all ages and typically have a marketing or research background.

4.2.5. Summary

Ciba's exploration efforts are concentrated on the New Growth Platform which is implemented as a separate organizational unit and which directly reports to the Chief Innovation Officer who is a member of the management board. This structure ensures full dedication to exploration activities pertaining to the identification and development of entirely new business opportunities. This engagement is also reflected in *Ciba's* spending policy, where 25% of the group's entire R&D budget is invested in NGP and thus in exploration activities. This engagement also is a signal to the entire organization which emphasizes *Ciba's* efforts to develop exploratory innovations.

NGP's exploration activities are conducted within the boundaries of the corporate vision but beyond the limits of its core business strategy. While corporate vision is also about the firm's future positioning, the core business strategy entails guidelines for the improvement of existing technologies in its current industries. Furthermore, NGP's exploration strategy is based on adjacent moves around its core business. After an opportunity has been identified, subsequent activities follow a process entailing regular assessment gates until the project is eventually turned over to an existing business line or spun out to external parties. Overall, key findings from *Ciba's* exploration approach are as follows:

- NGP's exploration activities are conducted within the boundaries of the corporate vision but beyond the limits of its core business strategy
- Separation of exploratory and exploitative innovation activities
- Distinct top management support for exploration activities which is demonstrated by strong investments
- Exploration is conducted based on existing core competencies, ensuring a link between new knowledge and current business

4.3. Case 2: W. L. Gore & Associates

4.3.1. Company profile

W.L. Gore & Associates (*Gore*) is a multinational and privately held company founded 1958 in Newark/Delaware in the United States of America by Wilbert (Bill) Gore and his wife Genevieve. Bill *Gore*, a former DuPont employee, pursued his conviction of the untapped potential of the polytetrafluorethylen (PTFE) technology, and developed the MULTI-TET™ insulated wires and cables as their first product. In 1966, *Gore* rented a facility for its wire and cable production in Ottobrunn near Munich in Germany. The same year *Gore* supplied cables for the NASA Surveyor mission, which marks the first U.S. effort to land a vehicle softly on the moon. One year later, in 1967, *Gore* began to operate large plants in Flagstaff/Arizona and near Edinburgh/Scotland. The success story of GORE-TEX® started in 1969 when Bob Gore, the son of Bill Gore, in a moment of frustration quickly stretched PTFE and discovered the unique and versatile characteristic of the expanded PTFE (ePTFE). In 1976, the first textile with GORE-TEX® technology was sold. In 1996, *Gore* passed the 1 billion USD mark in annual sales, achieved by a large and versatile product palette. Today, *Gore* has more than 8.000 employees (called associates) and is present in more than 45 plants, development and sales locations worldwide. Today, *Gore* is the global product leader for PTFE-based products.

Gore is organized in four divisions - fabrics, electronics, medical, and industrial products. Within these four divisions, a wide range of products are developed. Each division is again subdivided in distinct business units. For example, the fabrics division, which is the second largest with respect to turnover and which is best known for its brand GORE-TEX®, is further organized in 'Consumer Oriented Fabrics' (COF) and 'Technical Oriented Fabrics' (TOF). Both are again divided in sub-business units. In COF, products are developed for e.g. outdoor, running & cycling, hunting, motorsports, citywear, snowsports, footwear and accessories. In TOF, products for the military, police, general workwear, fire fighting, medical fabrics, and solid waste treatment are developed.

4.3.2. R&D organization and resources

R&D organization

Gore's research and development is conducted in all four divisions as well as on corporate level. Each of the four divisions maintains its own research and development which contributes directly to their respective product platforms. Furthermore, each division maintains a new business development (NBD) unit whose goal is to identify so called 'white spots' and develop entirely new business opportunities. This structure is also resembled on corporate level, where *Gore* maintains a corporate R&D and a corporate NBD unit. As with all corporate units at *Gore*, their task is to both pursue activities which are beneficial for all divisions as well as supporting single divisions with special tasks such as exploring specific technologies important for them. While corporate R&D is rather technology push oriented based on *Gore's* core technology, NBD is more market pull oriented and provides information about future markets, that is, providing directions what capabilities and solutions should be investigated by R&D. However, NBD is not entirely a unit with permanent staff but recruits itself from R&D people who are pursuing new technologies and who basically return to the function they originally came from once the exploration project is finished. As a consequence, the entire *Gore* organization is very flexible and unlimited regarding the exchange of people within different organizational units.

The mission of the divisional NBD is the identification and development of new business opportunities aimed at significantly increasing turnover. On corporate level, however, the NBD mission is to explore entirely new markets which are not in the scope of the divisional NBD activities. Most people in corporate NBD have a background from one of the divisions. In contrast to NBD, R&D is more technically oriented and engages in exploration activities mainly regarding new technologies and the development of new technology platforms. NBD is more focused on new business opportunities and thus engages mainly in exploration activities which aim at entering new markets and gaining entirely new customers. However, NBD and R&D closely collaborate, and insights from exploration activities from either of the units can spur respective development activities in the other unit. For example, if R&D is developing a new technology platform, NBD would try to explore respective markets and applications where this new technology could be applied. Vice versa, if NBD explores new markets or applications and identifies new business opportunities, R&D would develop respective technologies that would meet the requirements. Therefore, there is frequent exchange between and interaction of NBD and R&D units within *Gore*.

Furthermore, *Gore* maintains a centrally organized group called 'Core Technology Group' with main hubs in the USA, Germany, Japan, and some smaller hubs around the globe. This group is in charge of understanding, processing, and implementing fluor polymer (primarily ePTFE today) technology into *Gore* products. Thus, this group, to which about 1.000 people worldwide are associated, is not only in charge of looking into mere product innovation, but also how this affects for example manufacturing technologies. As such, it is a distinct group in charge of nurturing and advancing *Gore's* core technologies, and it closely collaborates with corporate R&D and NBD.

The pursuit of new technologies and markets is divided between the different organizational levels. The business units engage mainly in product development for current markets based on current technologies and occasionally engage in the investigation of related technologies. The divisional R&D has an explicit technology focus and therefore engages in research on related and new technologies, which, however, have a strong relationship to the current market and products. The divisional NBD unit tries to identify 'white spots', that is new markets and application opportunities for current and related technologies and thus to multiply existing competencies to new markets. These activities typically have a longer time horizon and are 'more bold', and they reach out for markets where *Gore* has no current presence. In parallel, its task is to explore adjacencies and related markets as well as technologies which not necessarily have to have a direct product relationship. Thus, the degree to which *Gore* engages in exploration depends on the single organizational units. Figure 9 exemplary illustrates this for a division at *Gore*.

4.3 Case 2: W. L. Gore & Associates

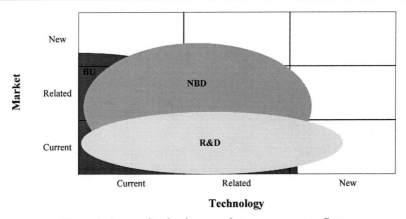

Figure 9: Scope of technology-market engagement at Gore

Gore does not officially maintain organizational charts but staffs projects according to content and commitment. For example, if the context of a new innovation project touches the responsibilities or competencies of several business units or market segments, the corresponding project team is staffed from all involved units. To *Gore*, this organizational flexibility has been a key success factor in the past.

R&D resources
Gore's R&D budget is built based on a bottom-up approach based on the forecasts from all business units. The accumulation of all forecasts thus resemble the yearly R&D budget. About 50% thereof is invested in 'fixed assets' such as overhead while the remainder is invested in research and development activities. Thus, the R&D budget covers all activities from product improvement, activities that aim at identifying and developing new business opportunities, and activities that aim at identifying and developing entirely new products and technologies. *Gore* does not maintain specific strategies how much resources will be spent on specific types of activities. Although all projects are managed in a project portfolio, which distinguishes between the type of project (e.g. maintaining the core business, differentiating from core business and NBD/new technologies), there are no guidelines with respect to how the R&D budget is distributed. However, *Gore* aims at allocating resources evenly across the above mentioned project types. Reflecting the open and flexible organizational structure of *Gore*, both exploration and exploitation projects can be initiated at any time and based on opportunities, and granting resources for either of the activities is a flexible process.

Thus, whenever an opportunity opens, *Gore* decides if additional budget is granted. Typically, additional budget is required for purchasing external market research results, for collaborative work with externals, or for experimental material and new assets for detailed experiments.

4.3.3. Exploration: strategy and procedure

Gore's corporate and innovation strategy is driven by its vision to be the globally leading supplier of high-quality innovative products and services. That is, *Gore* aspires to be the global product leader in terms of quality and uniqueness. Unless this criterion is met, *Gore* typically does not even consider marketing and selling the product. Therefore, PTFE is only applied in products that are very distinct from competitor products. For example, the fabrics division core competency for its products is to deliver durable comfortable protection. However, as *Gore* has four divisions, divisional core competencies might differ from each other. In general, *Gore* will not engage in projects where they believe that a distinct competitive position can't be achieved, or where competitors could easily imitate them. Furthermore, the development of new technologies typically takes place internally focusing on *Gore's* core technology, although *Gore* also cooperates with external partners prior to any physical development activities. This company-wide aspiration is the starting point for any innovation activities at *Gore*.

Gore's core technology strategy considers fluoro polymers, expanded PTFE and composites of ePTFE as a fundamental material set and as part of the overall innovation strategy. *Gore* does strategic investments in its core technology, and is quite cautious about developing outside of core technology. In addition to the core technology, *Gore* has what is called 'strategic enabling technologies' and 'enabling technologies'. Strategic enabling technologies are IP protected and differ from enabling technologies in their uniqueness and IP protection. Strategic enabling technologies have distinctiveness themselves or are combined with core technology to form new products, and thus are technologies at which *Gore* has a very deep expertise and which help accomplish sustainability of *Gore* products in the market. Therefore, although *Gore* is built on its core technology PTFE, there is no narrowly defined core business. Rather, *Gore* has managed to employ its competencies and know-how into a wide range of product markets around PTFE. As a consequence, innovation and entrepreneurial activities happen in a broad scope and can take place virtually in any industry.

Each division tends to have a different core competency but there is a common innovation strategy, which is about product leadership and products fit for the end use. Furthermore, *Gore* engages in active project portfolio management which is based on strategic directives. For example, divisions which pursue a growth strategy target double digit growth rates which consequently is implemented by a sufficiently high amount of exploratory projects. In other cases, where divisions are expected to grow only by a single digit, divisional strategy prescribes that the respective project portfolio emphasizes more exploitative and less exploratory projects.

Exploration strategy
The exploration and innovation strategy is conducted around the current core business. Every business unit has its own core, which is defined by a set of central characteristics such as current products, current customer segments, current sales channels or current geographies (see figure 10).

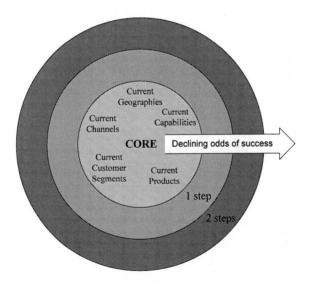

Figure 10: Gore's exploration strategy

Because of this multilayer definition of the core business, exploration is conducted anywhere within the core, that is, exploration does not only include R&D aspects but also exploring new markets, sales channels, geographies, or general capabilities. While the business units typically engage in innovation activities which are initiated by rather concrete customer problems and which improve the core business, exploration is typically conducted by NBD in all related segments that are adjacent to the current core. Thus, NBD either explores new application possibilities for a new technology or new business opportunities for which respective technologies still have to be developed. Thus, in the case of exploration, an existing technological solution is often looking for a problem, and it is then the task of NBD to explore new domains where this solution could be applied. As a consequence of strengthening and extending the core business, the core can be fundamentally redefined over time as sequenced moves as a result of successful exploration.

Gore's tactic is to explore a controlled amount of dimensions adjacent to the core at a time. *Gore* knows from experience that exploration into more than three dimensions at the same time is typically quite risky, and that trying to develop respective innovations which correspond to all dimensions concurrently lead to declining odds of success. Therefore, business units typically engage in activities which consider one step from the core, while NBD exploration activities often involve three to four steps simultaneously. Once several steps are considered at the same time, *Gore* is very cautious and often sets up a task force which exclusively engages in further exploring these dimensions.

Conducting exploration at Gore
Exploration activities at *Gore* are pursued both in the R&D of the business units as well as in NBD, however with different emphasis either on technologies or on new business opportunities, and furthermore are conducted more or less systematically depending on where and by whom exploration is conducted. For example, certain divisions and consumer product units tend to be rather systematic with respect to exploration, while NBD groups operate much more intuitively. This is due to the fact that NBD looks much more at big trends which have an effect that go beyond *Gore's* immediate products. Thus, people at NBD look at how certain things evolve and translate this into how this might affect *Gore* products, and they are dealing with aspects for which often no markets exist. Exploration activities conducted in R&D tend to be more technology driven while NBD exploration activities typically focus on consumer and market driven aspects.

Exploration at *Gore* is manifold depending again on where and by whom it is conducted. Throughout the entire organization, technology, consumer and market scanning is conducted which often happens in collaboration with external service providers. Furthermore, scenarios are regularly built together with consultants, futurists, and other people to see where the world is headed and how future trends are emerging. For example, the NBD unit of the fabrics division regularly conducts creativity sessions which they call 'arenas'. One arena in the past has been the investigation of potential application of the PTFE membrane in the medical sector. NBD then engaged in a three week field observation of the medical sector, including visits to hospitals and observing and talking to medical doctors about their work. By this, many opportunities were identified and much knowledge accumulated.

Furthermore, NBD and R&D regularly conduct brainstorming sessions which are conducted within the space opened by 'vectors' that are provided by R&D. These vectors entail strategic directives based on *Gore's* technological core competencies, and which are important for the entire division or which are broken down to the specific needs for e.g. a particular market segment. On the divisional level of fabrics, for example, such directives include terms like 'comfort'. In the specific case of the market segment 'gloves' as a sub-unit of the fabrics division, terms are for example 'tactility', 'flexibility', or 'warmth', which represent fundamental core competencies of *Gore* within this market segment. Typical investigations within the scope of brainstorming sessions of a medical arena pertain to exploring what needs to be protected from what and why. These vectors or search terms are then used by the associates to search for new opportunities to come up with ideas in the brainstorming sessions. As a consequence, every associate has a different approach how to cope with these terms and how they ultimately come up with new ideas.

Based on insights and ideas resulting from both activities, *Gore* typically develops a first basic concept, which often takes the form of a one-page summary sheet with all relevant information about the idea. An implicit condition for developing this page is that the idea meets the general criteria provided by *Gore's* overall innovation strategy. Thus, a precondition for the idea is that it must be based on, strengthens or extends *Gore's* existing competencies. Apart from a basic description of the idea, the concept must correspond to three main *Gore* questions, which is called the 'Real-Win-Worth':

- Is it real: Is the market real? Is the product real?
- Can we win: Can the product be competitive? Can our company be competitive?
- Is it worth doing: Will the product be profitable at an acceptable risk? Does launching the product make strategic sense?

The 'Real-Win-Worth' concept contains a set of sub-questions which need to be answered by every idea concept to be further considered. For *Gore*, an honest answer to this often provides already very good insights about the true potential of the exploratory idea. The exploration of an idea and the working out of a concept typically happens within the dabble time that is granted to each associate. These concepts are then presented to different people and boards in the organization, where the idea finder basically seeks support for his concept. Therefore, a 'board' which has the power to provide resources can consist of a single person such as a technology leader, but typically also involves several business unit leaders. If the concept sounds convincing to a board, it is further investigated and detailed. This entails in case of a new technology specific research on the technology, and concrete tests and experiments. After this exploratory phase, the idea is located in a risk matrix to illustrate how far away the idea is from current technology and markets (see figure 11). The risk matrix' y-axis is a continuum from 'same as current offering' to 'new to the company' pertaining to the technology or product at question. The x-axis resembles a continuum from 'same as present' to 'new to the company' pertaining to the intended market. The evaluation where a specific project is located is determined by the same board where the concept has initially been presented. The team members evaluate individually by using a set of five to six questions pertaining to the product/technology and the intended market. Afterwards, all individual assessments are discussed in the team and a consensus is reached.

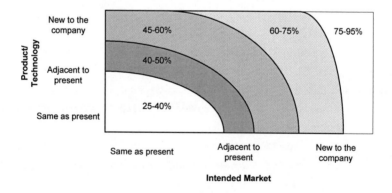

Figure 11: Project risk matrix at Gore

After the initial exploration phase of gaining entirely new knowledge, a project is formed which transforms into the standard product innovation process which is organized as a stage-gate process. From this point on, the project needs to meet time and quality criteria against which it is constantly assessed.

4.3.4. Environmental aspects conducive to exploration

Gore has a culture based on four principles. First, fairness is a principle that is shown towards everyone, both internally and externally. Second, all *Gore* associates have the freedom to accumulate new knowledge, skills, and responsibilities, and are encouraged to ask other associates to help them achieve their goals. Even more, *Gore's* philosophy is that each and every employee has the freedom to pursue those kind of activities which he is good at and enjoys working with, instead of seeking the weakness in oneself or other associates and rather use the strengths of the individual. Therefore, everyone will allow, help, and encourage other associates to grow in knowledge, skill, scope of responsibility, and range of activities. Consequently, every associate is in charge of attracting fellow employees to his idea and ultimately form a group where all members contribute to a common goal. Thus, *Gore* is organized around opportunities and people work by projects and contents rather than in rigid organizational structures. Third, commitment towards tasks and fellow associates is valued very high. Finally, every associate is asked to consult with other associates before taking activities that could hurt the image of the entire company. Thus, the *Gore* culture paired with a low hierarchical structure that knows no bosses encourages people to pursue what they are best at and also excel at this.

Probably the most important aspect that enables an environment very conducive to internal entrepreneurship and innovation is *Gore's* organizational structure. First, *Gore's* structure with sites which are not supposed to grow larger than 200 to 250 people ensures near and direct communication. This furthermore enables the integration of all sorts of people (e.g. marketing and R&D people) within the entire organization without having to fear that specific competencies are not included because of too large and complex organizational structures, as is often the case with larger and decentralized companies. Second, *Gore* does not have any management layers or traditional organizational charts, only few people have titles, and no one really has a boss in the conventional sense. As a consequence, everyone is free to talk with anyone else, as there are no lines of command. However, individuals who have been repeatedly asked by other associates to serve as chief are called 'leader', which is an award that shows the individual's capacity to lead people and do things well. Thus, associates will make their own commitments and hold on to them.

As a consequence, project teams at *Gore* are small and self-operating. For example, the initiator of an idea is required to recruit his own team across the entire organization, and tries to bundle the competencies required. If asked, each associate has the choice to join or to decline dependent on workload and skills or if other commitments are more urging. If the associate believes that the project is both interesting (i.e. matches with the skills and strengths) and could help advance business (i.e. that the project is of strategic importance in the portfolio discussion), he tries to join the project. Therefore, associates are responsible to their teams rather than to single bosses, which represents one of *Gore's* core principals of a high-trust, low-fear organization. Finally, the 'waterline principle' entails that employees are encouraged to take risks, and do not face detrimental consequences if a project should fail. *Gore* only expects his employees to apply common sense when it comes to the question what might be harmful to the entire company. This also entails the allowance for mistakes and to learn from mistakes. *Gore* also nourishes internal and external relationships that are based on mutual trust, honesty, and respect, and which happen in a personal and direct communication rather than other communication media.

Gore encourages its employees to think innovatively, to explore new things, and empowers entrepreneurial activities. This is undermined by granting its employees dabble time of about 10% of the regular work time to be spent on interesting ideas and projects outside of daily business. Although established in the entire R&D organization, it is the specific goal of the new business development units to maintain and nourish a network that supports employees who are interested in business and product innovation.

Although it is free to anybody within *Gore* to engage in exploratory activities, people who tend to engage more often are naturally the ones who have an entrepreneurial spirit. As a consequence, they migrate more often to units whose task is to identify white spots, such as NBD. For example, when the global NBD group was initiated, people came together who had a downright intrinsic motivation to make something happen, even though they had no idea about where the journey would take them. Instead, all they had was their core technology, and they started exploring into all kinds of directions to see where this technology could be applied.

4.3.5. Summary

Exploration at *Gore* happens across all organizational units and levels and thus within a hybrid organizational structure. While R&D rather engages in exploration activities pertaining to researching and developing new technology platforms, NBD engages in exploration activities which aim at identifying and learning new markets and business opportunities. As a consequence of close collaboration between R&D and NBD across all levels and divisions, there is intense communication between all associates who also frequently change their original unit for the time they pursue a specific project. Furthermore, *Gore* appropriates this structure by being able to pull together the most capable people for exploratory activities from the entire organization, who typically show an intrinsic motivation to innovation and who are willing to engage in projects with uncertain outcome.

Exploration is carried out within the defining boundaries of strategy and existing competencies. Based on *Gore's* existing core competencies, which are clearly defined, NBD and R&D engage in exploration activities adjacent to their core business. In doing this, *Gore* takes one step at a time, that is, they entirely explore one dimension (e.g. a new sales channel) before they engage in a second exploratory activity such as identifying new markets which are created through that new sales channel. Apart from a clear exploration strategy, *Gore's* concrete procedure is more or less systematic depending on where in the organization exploration is conducted, and ultimately even by who it is conducted. Typical procedures range from initial brainstorming sessions within a previously defined 'arena' to learning new knowledge within these arenas by observing e.g. an industry up front for several weeks. Key findings for *Gore's* exploration approach include the following aspects:

- Hybrid structure of exploration activities allows and encourages everybody to engage in exploration activities
- Exploration is carried out within the defined limits of strategy and existing competencies and are always adjacent to the existing core business
- *Gore's* lattice structure of organization is very conducive to exploration as it encourages everybody to become involved in such activities

4.4. Case 3: Hilti AG

4.4.1. Company profile

Founded in 1941, the worldwide *Hilti* Group evolved from a small family company to a global leader in products for professional customers in the construction and building maintenance industry. Today, *Hilti* is the global leader in the development, manufacturing, and marketing of high-end quality products and services for professional customers. With about 20.000 people in 2008 in more than 120 countries worldwide, *Hilti* had total revenues of 4.2 billion Swiss Francs. Two thirds work directly for the customers in sales organizations, engineering and customer service, while about 2.000 people are located in the corporate headquarters in Schaan in the Principality of Liechtenstein. *Hilti* maintains production plants and research and development centers in Europe and Asia. Since its founding, *Hilti* has been tremendously influenced by the values, tradition, and spirit of its founder, Martin Hilti. Still today, corporate management maintains the principles and core beliefs such as keeping the company in a constant state of evolution where people come first, product quality is of utmost importance, and products are exclusively sold via direct sales in direct interaction with the customer. As a result of *Hilti's* direct selling approach, most of its employees work in the market organization (i.e., sales, consulting, or service) and are in direct contact with customers. *Hilti* was one of the first companies worldwide to receive an ISO 9001 certificate in 1996. *Hilti* is still controlled by the *Hilti* family, and since 2000, all registered shares of the *Hilti* corporation are held by the Martin Hilti Family Trust (nonvoting participation certificates have been listed on the stock exchange since 1986).

Hilti's product range covers drilling and demolition, direct fastening, diamond and anchoring systems, fire stop and foam systems, installation, positioning and screw fastening systems, and cutting and sanding systems. *Hilti* also provides service offerings including devices with corresponding tools and consumables, consulting, application instruction and training, technical documentation, and customer-oriented service after sales. They serve worldwide professional customers in the construction industry, including construction experts, electricians, fitters of sanitary facilities and elevators, metal workers, carpenters, general entrepreneurs, and civil construction authorities. Products, services, sales, and consulting are all typically tailored to different customer segments, from independent construction workers to building (sub)contractors. This differentiation leads to a very broad assortment of premium-quality and premium-priced products.

Martin Hilti believed that "market share is more important than factories", which has ever since been a driving factor for understanding and responding to customer needs. Recognizing that customers value knowledgeable advice on how to best use *Hilti* tools, the company established a direct sales force rather than using distributors or dealers. Almost without exception, *Hilti* products offer the highest quality and highest price in each product category in which the firm competes. These price premiums have been justified by not only the enhanced durability and productivity of *Hilti* equipment but also by the reliability of *Hilti* services.

4.4.2. R&D organization and resources

R&D organization

In general, *Hilti's* research and development activities are divided between technology development on the corporate level, pre-development on the business area level, and product development on the business unit level. As a consequence of this - at the extreme - separation of technology development from product development, both activities are conducted by people with differing competencies. In the business units, there rather are engineers who have design competencies, while there are more basic scientists on the corporate level.

Hilti's technological competencies are bundled in 'Corporate Research & Technology' (CR&T) and in the two business areas 'Electric Tools & Accessories' and 'Fastening & Protection'. CR&T is responsible for corporate innovation management which includes the definition of corporate innovation processes, global product portfolio management, and corporate technology. In addition, CR&T supports business area and business unit R&D with respect to researching and pre-developing new product technologies. CR&T is furthermore divided in several competence groups which are responsible for research on fundamental disciplines such as mechanics, physics, material science, and manufacturing technologies.

Each business area consists of several business units and maintains its own marketing and development department. In the business areas, pre-development activities are carried out while product development is carried out in the business units. However, for historical reasons, there are also business units which engage in basic research as they have very specific technological know-how. For example, research activities in the chemical area (e.g. for chemical anchors) are conducted in the business area 'Fastening & Protection', and research in measuring technology is conducted in the business unit 'Measuring' (which among other involves basic laser technology) which is part of the business area Electric Tools & Accessories. *Hilti's* organization is illustrated in figure 12.

Figure 12: Hilti organization

In addition to the R&D organization, *Hilti* maintains its own marketing organizations at its disposal in approximately 50 countries that produce 90 percent of the turnover. In another 70 countries, *Hilti* is represented by sales partners and agents. *Hilti* headquarters aspire to realize close cooperation among the market organizations to combine experiences and facilitate the extensive exchange of know-how.

R&D resources
Hilti deploys resources for product innovation activities based on its R&D budget. The R&D budget, which is more or less constant over years, is calculated as a percentage of sales turnover and amounts to approximately 4%. Pertaining to the organizational distribution of the R&D budget, about 10% is distributed to CR&T while the remainder is equally distributed to the two business areas. The business areas are autonomous in how the money is spent, and they redistribute the budget according to their own strategic portfolio management and needs, that is, what is needed for pre-development and development activities. Of the CR&T budget, 20% is spent on short-term topics which have a time horizon of up to one to two years, 50% on mid-term with a range of

about three to five years, and 30% on long-term topics with a horizon of about eight to ten years. All activities at CR&T are conducted in close collaboration with the business areas and business units which CR&T supports with research and pre-development activities. As a consequence, the largest portion of CR&T's R&D budget is invested in the research and development of technologies that help advance all business areas. Long-term topics with an exploratory character are mostly conducted exclusively in CR&T. As long-range exploratory activities at *Hilti* are typically highly risky, investments in such activities are internally considered as 'play money'.

4.4.3. Exploration: strategy and procedure

Hilti's corporate strategy 'Champion 3 C' (C3C) focuses on
- helping customers to reach their goals by responding to their requirements and through this to increase market reach and market share
- competencies pertaining to excellence in core activities such as innovation, quality, direct customer relationships, and effective marketing, and
- concentration on products and markets where *Hilti* can achieve a leadership position.

The C3C strategy is embedded in *Hilti's* overall business model which targets to achieve sustainable and profitable growth (see figure 13). *Hilti's* core belief is that people who live by the firm purpose and values ultimately contribute to reaching the company's goals. With a distinct focus on customers, existing competencies, and a concentration on product leadership, *Hilti* is able to meet customer needs by offering a high-quality product portfolio supported by efficient supply chain management and after market service. As a consequence of this, not only innovative products are developed, but everybody involved in the process (i.e. customers, employees, partners, as well as the external socio-economic environment) are satisfied. While *Hilti* has specific growth and profit targets, the *Hilti* business model is the vehicle through which these targets shall be achieved.

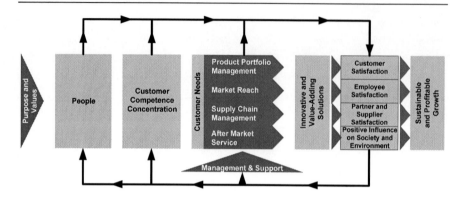

Figure 13: Hilti business model

Hilti targets to be the global market leader in products and applications for professional customers in the construction and building maintenance industry. Thus, for all product systems, *Hilti* analyzes how the product (a drilling machine for example) is actually used by customers and what further applications are involved in the use and the purpose of the product. For example, *Hilti* not only offers the highest quality product to set an anchorage point, but they also provide the highest quality solutions necessary in the application chain such as e.g. chemical anchors. In summary, *Hilti* targets to cover the entire chain which leads to the successful outcome of the application 'setting an anchorage point'. Thus, any product innovations must not only meet customer needs but also clearly add value by providing additional customer benefits. As a consequence of this strategy, *Hilti* does not become active in new domains or engage in the development of products where first assessments indicate that they are unlikely to achieve leading competence in product quality and service.

Exploration strategy

Hilti's overall exploration activities are conducted within corporate innovation fields which are derived based on specific growth targets and based on *Hilti's* brand image. Although *Hilti* is mainly a product and manufacturing technology-intense company, these innovation fields concern both organizational and technological exploration activities. Corporate innovation fields are then further delineated to the level of the business areas and business units, where more differentiated innovation fields are derived. The heads of pre-development of the business areas are foremost responsible for breaking down and implementing corporate strategy and processes to fit the competencies of the business area and to meet corporate goals. All innovation fields are communicated and made transparent within the R&D and marketing organizations and are fairly stable over time.

On an abstract level throughout the entire organization, central questions that drive *Hilti's* technology exploration activities are: "how can we accomplish best what the customer wants to accomplish", "how can we make a hole", or "what other energy principles exist". Each business area and its business units have several approaches to answering these questions depending on their specific competence in the application. As a consequence, different organizational units have differing innovation fields in which exploratory activities are conducted. From a strategic point of view, a strong focus on customer goals is very crucial to *Hilti's* exploration activities. This enables *Hilti* not only to think in industry or product categories but puts an emphasis on outcomes with respect to customer benefits. As a consequence, *Hilti* permanently explores how specific outcomes (such as e.g. 'making a hole') can be achieved best regardless any underlying technologies. After this abstraction, they are better able to engage in exploring analogous technologies in, for example, entirely different domains. As another consequence, CR&T also investigates which other or new technologies could potentially substitute existing ones, even if existing technologies might be jeopardized.

Conducting exploration at Hilti
Technology exploration is a continuous activity which runs parallel to all other research and development activities in the firm. However, from a process perspective, technology exploration is a part of the front-end of the early innovation phase. In general, *Hilti's* innovation process can be split into three categories: research process, technology and platform development, and product development. These three categories are then followed by the product care and phase-out process. The overall innovation procedure - called the 'Time To Money' (TTM) process - reflects a stage-gate process with five gates (see figure 14). At every gate, the company makes a 'go' or 'no-go' decision. The TTM process is planned in detail for every project, and significant efforts are undertaken to meet the planned deadlines.

Exploration happens within the front-end of the TTM innovation process which includes Gate 1 (opportunity, providing detailed information about whether the subject investigated represents a business opportunity) and Gate 2 (task, providing the product concept and a project plan). The stage between the gates is referred to as the 'product definition' phase. Gate 2 is followed by the 'concept' phase, which leads to Gate 3 (targets, providing key results in the form of a product solution and marketing concept). At Gate 3, the product board, which consists of a committee of executive managers, reviews the final product concept and makes the final 'go' project decision. After the subsequent 'design' phase, Gate 4 requires a tested system, from which the 'launch preparation' phase initiates. Gate 5 aims to initiate the market introduction. During the product life-cycle, product-care activities are conducted which are eventually followed by the product phase-out.

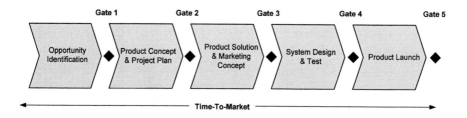

Figure 14: Time-To-Market process at Hilti

Exploration at CR&T includes the investigation of a technology that is new to *Hilti* and – when promising – a subsequent development of a functional prototype (as opposed to a product prototype) to assess the feasibility of the technology. Exploratory activities in their first stage include mere desk-research such as technology monitoring and scanning of new technologies or the investigation of a specific type of hardware. If first results from such exploratory activities seem promising, an official research project with a corresponding budget is started. For the activities in these stages, *Hilti* typically deploys dedicated people to investigate new technologies and new business opportunities which *Hilti* has not particularly focused on before.

As a continuous activity, *Hilti* conducts both monitoring and scanning of technological developments in the immediate environment across all organizational levels. On corporate level, CR&T monitors technologies within corporate innovation fields. However, technology monitoring is not necessarily driven by a specific application but serves to learn about new technologies and their application potential for *Hilti*. CR&T regularly conducts application and value chain analyses, so-called 'trade studies', where new applications or new industries are analyzed regarding players in the market, market structures, used technologies, location of value creation, and where first market potential estimations are made. These studies are conducted detached from current problems or challenges with the goal to learn about the application, its underlying structure, and the context in which it is applied. This exploration effort leads to in-depth insights into the respective application from different angles, and they serve as a basis for deciding if the application will be further analyzed and thus if subsequent innovation activities such as developing a prototype are conducted. Apart from trade studies, *Hilti* regularly questions its core technologies and explores fundamental and overarching applications important in the construction industry. For this, up to three people for three or more months investigate in entirely different industries if and where *Hilti's* core technologies are an issue, disregarding the fact if it is related to construction or not.

In contrast to CR&T, the business units conduct monitoring activities from a rather problem driven perspective, that is, they monitor emerging technologies which are immediately relevant for the specific application that the business unit deals with. On the business area and thus pre-development level, exploration often entails identifying industries where similar technologies are applied. This happens by associating similar industries and applications to the own field of application and is strongly driven by the ideas and creativity of the individual. These industries are then the base for further monitoring and exploratory projects and are started to find out about new technologies in more detail.

In parallel, *Hilti* also maintains a sophisticated market intelligence, where customer needs, market trends and new application potential are consistently monitored and fed back to the corporate headquarters. Although technology monitoring and scanning is conducted across all hierarchical levels, differences between the levels concern the time horizon of monitored technologies, i.e. CR&T has a time horizon up to ten years and more, while the business areas pursue topics with a horizon up to five years, and the business units rather focus on time horizons up to one to three years. Also, as a general and continuous activity, *Hilti* conducts scenario analyses to see where and how future construction applications evolve, and what technological solutions might meet these future demands. Another approach for exploring new knowledge is employing external partners to conduct studies pertaining to a specific question and investigating what technologies could possibly replace current ones.

4.4.4. Environmental aspects conducive to exploration

One of the main pillars on which the overall success of *Hilti* in the past decades has rested is its unique corporate culture. In the past, *Hilti* has undergone several culture definition processes, which sustainably strengthen the values already imposed by Martin Hilti when the firm was founded, and by which all employees and management abide. These values include

- to foster a company climate in which every team-member is able to grow,
- the development of mutually beneficial partner and supplier relationships,
- a high responsibility towards society and environment, and
- securing freedom of action by achieving sustainable and profitable growth.

Furthermore, the *Hilti* culture is characterized by a constant reconsideration of the status quo and responsibility and unreserved commitment towards fellow employees and tasks. The constant questioning of established procedures is born out of the belief that the organization must commit to life-long learning to excel as well as that it must challenge itself constantly and not attribute their performance reasons to external circumstances. In 2002, *Hilti* has set up a corporate culture program named "Our Culture Journey", which is a regularly held corporate-wide event to achieve a shared philosophy of the values of the firm among all employees. Explicit goals entail raising the employees' awareness of freedom of choice, their ability to actively shape their environments, and their personal responsibilities for their actions. Within this culture the first event, which was held at an offsite place, all 15.000 (in year 2002) *Hilti* employees participated in several days lasting sessions including top management consisting of the board of directors and the executive board. In general, *Hilti's* executive board and the board of directors are heavily involved in all activities within the firm. For example, top management members participate in culture-building events just like every other employee, and they spend a considerable amount of time per year in the marketplace with sales people and talking directly to customers. For them, pursuing egalitarian values is very important and this attitude is lived and communicated throughout the organization.

Because of the strong belief in the corporate values and in the culture, *Hilti* is very open-minded to new and 'strange' ideas that are outside of today's strategy. New ideas are constantly introduced to colleagues and management across all R&D levels, and the entire organization welcomes ideas and technologies that have not been invented in-house.

4.4.5. Summary

Exploration at *Hilti* is a quite strategic process which is conducted mainly at the corporate level and to the extent of pre-development activities at the business area level. All exploration activities are conducted within the limits of corporate strategy and corporate innovation fields. These overarching innovation fields are broken down by each business area and business unit and consequently contain guidelines where to explore with respect to the respective application.

In summary, *Hilti's* main approaches pertaining to exploration include:
- Clear corporate strategy with emphasis on sustainable and profitable growth by means of innovation, operational excellence, and product leadership
- Separation of technology development from product development
- Exploration is driven by focusing on applications and outcomes rather than mere products
- Exploration is enhanced by conducting trade studies, scenario analyses, and intelligence methods with respect to new technologies and markets
- Dedicated support for exploration activities with corresponding budget and distinct failure tolerance
- Distinct culture throughout the entire organization which emphasizes the importance of innovation

4.5. Case 4: Bühler AG

4.5.1. Company profile

Headquartered in Uzwil in Switzerland, *Bühler* is the global market leader in food processing, chemical process engineering, and die casting. Since its foundation almost 150 years ago, *Bühler* has developed from a pure raw material processing company to a sophisticated technology and service company, which also entails consulting other companies in their processes. *Bühler* has built its first flour mills, pasta production lines, or brewing equipment more than 100 years ago, and still today the processing of food is *Bühler's* core business. During time, *Bühler's* process know-how has been successfully applied in nonfood applications as well. Today, *Bühler* is located in more than 140 countries and employs 6.900 people. In 2007, the entire group generated revenues of 1.77 billion Swiss Francs. Of this, the division 'Grain Processing' generated about 57%, thus representing the largest division with respect to turnover, followed by 'Engineered Products' with 30% and 'Die Casting' with 11%.

Bühler's competencies cover the field of mechanical and thermal process engineering, plant design and construction as well as respective services for the transformation of renewable and synthetic raw materials into high-quality functional products and substances. *Bühler* is leading in the know-how and competencies in the basic technologies of grinding, blending and mixing, bulk handling, thermal treatment, and shaping for processing cereal grains and foods, producing and upgrading engineering materials as well as die casting. These competencies are bundled in *Bühler's* three divisions 'Grain Processing', 'Engineered Products', and 'Die Casting', where each division further consists of several business units which are in charge of a specific product (see figure 15).

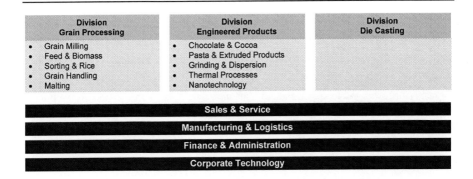

Figure 15: Bühler Organization

4.5.2. R&D organization and resources

R&D organization

Research and development is conducted both on the divisional and business unit level and is furthermore supported by a unit which is called Corporate Technology. In general, *Bühler* separates explorative activities from activities that aim at meeting current demands and improving existing product and technology platforms. Thus, Corporate Technology, which consists of about 35 employees, is responsible for investigating new and long-term technologies and new business opportunities, but also supports product development activities across all divisions. Corporate Technology is thus the pro-active driver of innovation and explores areas which do not fit in any of the existing business areas and which might have application potential for more than one business unit. Product development on the divisional and business unit level focuses exclusively on current core business and product and technology improvements in the existing business lines. Since *Bühler* does not engage in basic research activities, Corporate Technology mainly focuses on searching for new technologies which can be applied in the business context while the divisions and business units focus on the further development of existing products and technologies.

Corporate Technology also serves as an incubator by financing exploration projects pertaining to new technologies with uncertain outcome. For example, when *Bühler* was investigating the potential of nanotechnology for the company, a group was set up within Corporate Technology with the full-time task to investigate its potential for *Bühler*. If, as was the case with nanotechnology, the technology proves to be valuable for the entire company or for one of the divisions, a new business unit is spun out and transferred into one of the divisions. The point when a new business unit is spun out depends on the turnover that the new unit is independently making. Then, the project leader for exploring the new technology under the roof of Corporate Technology typically becomes the leader of the new business unit both as an incentive as well as to ensure that the new knowledge continues to be present in the new business unit. Furthermore, if a technology is replaced by another, *Bühler* resolves and reintegrates the business unit where the technology was maintained.

Furthermore, *Bühler* maintains new business development units on the divisional level. While R&D development activities focus on product and process innovations, NBD activities focus on leveraging existing competencies to new markets and on developing new business models around currently existing technologies and businesses. However, NBD activities are typically conducted in close collaboration with Corporate Technology. To increase NBD efficiency even more, *Bühler* also posts rewards for business model innovations which have been proposed by employees. However, technology and new business development typically are mutually dependent, so that both activities are conducted in close collaboration despite being managed by different organizational units. This allows *Bühler* to innovate technologies which have been 'in stock' for a while, leading to increased growth and overall turnover.

R&D resources
Bühler invests about 4% of its turnover in exploration, innovation and development activities. This overall R&D budget is invested to about one third in product improvements on the divisional and business unit level and to about two thirds in exploration and innovation activities. From Corporate Technology budget as part of the overall R&D budget, about 15% is spent for 'trouble-shooting' activities, 20% is invested in development projects in collaboration with the divisions, and the remainder of 65% is invested in exploration activities. Exploration is almost exclusively conducted on Corporate Technology as the divisions typically do not have the resources to engage in more than incremental product innovations.

The divisions are autonomous in the investment of their R&D budget, however, regular strategy meetings with Corporate Technology ensure that the divisional project portfolio is balanced with respect to the amount of mere product and technology improvement projects and product innovation projects.

4.5.3. Exploration: strategy and procedure

Apart from the general goal to be market leader for most of its products and technologies, *Bühler's* exploration strategy is strongly affected by the so called 'innovation guideline', which is a major component of the overall corporate strategy. This guideline entails goals about the time and frequency of introduction of new products in general as well as guidelines as to how corporate entrepreneurship is to be fostered. Based on this guideline, the divisional innovation strategies are derived by the single divisions and afterwards consolidated on corporate level and revised if necessary. Furthermore, *Bühler's* innovation guideline entails that 50% of turnover shall be generated by new products younger than 5 years, which, however, internally is considered a quite ambitious goal. *Bühler* defines something new if the product contains components that have not been previously applied and which lead to a marginal return of more than 40%. To reach this goal, *Bühler* has shifted its emphasis from product maintenance to basic research and the development of new products. *Bühler* tries to maintain a balanced innovation portfolio including applied research, product development, product maintenance, and developments in customer and business models. With respect to new business models, *Bühler* pursues a clear strategy entailing that new technical innovations increasingly more often need to be supported by the respective business models to successfully commercialize the innovation. Thus, innovation for *Bühler* means both technical and business model innovation. As a consequence, *Bühler* is constantly investigating how newly developed processes can be turned into market innovations.

Furthermore, *Bühler* is aware that future competitiveness is only sustainable by moving down along the value chain towards increased service and even consulting in addition to its current main business of 'selling hardware' (see figure 16). Although hardware will always be a main pillar of *Bühler* business, *Bühler* increasingly explores into new service opportunities as well as engages in consulting based on the long experience that *Bühler* has accumulated. As a consequence of this strategy, *Bühler* has both the mandate and direction for exploration activities.

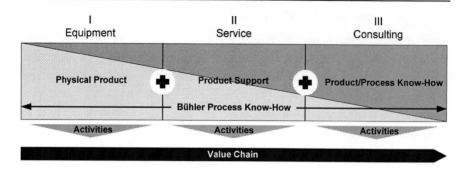

Figure 16: Core business and value chain at Bühler

Exploration strategy

Corporate Technology has made a strategic decision by defining search fields in which almost all exploration activities are subsequently conducted. Thus, based on the framework provided by the innovation guideline and corporate strategy, exploration is conducted within two general search fields which pertain to socio-economic trends and technical trends. These general trends are defined by Corporate Technology in a first step and are subsequently broken down to more specific search fields in collaboration with the R&D heads of the single business units. Trends and search fields are reviewed once per year and adjusted if necessary. *Bühler* has arrived at these search fields in a very analytic approach by considering the business environment that *Bühler* is competing in. The result from this analysis is the reinforced awareness that *Bühler* operates in the food industry, in food processing technology, is active in the coating business where it is important to look into matters of life style, or in the energy business where *Bühler* investigates the consumption of energy for the development of die cast components for the automotive industry, and the like. As a result of this, so called 'scouting fields' were derived in a second step which belong to the socio-economic and technical search fields which in turn include life science, material science, the digital world, and the natural environment.

Based on these scouting fields, Corporate Technology subsequently breaks the two main search areas down into even smaller and more concrete search fields which are subsequently scouted by the entire organization (see figure 17). For example, health and nutrition is an important scouting field under the socio-economic umbrella, while *Bühler* considers interesting anything connected with electronics under the technical umbrella. In fact, *Bühler* generates about 60-70% of all later innovation projects out of this initial exploratory search strategy within the search areas. As another consequence of this scouting activity, many topics pop up which are not directly connected to current *Bühler* business, and which would not have been identified otherwise. Thus, the range of technologies considered and explored is naturally very broad. Furthermore, a timeline ranging from today until 20 years in the future indicates where the respective topic or technology stands today, which serves as an indicator for *Bühler* with respect to the intensity of exploring the technology.

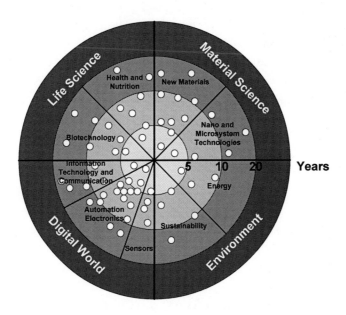

Figure 17: Search fields at Bühler

Conducting exploration at Bühler

The innovation strategy imposed by the innovation guideline serves as the basis for all innovation activities in the *Bühler* group. Thus, this guideline is a framework for both incremental product improvements as well as any exploratory search activities. All activities and projects are monitored in Corporate Technology, and the CTO is responsible for maintaining a sound balance between all type of projects. Thus, if short term projects or improvement projects outbalance long-term projects and exploration activities, the CTO reviews the single divisional strategies together with the R&D Heads of the single divisions to readjust strategy to pursue more exploration activities.

Exploration activities at *Bühler* are conducted pertaining to the identification of new technologies and pertaining to new business opportunities. With respect to new technologies, the search fields under the two main search areas are scouted on a regular basis by employees from Corporate Technology. For each scouting field, there is a dedicated person responsible for scouting that field and spreading any relevant information throughout the entire organization to other organizational units. *Bühler* engages about half a day per week in such type of exploratory search activities. Objects for scouting activities are technologies which range from product to process technologies and applications in which these technologies are incorporated. Insights resulting from these scouting activities are also summarized in a scouting newsletter which is distributed throughout the entire organization. Any potential business opportunity is usually directly evaluated by the scout regarding its fit with both divisional and corporate strategy. If an idea generated out of this exploratory search is deemed interesting and fits strategy, a feasibility study is initiated to explore the details of the idea. With respect to the identification of new business opportunities, the divisions explore if and how existing technologies have an even higher exploitation potential. As the divisions and business units are fairly close to the customer and the 'final products', they are constantly confronted with improving their offers to the customers. Thus, the divisions explore how new services or new technologies could improve current business. As a consequence, the divisions develop business models around specific technologies which are presented and assessed in Corporate Technology.

Exploratory ideas which are assessed interesting and potentially beneficial are pursued in a separate unit. Thus, when *Bühler* engages in exploration activities which look promising with respect to commercial impact, new organizational units within Corporate Technology are established to explore the new knowledge in even greater detail. Corporate Technology then serves as an incubator and supports the new unit in financial terms until the exploration project is cancelled or until the new unit can sustain itself and can be annexed to one of the existing divisions. In the case that a project is cancelled, this organizational unit can be flexibly and quickly dissolved.

A typical approach by *Bühler* to spur exploration apart from scouting activities is inviting external experts on specific areas to participate in workshops. As the two main search areas are broken down into specific search fields, *Bühler* regularly carries out workshop series on topics within these specific search fields. By this, *Bühler* learns new insights and understanding on that topic and absorbs knowledge which might be used for innovation activities later on. For example, *Bühler* invites external experts on how *Bühler* connects to the topic 'health' and what *Bühler* might be able to do within this context.

Exploration activities in Corporate Technology are conducted by both experienced engineers as well as young university graduates to ensure continuity and a link between existing competencies and products and future technologies and applications. For the same reason, Corporate Technology closely collaborates with people from business unit R&D by building joint teams. In contrast to development people on the divisional level, Corporate Technology people tend to have a broader experience background and tend to be more energetic and enthusiastic about novel ideas and projects. This includes better skills in communicating with people, advertising specific ideas more fiercely, and digging deeper into questions pertaining to innovation. Therefore, they have a much broader innovation focus and are better suited to conduct exploration activities. Furthermore, as it is the explicit task of Corporate Technology to engage in exploring new domains, Corporate Technology actively employs people with both broad and deep knowledge backgrounds for this type of activity as well as university graduates to integrate the latest knowledge in relevant technological areas and to embrace the entrepreneurial spirit that these graduates typically bring to *Bühler*. Many people in Corporate Technology are therefore new to the firm and typically stay there for about three to five years before moving into a divisional or business unit function.

4.5.4. Environmental aspects conducive to exploration

Ever since introducing the innovation guideline and defining general search areas and the search fields, *Bühler* has managed to implement a culture of innovation where bold ideas are fostered and failure is accepted. By this, the importance of innovation is spread throughout the entire organization, and exploratory search activities and innovative ideas are rewarded. *Bühler* lives the conviction that a true innovative edge requires the courage to accept risks, the ability to identify and seize new opportunities, the potential for differentiation, leadership, and an open mind toward change and growth. As a consequence, exploration activities are conducted across all levels of the organization, tapping virtually every learning and innovation source. This is furthermore facilitated by communicating the *Bühler* vision to all organizational levels with the target to involve every single employee in the task of innovation. As the vision is rather abstract and includes questions such as where *Bühler* will be in 20 years from now, imagination and creativity and therefore also exploration activities to answer that question are spurred.

Bühler has changed from developing nearly all technologies internally to absorbing and proactively integrating externally generated knowledge. As a consequence, *Bühler* is not only open-minded for externally generated knowledge, but pursues strong exposure to external developments of any kind, which facilitates exploration in terms of the source and quantity of new knowledge. This includes strategic partnerships with research institutes, universities, or the collaboration with lateral thinkers.

4.5.5. Summary

Exploration at *Bühler* happens across the entire organization from corporate level to the business unit. However, exploratory activities which are of high uncertainty and which do not fit in the strategy or project portfolio of any of the divisions are typically conducted in Corporate Technology. In contrast to R&D, the new business development units across all hierarchical levels engage in exploring new business models for marketing new technologies and processes. Thus, despite close collaboration between Corporate Technology and NBD, there is an organizational distinction between technology and business development.

Activities pertaining to exploration are conducted within clear strategic boundaries. Thus, *Bühler* has identified global megatrends and derived scouting areas and search fields in which regular exploration with respect to new technologies and knowledge is conducted. Corporate Technology people engage approximately half a day per week in this task.

Bühler strongly emphasizes the importance of long-term innovations throughout the entire organization and has established incentive systems for exploratory ideas. This has resulted in business units implementing dedicated innovation cells to engage even more in exploration.

Key findings for *Bühler's* exploration approach include the following aspects:
- Exploration is conducted across all levels and divisions with a focus on technology and trend exploration in Corporate Technology
- *Bühler's* innovation strategy sets clear boundaries as to where, i.e. in which areas (both trends, technologies, and markets) exploration is engaged in
- Exploration is encouraged through strong corporate communication and supported by respective incentive systems
- Apart from pure scouting activities, *Bühler* typically collaborates with external partners in the further pursuit (i.e. prototype development) of exploratory projects to minimize uncertainty

5. Conceptualizing firms' exploration approach

This chapter captures and refines tentative constructs and relationships that emerged during the single-case analysis. Thus, chapter 5.1 provides a focused data summary of the cross-case similarities and differences. Based on the initial insights gained from this summary, chapter 5.2 develops a conceptual framework which guides the subsequent cross-case analysis. Chapter 5.3 entails the cross-case analysis which discusses the findings from the cases and reflects them based on existing literature on exploration. Ultimately, this leads to the development of a conceptual model of exploratory search based on the identified constructs and relationships from the cross-case analysis, which will be presented in chapter 5.4.

5.1. Single-case summary

During the interviews, many new insights emerged which were not covered by the original conceptual framework. As a consequence, to concentrate, harmonize and facilitate the subsequent single-case summary, the most significant results are presented according to the following guiding questions:
- Conducting exploration
  - What are the main strategic directives for conducting exploration activities?
  - How is exploration conducted from a process perspective?
- Organization of exploration
  - How is exploration organized in the company?
  - What people are involved in conducting exploration activities?
  - What are the premises for conducting exploration activities?
- Influence of exploration approach on R&D effectiveness
  - How does the exploration approach affect the performance of overall R&D and new business development efforts?

5.1.1. Strategic and procedural approaches

Strategic directives for exploration

The case firms have in common that exploration is a strategic issue which has a close connection to corporate strategy. In all firms, existing capabilities build the foundation for exploration activities, which becomes most clear in the cases of *Ciba* and *Gore* which have a defined exploration strategy around existing core business. Furthermore, with the exception of *Ciba*, all firms work with abstract search terms to facilitate exploration activities. These terms are often based on the firm's capabilities (e.g. such as 'outlast' in the case of *Hilti*, 'protection' in the case of *Gore* or 'health and nutrition' in the case of *Bühler*) or brand image, which ensures that exploration activities are related to existing business. Another commonality is the fact that exploration from firm perspective mostly pertains to learning new knowledge about markets and finding business opportunities, while exploration for technological knowledge is often considered as 'daily business'. In fact, the case firms are all product developing firms where research and development plays a key role for competitiveness. Thus, exploration efforts are mainly targeted at generating additional growth in form of new business around existing technological capabilities. Therefore, in the following, exploration pertains to searching new knowledge about markets and new business opportunities, if not otherwise stated.

The scope and breadth of exploration activities at *Ciba* is strongly affected by corporate vision and corporate growth targets. Corporate vision specifically entails the goal for the organization to explore into new markets and business models for increased leverage of existing technologies and thus to develop innovations with greater economic impact. As basic research pertaining to new technologies and chemical compounds is critical for daily business anyways, *Ciba's* strategy emphasizes exploration pertaining to new markets and business models around existing and new technologies. Apart from a general strategic intent and corporate commitment to exploration activities, *Ciba's* exploration strategy rests on stretching existing competencies to new markets. Thus, *Ciba* explores in areas which are adjacent to the existing core business to ensure a link between current and future competencies. By this approach, *Ciba* effectively limits uncertainty inherent in exploration and increases its chances for innovation success. Furthermore, this approach ensures that *Ciba* goes beyond the development of mere incremental innovations.

Gore's exploration strategy is about the identification of new business opportunities for existing or new technologies. New business opportunity exploration is conducted around the core business (which is different for each of the four divisions). Thus, exploration is based on existing competencies pertaining to markets, customers, geographies, or sales channels for example. Since PTFE is *Gore's* core technology, exploration activities are focused on the identification of new opportunities for leveraging PTFE. By exploring around the core business, *Gore* ensures that future innovation projects do not depart too far from today's business to avoid a too big stretch of existing capabilities. Furthermore, *Gore* only explores one dimension of the core (e.g. new geographies) at a time, as experience from the past has shown that exploring several dimensions concurrently drastically decreases chances for successful innovation.

The brand image and brand promise of *Hilti* products resembles - more or less consciously - the starting point for exploration for new knowledge. The company motto "*Hilti*. Outperform. Outlast." resembles the corporate vision for the quality and performance of all *Hilti* products. In addition, *Hilti's* innovation strategy entails being product leader in all of its products. Product leadership to *Hilti* means a strong focus on applications rather than specific technologies. Thus, *Hilti's* strategy is to explore entirely new technologies no matter if they might jeopardize existing technologies, as long as they lead to improved quality and performance, or even replace existing products. Therefore, *Hilti's* exploration scope and breadth is based on its strategy to be product leader in all applications that *Hilti* offers. In parallel to this technological exploration, *Hilti* conducts 'trait studies' which analyze markets in which *Hilti* is currently not active. This is done to find out if existing or new *Hilti* applications could potentially be applied in these markets.

At *Bühler*, the corporate goal to be the global leader in its technologies and process know-how affects the intensity and direction of exploration activities. On the one hand, exploration activities pertaining to new technologies such as new sensor technology to improve the control in e.g. food processing is considered natural and logic as it is directly related to the core business. However, in addition to that, *Bühler's* exploration activities are targeted at environmental developments such as mega trends and the question how this affects future *Bühler* business. As a result of such activities, *Bühler* tries to match future requirements with current competencies. Thus, *Bühler* tries to secure future competitiveness by considering and forecasting environmental developments (regarding both technologies and overall trends) and adapting to these developments.

Process perspective of exploration
An overall commonality between all firms is their engagement in scanning the environment within the boundaries as imposed by exploration strategy. Thus, the firms conduct e.g. scenario analyses or carry out workshops with external experts to obtain more knowledge about a specific field of interest. Initial ideas are often further explored by individuals or a small group of people who subsequently develop a brief summary which is presented to a board that decides if the idea is further pursued or not.

At *Ciba*, opportunities for exploration emerge throughout the entire organization but are mainly pursued on corporate level. As *Ciba's* core competence is researching and developing new chemical compounds to serve new applications, additional exploration activities typically concentrate on new business opportunities, where *Ciba* believes to be able to generate the most sustainable and radical innovations. These emerge by scanning developments and adjacent markets in the business environment. On corporate level, exploration activities are systematically conducted by fully dedicated people within the New Growth Platform while on the business unit level, opportunities often emerge out of concrete problems. In a first step, exploration typically entails desktop research and acquiring information through expert contacts. The results are presented to the divisions and the management board, and if there is an interest, a project is formed within NGP and worked out to a concept. This concept is permanently assessed by the management board and presented to the divisions and finally transferred again to a business line or spun out in a new organizational unit.

Exploratory activities at *Gore* are conducted both by research and development and by new business development people. While NBD people engage in exploration which aims at identifying entirely new markets and business opportunities, R&D people explore technologies which complement or enhance the core technology PTFE to serve new markets or business opportunities. Within NBD, exploration is conducted by fully dedicated people. In contrast, exploration within R&D is conducted within the dabble time of about 10% of each employee's regular work time. While R&D people generate many new business ideas through the creativity of the individual, exploration at NBD is more structured based on adjacency explorations from the core. If an idea attracts fellow colleagues, a small team typically continues to pursue the idea and works out a business plan. The business plan is ultimately presented to internal 'investors' such as R&D and business line leaders and assessed.

Exploration at *Hilti* is typically conducted on corporate level in 'Corporate Research & Technology'. Based on a set of hierarchical innovation fields derived from corporate strategy, CR&T conducts scenario analyses, scans emerging trends, markets, and technologies, and conducts 'trait studies' which deliver in-depth insights about industries where *Hilti* has no prior experience at all. The results from these exploration activities are presented and discussed in the 'technology board' which consists of board members, the CTO, and the heads of the business areas. All ideas are assessed against the *Hilti* strategy, and if deemed promising, the idea or technology is further worked out to a business plan. The resulting exploration project is continuously presented and assessed in the technology board.

Exploratory activities at *Bühler* are conducted on all organizational levels, however with full dedication only in the Corporate Technology unit. *Bühler* has derived scouting fields from a detailed analysis of the business environment, in which *Bühler* regularly and systematically scans specific topics. In addition, *Bühler* systematically analyzes current and future trends to see how future development might impact current business and what future technologies might have to be developed. Technologies which are explored in this context are analyzed with respect to their fit with current strategy and the competencies in the entire organization.

Table 7 summarizes the findings pertaining to exploration strategy and procedure within the case firms.

	Ciba	Gore	Hilti	Bühler
Exploration strategy	▪ Exploration is conducted pertaining to new markets and business opportunities ▪ Exploration is conducted according to adjacent moves from the existing core business	▪ Exploration is conducted pertaining to new markets and business opportunities ▪ Exploration is conducted according to adjacent moves from the existing core business	▪ Exploration is conducted both pertaining to new technologies and new markets ▪ Vision and brand image serve as foundation for exploration activities	▪ Exploration is conducted pertaining to new technologies and new business models ▪ Global trends and immediate business environment determine direction of exploration activities
Exploration procedure	▪ Matching existing technologies with new markets	▪ Matching existing technologies with new markets ▪ Conducting of 'arena studies'	▪ Scanning of technologies and trends ▪ Conducting of 'trade studies'	▪ Scouting of technologies and trends within specific search fields

Table 7: Comparison of exploration strategy across sample companies

5.1.2. Organizational set up

Locus of exploration

Basic exploration at *Ciba* with respect to new chemicals is conducted throughout the entire organization on corporate, divisional, and business line level, and represents more or less 'daily business'. Exploration activities pertaining to new markets and new business opportunities are conducted on corporate level in the unit 'New Growth Platform'. The New Growth Platform as a fully dedicated unit is concerned with learning about new markets and new business opportunities, and, more generally, in learning about business which does not fit in any of the current businesses. At *Ciba*, exploration is rather a top-down approach which is mainly conducted in the NGP as a separate organizational unit which also directly reports to the Chief Innovation Officer.

At *Gore*, both R&D and NBD engage in exploration. R&D people engage in exploration for the development of new technology platforms while NBD people explore new business opportunities for already developed technological solutions or for providing R&D with directions for technology development. This approach is reflected both on divisional and corporate level, as *Gore* maintains R&D and NBD units on both levels. However, the identification of new business opportunities affects the development of new technologies and vice versa, which is why NBD and R&D work closely together. *Gore* does not have a clear organizational distinction between exploration and exploitation units. Rather, teams gather around opportunities and resolve again after the exploration activities are finished.

Hilti's organizational structure with respect to exploration activities is directly influenced by the corporate innovation strategy. Business lines are responsible for conducting development activities and thus improving existing products, and thus do not engage in exploration activities. Predevelopment activities on the business area level focus on the advancement of technologies that benefit several business units. Exploration in its most distinct way is conducted exclusively in Corporate Research & Technology, and focuses on the identification of entirely new technologies and business opportunities. Thus, *Hilti's* exploration activities are clearly distinguished from exploitation activities and happen on corporate level. Although by other circumstances a large portion of CR&T budget is spent on supporting specific tasks for other organizational units, CR&T people are otherwise fully employed to explore new technologies and to identify future business opportunities.

Bühler pursues a hybrid exploration approach which entails that exploration activities are conducted on corporate and divisional level. However, while technology exploration is exclusively conducted in the unit Corporate Technology, exploration pertaining to new business opportunities and business models around existing technologies is conducted also on the divisional level. Thus, corporate R&D is in charge of scouting trends and technological areas as well as new business opportunities, all of which typically have no immediate application potential in one of the business units. Therefore, exploration is, although encouraged throughout, a rather top-down approach with a clear mission for corporate R&D. *Bühler* is aware that business lines usually do not have the time to engage in exploration, which is why corporate management provides Corporate Technology with distinct resources to be invested in exploration.

People involved in exploration activities
Although exploration activities can occur throughout the entire organization, dedicated exploration is typically conducted in separate organizational units. In contrast,

exploration on the level of product development typically happens on occasion and is based on a specific problem. Therefore, people from upper management are typically responsible for designing exploration strategies while people in dedicated organizational units actually conduct the search for new knowledge. People who actually engage in exploration are often characterized by a broad knowledge background and/or show distinct entrepreneurial behavior.

At *Ciba*, the exploration strategy is designed by corporate managers including the Chief Innovation Officer and the heads of the divisional R&D. People in NGP have diverse educational and industry experience backgrounds such as e.g. chemistry, different kinds of engineering, as well as marketing. The same is true for business opportunities emerging in business units, however, people here mostly have an engineering background. These people are officially employed by NGP for the time of the exploration project and reintegrated in their original unit afterwards.

Gore encourages all of its employees to engage in exploration activities. Although there is no central unit which designs exploration strategies and activities, all employees are supposed to engage in exploring new business opportunities, ideas, or technologies. This happens by fully dedicated people in new business development and to 10% of the regular work time in research and development units. The typical approach is that small teams organize themselves around opportunities both within NBD and R&D and then engage in exploring an opportunity in detail. Thus, in general, people from new business development, research and development, as well as product management and sales are involved in exploration activities, by that forming an interdisciplinary team. After an exploration project has been successfully conducted or terminated, the group dissolves and people 'return' to their original organizational unit.

At *Hilti*, exploration is a corporate strategic issue which is why respective strategies are designed by the technology board which includes the board member who is responsible for technology and innovation, the head of Corporate Research & Technology, as well as the heads of the business areas. As CR&T is organized according to *Hilti's* main technical disciplines such as mechanics, physics, material science, or chemistry, exploration activities in CR&T are conducted by people with respective backgrounds. In addition, these people typically have work experience in a *Hilti* line function to maintain a close link to existing business as well.

At *Bühler*, the exploration strategy is designed by the CTO, the Corporate Technology unit, and the R&D heads of the single divisions. In general, exploration is exclusively conducted on corporate level. In Corporate Technology, which consists of 35 people, a large portion of the unit members are fresh university graduates. Most people are therefore comparably young and stay approximately three years in this unit which thus serves as a springboard for later line functions. People in this unit have a diverse background ranging from disciplines such as physics and chemistry to process and mechanical engineering. By this approach, *Bühler* ensures that latest knowledge is incorporated and absorbed in the organization. Furthermore, as new people are typically not so familiar with existing business, *Bühler* is able to benefit from seemingly odd ideas which at first might not seem to fit current strategy but which often entail exploratory innovation potential.

Premises conducive for exploration activities
As innovation plays a key role in all case firms, they try to establish an environment which is conducive for innovation and which allows for sufficient time and resources to engage in exploration activities. Thus, all firms have financial and other incentive systems for innovation in general and more radical ideas stemming from exploration activities in particular. Also, all firms provide distinct resources for exploration activities such as separate organizational units with own budgets or 'dabble time' to be spent for exploratory activities. However, all firms have somewhat different approaches about how to establish an innovation culture conducive to exploration.

Ciba signals the importance of innovation in general and exploring new business opportunities in particular in the entire group by dedicating 25% of overall R&D budget to exploration. According to the CIO, an effect of this is that *Ciba* by that also establishes a culture conducive to innovation in general. Furthermore, by separating exploration projects on the New Growth Platform from any activities which aim at further developing existing product platforms, *Ciba* ensures that exploring new knowledge can be fully enabled without being influenced or distracted by daily business.

Innovation culture is a main lever at *Gore* to spur innovation in general and to enable exploration activities. Already during the recruiting process for new employees, *Gore* ensures that applicants have a distinct entrepreneurial mindset, are willing to take initiative, and are distinct team players. Because of this, and because of *Gore's* encouragement for all employees to engage in exploration, indeed people from all organizational units are somewhere involved in exploring new ideas and learning new knowledge in general. Also, *Gore* regularly conducts internal 'capability shows' to cross-fertilize knowledge and, in fact, to show internally what the single business units are capable of doing. Furthermore, exploration activities are organized around opportunities rather than within rigid organizational structures. Because of this, *Gore* is able to pull together the most capable people of the entire organization to pursue a specific task.

At *Hilti*, innovation and exploration projects are communicated throughout the entire organization by internal fairs and presentations as well as announcements on the intranet. By this, *Hilti* manages to establish an innovation culture and raises awareness for the importance of exploration in general, which in turn leads to increased innovation ideas and spurs creativity in general. In particular, *Hilti* conducts camps which last several days in a location outside the company to familiarize new people with the unique *Hilti* culture.

Bühler conducts exploration activities foremost in the Corporate Technology unit. CT serves as an incubator for entirely new technologies which might be spun out later to specific business lines once they are able to sustain themselves in terms of financial turnover. In this light, *Bühler* is very flexible regarding the establishment and disassembly of organizational units which engage in exploration. Thus, new units are taken under the umbrella of CT and grown there until they can be integrated in an existing division or spun out. Table 8 provides an overview of the premises conducive for exploration across the sample companies.

	Ciba	*Gore*	*Hilti*	*Bühler*
Structural organization	▪ Technology exploration on business unit level ▪ New business exploration on corporate level	▪ Technological exploration in R&D and new business exploration in NBD across all organizational units	▪ Both technology and new business exploration exclusively on corporate level	▪ Technology exploration on corporate level ▪ New business exploration on corporate and divisional level

5.1 Single-case summary

	Ciba	*Gore*	*Hilti*	*Bühler*
People involved in exploration	▪ Corporate and divisional people for new business exploration ▪ Divisional people for technology exploration	▪ All employees	▪ Corporate people for technology and new business exploration ▪ Divisional people for technology exploration	▪ Corporate people for technological exploration ▪ Corporate and divisional people for new business exploration
Facilitators for exploration	▪ Dedicated funding for exploration ▪ Separation of exploration and exploitation enables full concentration	▪ Distinct innovation culture with focus on exploration and innovation ▪ Explicit dabble time for exploratory activities	▪ Dedicated funding for exploration ▪ Separation of exploration and exploitation enables full concentration	▪ Quick assembly and disassembly of organizational units for more efficient exploration

Table 8: Comparison of exploration facilitators across sample companies

Exploration activities pertaining to new technological knowledge are typically conducted across all hierarchical levels of the organization. Also, exploration is typically both a top-down and bottom-up approach which is a consequence of purported strategic directives across all organizational levels. Exploration pertaining to the identification of new business opportunities and to learning about new markets is mostly conducted in separated organizational units. There, people usually work full-time to find out about new markets and how the firm can generate new business based on existing capabilities.

5.1.3. Influence on R&D performance

Without exception, all case firms have been market leaders for decades and/or rank among the top global performers in their respective markets. Therefore, it is reasonable to assume that these firms have implemented approaches by which they can stay abreast of their competition. For this reason, meaningful measures with respect to the relationship between exploration activities and R&D performance can be analyzed only on a macro level. Thus, instead of analyzing the impact of single exploration efforts on

R&D performance for a single time span, a more general approach is chosen: a proxy is used for the assessment about changes in R&D performance which relies on company-specific measures and interviewee's statements about the input/output ratio of exploration efforts and the contribution of innovation activities to the firm's overall success.

Before *Ciba* implemented the corporate innovation strategy of adjacent moves, exploration was conducted haphazard throughout the entire organization detached from any strategic directive. As a consequence, efforts were made which later resulted in failed projects as they would often overstretch existing competencies pertaining to technologies and/or markets. Today, *Ciba* considers exploratory efforts only positive when the learned new knowledge can be utilized for innovation. Since exploring starts based on the core business, both the quality and the quantity of exploratory projects have increased which reassured *Ciba* in their exploration strategy. Thus, since the implementation of the new exploration strategy, the balance of the project portfolio consisting of exploratory and exploitative innovation projects has shifted more toward exploration projects. As another effect, people are much more content with having a strategic directive, because they are now able to steer their exploration efforts effectively in alignment with corporate strategy.

Gore has time and again proved its dominant global position in virtually almost all of its product categories. The base for this success story is manifold and to a large amount due to *Gore's* extraordinary company culture. Exploration activities are always conducted based on existing competencies and on the existing core business. With this approach, *Gore* has managed to constantly introduce new products that are distinct in performance and/or quality. A major difference to earlier approaches is that uncertainty is effectively reduced, leading to more successful exploration projects which are aligned with existing strategies and which enable the leveraging of existing capabilities. This constant extension of the core has led to major business success in the past decades. As a consequence, *Gore* is able to invest exploration resources more effectively than before.

Hilti has been the global leader in its product platforms for decades. This success story is owed to the consequent implementation of corporate strategy. Based on the exploration strategy, *Hilti* constantly learns new knowledge about future trends, emerging technologies and markets, and new industries where they have no prior experience but where there might be future business potential. Throughout *Hilti's* history, they had to overcome barriers imposed by changes in technologies and by fierce competition. However, *Hilti* has successfully managed to leverage their core capabilities, which puts focusing on applications in the center. Strategic investments in these capabilities have enabled *Hilti* to enter new market segments and to constantly integrate new technologies in their applications, which allows them to maintain the global market leadership.

The constantly high global market shares between 70% and 80% in specific technologies at *Bühler* are both evidence and commitment for past and future successful exploration activities. By engaging in exploration activities aiming at new technologies and new business opportunities, *Bühler* has managed to stay abreast of its competitors. Exploration activities are conducted within defined search fields and lend a guideline to avoiding exploring unknown territories where uncertainty is unjustifiably high. Furthermore, by separating exploration activities from daily business, particularly incremental product improvements, *Bühler* is able to fully focus on its activities without being distracted from divisional or product requirements. As a consequence of this focused effort, both the quality and quantity of exploration projects have increased over the past decade and tend to increase even more according to the CTO.

Table 9 summarizes the case firms' R&D effectiveness measures.

	Ciba	*Gore*	*Hilti*	*Bühler*
R&D effectiveness measure	▪ Number of exploration projects ▪ Outcome of exploration projects ▪ Contentedness of R&D employees	▪ Contribution of exploration projects to overall firm performance ▪ Quality of exploration projects	▪ Number of successful exploration projects ▪ Outcome of exploration projects ▪ Amount and quality of learned new knowledge	▪ Number of exploration projects ▪ Outcome of exploration projects

Table 9: R&D effectiveness measure of sample companies

5.2. Conceptual framework development

Insights from the cases indicate that the firms engage in exploration activities in areas where they are able to leverage existing technological capabilities. In doing so, their exploration strategy, however, still reaches beyond currently existing technologies, know-how, or market expertise. Exploration activities are conducted within the frame of a corporate innovation strategy or corporate vision, which might be a means to increase the likelihood of commercially viable outcomes. Also, exploration activities, from firm view, typically involve learning new knowledge about new markets and identifying new business opportunities. In contrast, technology exploration is mostly considered 'daily business', and thus happens across all hierarchical levels.

The fact that exploration activities are conducted based on existing capabilities moderates existing literature on exploration. This is true particularly from the perspective of organizational learning, which posits that exploration resembles distant search for knowledge that tends to be detached from existing business. Also, exploration with respect to learning new knowledge about new markets is conducted in distinct and dedicated organizational units which often are connected to corporate R&D or top management level. This separation of exploratory activities and daily R&D business ensures full concentration on exploratory activities. This result supports literature on ambidextrous organizations which posits to separate exploratory from exploitative activities to avoid crowding out effects in favor of exploitation (Tushman and O'Reilly III 1996).

The main target of this research is to understand how firms engage in exploration and why they might be more successful in doing so than other firms. Therefore, it is important to understand the relationships between exploration with respect to strategy, organization, and processes and the outcome of these activities on exploration effectiveness and efficiency. Insights from the cases reveal that, in particular, corporate innovation strategy has an impact on how and where exploration activities are conducted. Therefore, search direction is especially determined by higher order strategies, and can furthermore only be effectively conducted when specific facilitating factors such as financial and human resources are in place. In turn, outcomes of a specific search strategy in terms of positive or negative performance feedbacks have an impact on the alignment of innovation strategy. To implement innovation and search strategies, firms need respective financial assets and competencies. These relationships are illustrated in figure 18 which summarizes the conceptual framework.

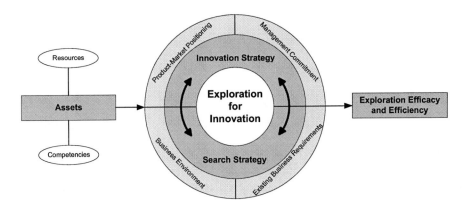

Figure 18: Conceptual framework of exploration for innovation

To better understand these relationships, the constructs which are identified from the case summary are in the following further discussed and reflected on existing literature on exploration, thereby extending existing literature. This procedure enhances internal validity, generalizability, as well as the quality of the theory building from case study research (Eisenhardt 1989). As a consequence, the identified constructs are investigated from the perspective of existing literature as presented in chapter 2. The conceptual framework developed in this chapter is further elaborated in the subsequent sections and finally developed to a concluding conceptual model.

5.3. Cross-case analysis

Although the initial reference framework is based on existing literature pertaining to exploration and served as a guideline for conducting interviews and thus investigating the companies' exploration activities, results from the interviews typically entail new insights not yet covered by literature. Therefore, for a cross-case analysis in general, the researcher must take a new perspective toward the case study data by applying other case comparison criteria than those used in the initial framework (Eisenhardt 1989; Eisenhardt and Graebner 2007). By using structured and different perspectives on the data, the likelihood of accurate and reliable theory is increased, allowing for extending literature and the development of new theory which has an even closer fit with the data. As a consequence, tentative constructs and relationships serve as the analysis criteria during the cross-case analysis.

Also, in contrast to a single-case analysis, a cross-case analysis offers a wider variety of insights and therefore possesses bigger validity than a single case. To increase internal validity, generalizability, and the theoretical level of theory building from case study research, the cross-case analysis is conducted by continuously referring back to existing theory about exploration (Eisenhardt 1989).

In the following chapters, constructs which emerged during the case studies are analyzed which have emerged to be particularly conducive to successful exploration. The case studies reveal that exploration is a strategic activity which is a key factor for future competitiveness for the firms. Furthermore, insights from the cases support the arguments that exploration posits an organizational challenge because of its inherent uncertainty. However, the case firms seem to have established approaches which avoid the negative effects exploration might have, and focus instead on the benefits of exploration activities. The firms have implemented mechanisms by which exploration is enabled in the first place, and how exploration can be conducted more effectively. Furthermore, the cases reveal that organizational aspects pertaining to the capabilities of the individual are important for successful exploration. Therefore, the following chapters analyze constructs pertaining to the
- firms' propensity to engage in exploration,
- firms' approaches for effective exploration, and
- firms' organizational elements for efficient exploration.

While firms' propensity to engage in exploration analyzes how firms enable exploration in the first place, firms' approaches for effective exploration analyzes how they ensure that exploration activities conducted in the organization will have a high likelihood to lead to beneficial results. Finally, firms' organizational elements for efficient exploration analyzes variables which allow them to execute exploration activities efficiently.

5.3.1. Elements impacting exploration propensity

According to the case studies, firm values and the overall corporate innovation strategy have tremendous impact on the propensity and direction of exploration activities and consequently and on the way these activities are conducted. The case firms are aware that future growth and leading market positions are not sustainable if they do not engage in the search and integration of new knowledge to develop more radical or exploratory innovations. Therefore, firms may be fairly willing to invest in exploration activities and provide corresponding resources to enable exploration in the organization.

Exploration and the search for new knowledge must first be enabled before people can actually conduct search. Therefore, firms need to create an environment which allows for exploration to happen in the first place. Furthermore, if firms do not create such an environment, exploration activities run the risk of being crowded-out in favor of exploitative activities (March 1991; Gupta, Smith et al. 2006). Finally, firms wishing to maintain their leading market positions in the future must invest in exploration activities to generate pathbreaking innovations. The cases reveal that the firms enable exploration by substantially investing in activities conducive to exploration. This positivistic attitude towards exploration may be anchored in the values, strategies, and culture of the case firms. In analyzing cause-effect relationships pertaining to the propensity and direction of exploration, two relationships emerge from the case studies:
- the impact of firm values on the propensity and intensity of exploration to enable exploration in the first place
- the impact of product strategy on the intensity and direction of exploration

These aspects are in the following analyzed in more detail to reveal their effect on exploration intensity and exploration direction.

Firm values
The decision to invest in exploration activities and grant the organization enough leeway to pursue activities which are not within daily business can be explained from a value perspective of the firm. Firms have values and beliefs that lead them to pursue one strategy, activity, or process more than another. Beliefs and values represent predictions about how things are (beliefs) and statements of how things ought to be (values) (Schein 1991). Values define which functions or activities should receive the most support in an organization, and values are argued to energize people to do better the things which matter most (Miller 2003). The case firms engage in exploration

activities because they believe that exploration is on the one hand a necessity, but which will on the other hand lead to beneficial outcomes for the firm. On the other hand, the case firms have always been successful in the past, which might be a responsibility and motivation at the same time to continue to excel in innovation.

Fundamental values pertaining to how an organization is managed, and on what strategies it competes in the market are a hallmark of all the case firms. *Hilti* founder Martin Hilti had very clear beliefs about how employees were supposed to be treated and what was important to a healthy organizational climate. One of the basic principles he had was to excel at everything *Hilti* was doing, which meant that *Hilti* would always focus on superior product quality, and which meant that innovation was the only viable pathway. Also *Ciba*, *Gore* and *Bühler* have long traditions of developing breakthrough innovations, and the companies thrive on that still today. In fact, all case firms believe that innovation is the most important driver for ensuring future competitiveness. Therefore, with the exception of *Gore*, all case firms invest a fixed fraction of the annual R&D budget in exploration activities to live up to their values. Thus, their firm values make them invest in exploration activities, because this is how they believe they can sustain their leadership. At the same time, signaling the importance of innovation also promotes the establishment of a specific mindset conducive for exploration (McGrath and MacMillan 2000). The cases reveal that exploration has an utmost high value, as exploration is seen as a means for generating innovation that will sustain their competitiveness.

From another perspective, the firms view exploration activities as a necessary premise for long-term competitiveness. As exploration activities are associated with high uncertainty, firms naturally tend to pursue more exploitative activities, where returns are much more certain and close in time (March 1991). In fact, the respondents in the interviews across all firms state that it is much easier to pursue daily business and advance existing products and technologies than engaging in activities where outcomes are uncertain and where the likelihood of approval by upper management is small. However, particularly interview partners from upper management level are well aware of the pitfalls of a one-sided focus on exploitation. The CTOs across all case firms are aware of the importance of exploration and the more radical innovations associated with this.

In summary, the firms show a fundamental attitude towards innovation and activities which are necessary to arrive at breakthrough innovation. Thus, the case firms want to engage in exploration to sustain their market leadership, and they want to be conceived as the technology and innovation leaders in the market. This attitude may strongly rest in the firms' core values and beliefs about who they want to be and how they can achieve their ambitions.

Product strategy

The strategy firms chose pertaining to their products may be closely connected to the firm values and beliefs. Thus, firms which define themselves by innovation may chose product strategies which will live up to their core beliefs. The cases suggest that there is a close match between firm values and product strategy.

Gore and *Hilti* both pursue a clear product differentiation strategy for all of its products. Their claim is to persistently deliver their customers the highest possible quality products in a specific application (such as e.g. comfortable protection against outer weather conditions in the case of *Gore* or the highest performing drill hammers in the case of *Hilti*), which both firms call 'product-leadership', and they will only engage in activities and develop products which are clearly distinct from competitor products. For example, the *Gore* fabrics division customer promise is to offer 'the *only* water and wind repellent textile for outer wear which lets the body breathe'. This statement is conferrable to most of *Gore's* other products in the same or other divisions. Therefore, *Gore* will not engage in the development of any products which could be easily imitated by its competitors, even though they might thereby achieve short-term competitive advantages. Likewise, *Hilti's* motto '*Hilti*. Outperform. Outlast.' is a statement about the quality and performance of all of its products. In contrast to *Gore* and *Hilti*, *Bühler* 'products' resemble in-depth knowledge about food processing including the technologies that are involved in it. *Bühler* manages to incorporate this knowledge in its final product, which is the planning and construction of food processing mills and plants. For *Ciba* it is more difficult to differentiate from competitor products and claim product leadership, as *Ciba's* products are chemical compounds which are assembled in products of their customers. Being in the chemical bulk ware business, for final customers like for example the automotive industry, it is not of major importance who provides the ingredients as long as they meet performance criteria. Thus, while all other companies control most of their value chains, *Ciba* has many intermediaries to the final customer and thus is not able to differentiate as much as the other case firms.

The potential to which the firms can reach product differentiation and product leadership has major implications for the direction and amount of exploration for innovation. For example, *Hilti* covers the entire value chain from developing and manufacturing the product to the final delivery to the end customer through its huge net of direct sales. Through this, *Hilti* ensures that all important parts of the entire application pertaining to product and manufacturing technologies is covered and controlled by *Hilti*. As a consequence of this, *Hilti* not only offers final marketable products, but also has a broad scope of exploration possibilities, ranging from exploring new product technologies to new manufacturing technologies and new markets. *Bühler* has a similarly large scope pertaining to exploration. They, too, cover the entire value chain from product development to plant construction and service and consulting for their final customers. As is the case with *Hilti*, *Bühler's* exploration scope therefore includes exploring new product and manufacturing technologies as well as new business models around existing hardware products. Because of *Gore's* extremely versatile core technology PTFE, *Gore* is able to carry over their tremendous know-how around this technology to many new markets and applications. As a consequence, exploration typically happens within *Gore's* new business development units, which explore new markets to find out if and how PTFE can be successfully applied. Although *Gore* does not cover the downstream part of the value chain, the versatility of the core technology and their brand name compensate for this. *Ciba's* scope for exploration activities is compared to the other case firms limited. Exploration, apart from basic exploration pertaining to new chemicals, is mainly confined to exploring new applications and markets for new business opportunities. As a consequence, *Ciba* has bundled its exploration activities on the New Growth Platform, which mainly explores new markets and new business models around existing technologies. However, recently, single business lines are trying to control larger portions of the downstream value chain to increase value generation. As a consequence of this, their exploration scope possibly increases in the future. Table 10 shows the characteristics present in the case studies.

	Ciba	Gore	Hilti	Bühler
Potential for product differentiation	▪ low	▪ high	▪ high	▪ high
Value chain coverage	▪ limited	▪ limited	▪ large	▪ large
Exploration potential based on value chain coverage	▪ limited	▪ medium	▪ large	▪ large
Exploration potential based on core technology	▪ large	▪ large	▪ large	▪ large

Table 10: Comparison of exploration scope across sample companies

Summary

Insights from the cases suggest a close relationship between the values and beliefs of a firm and its propensity to engage in exploration activities. According to upper management of the case firms, they all believe that a constant stream of innovation and the development of pathbreaking innovations is the key for future success. As a consequence, the firms invest a fixed amount of R&D resources in exploration activities. As this approach towards exploration has proved to be successful in the firms' past, it can be argued that exploration has become a basic activity within the firms' business that is not questioned in its purpose and benefits. Therefore, the case firms are likely to continue to invest in exploration activities in the future as well, as this is the key to continued competitiveness.

Furthermore, the cases show that the product strategy may be a direct consequence of the firm's values and beliefs. Because innovation is considered the key to success, a common pattern across the case firms is their strategy to be product leader in their respective markets. One way to implement this is exploring the value chain for improved value generation. As such, it shows that the more the firms are in control of their value chain, the broader is the range for exploration activities. Although other strategic motivations for engaging in value chain exploration cannot be ruled out, the firms state that increasing control in the value chain offers them new potential for exploration and thus subsequent innovation. This in turn has implications for the direction that the firms are exploring, that is, exploration is effectively conducted in the downstream part of the value chain.

5.3.2. Elements impacting exploration efficacy

A common pattern across all case firms is the fact that they do not randomly explore new domains. In fact, all interview partners were uniform in their statements that the exploration of random domains to which the firm does not have any relations bears too much risk. Instead, they align their decisions about where to explore with strategic imperatives and existing capabilities. Insights from the case studies show that, in particular, the following variables have a major impact on the efficacy of firms' exploration activities:

- alignment of exploration activities with existing business
- orientation to applications regarding technological exploration
- use of abstract search terms based on applications and outcomes
- leveraging and matching of existing capabilities

These relationships are in the following analyzed in more detail to reveal their effect on exploration efficacy.

Expanding core business

The cases reveal that the firms' core business is of utmost importance to all exploration activities that the firms engage in. *Ciba* as a specialty chemicals specialist explores exclusively in areas where existing technological competencies can be stretched and adapted to new external demands. Baden-Fuller and Volberda (1997) define competencies as involving shared knowledge among a large group of units within the complex firm. A competence therefore draws on several routines which have been refined, stored, and codified, or socialized. As a consequence of *Ciba's* exploration strategy, they will as a chemicals company not 'diversify' into completely different product-market offerings. As the head of innovation at Corporate Technology said: "we are a chemicals company and will not sell hamburgers tomorrow". This shows that even if *Ciba* was aware of a very profitable business opportunity, they will not engage in exploring this opportunity further if it is not to some extent connected to existing capabilities. The deep know-how that *Ciba* has accumulated over many decades has enabled them to become one of the global top players in the specialty chemicals business. As a consequence, *Ciba* aims at strengthening and extending their core business for further growth. *Gore* has virtually since the firm foundation in 1967 developed a stream of innovations across numerous industries which are all based on its core technology PTFE. It is the explicit company strategy to further strengthen existing core business and leverage the know-how of its core technology to new industries and applications. *Hilti* has been in the professional construction industry since the company foundation. They have accumulated a vast amount of process and product technology know-how pertaining to all of the applications offered. Underlying the focus on applications is the strategy to provide the best solution for a specific application regardless the underlying technology. Therefore, *Hilti's* strategy is to strengthen and expand its core business. The same is true for *Bühler* which will always remain in the 'equipment' business which is its main pillar while they continue to expand their service and consulting business. However, *Bühler's* know-how in food processing will always be its main competitive asset.

The firms in this study pursue a strategy which sustainably reinforces their existing core business. None of the firms has intentions to enter completely different product-market domains, but aim at strengthening and expanding their core business. The implication of this approach is that exploration activities will naturally not occur in areas where the firms have no prior experience, or where there is no potential for leveraging existing competencies. Sanchez, Heene et al. (1996) understand competencies to include all forms of available assets, capabilities, knowledge, know-how and skills, technologies and equipment in the organization, but also the coordinated deployment of these assets and capabilities. Furthermore, the experience of *Gore* and *Ciba* has shown that engaging in markets or technologies where respective competencies were missing the odds of success were drastically declining, ultimately leading to failed projects. Their experience is in line with literature on exploration, entrepreneurship, and diversification which has found that innovation activities which are based on existing competencies yield the highest chance of success (Afuah 2002; Miller 2003). This is because uncertainty with respect to new markets, technologies, and customers is reduced as the firm can adapt and stretch existing competencies to these new areas. Thus, the firm can use either existing market access and channels, beneficially use information about customers, or employ its knowledge about an existing technology in the new environment. These insights imply that even the most successful firms are unlikely to explore completely new technologies for use in entirely new markets, where the firm does not have any prior experience and where existing competencies are obsolete. Thus, literature on exploration with respect to an organizational learning perspective is moderated in the assumption that the long-term survival of the firm is only possible when the firm from time to time renews its knowledge and capability set.

Exploration around the core business is a strategy which impacts how and where the firms engage in exploration. Exploration is always conducted in domains which are either to some degree familiar to existing business, or where existing competencies could be stretched or adapted to. In this regard, McGrath and MacMillan emphasize the importance of setting challenging objectives pertaining to the value an opportunity should add to the existing business (McGrath and MacMillan 2000). These objectives must be challenging but realistic as well, or, in other words, activities may not simply target the probable but stretch to the possible.

Since the vision and corporate innovation strategy provides orientation for exploration, the firms are able to conduct a more effective exploration, because all activities are much more likely to yield beneficial outcomes than if no strategic directions are provided. This becomes particularly clear in the cases of *Hilti* and *Bühler*, which have provided the organization with strategic search fields (*Bühler*) or search terms which are based on the product brand image (*Hilti*). With respect to effectiveness, exploration activities will arguably have more value when they are conducted in conformity with overall strategies. From another perspective, the interview partners furthermore stated that it is too costly and risky to engage in domains where they have no relationship whatsoever. Here, the causal relationship may be the same: exploration activities which are conducted outside of strategic boundaries will probably meet internal disapproval and/or lead to project failure. This has been very obvious in the case of *Ciba*, where both people who were engaging in exploration efforts and management who was deciding about the potential of these activities were often frustrated because money for exploration activities had been spent in vain as they didn't concur with corporate innovation strategy.

Application orientation

The case firms focus on applications and thus on the outcomes of their products in the case of *Gore* and *Hilti*, on effects of the compounds in the case of *Ciba*, and on outcomes of their processes in the case of *Bühler*. Applications or functions are similarly abstract search terms in that they focus on outcomes instead of specific techniques. For example, *Hilti* has been exploring for quite a while what could come after the drill hammer, which has been the industry standard in drilling machines for decades. Although this represents one of *Hilti's* core technology competencies, *Hilti* continues to explore if there may be another technology which could better lead to the same outcome.

The degree to which the firms focus on applications in contrast to final products seems to have an impact on the space where exploration can be conducted. For example, *Hilti* exclusively thinks in applications, that is, their strategy is to provide the best solution to reach a specific goal. Thus, for instance, *Hilti* permanently ponders how a hole can be made in the best and easiest possible way. As a consequence, *Hilti* does not rely on currently applied technologies as the single means to make a hole, but are even willing to give up existing technologies and processes if there are better ways to reach the goal. This is in close congruence with *Hilti's* product leadership strategy, which posits to offer the highest quality products to its customers. The same is true for *Gore*, which also pursues a product leadership strategy. In the fabrics division, for example, the strategy is to be the only company that fulfills the promise of offering the only water and wind resistant and breathable membrane. Thus, also *Gore* thinks in applications and outcomes rather than products. For *Ciba*, thinking in applications and outcomes is virtually natural, as the nature of their chemical compounds is always a specific effect. Thus, chemicals and their respective technologies are means to a higher end, which enables *Ciba* to explore a broad range of applications where their technologies could be used. Application orientation at *Bühler* is very distinct as well in that its core business is the processing of food, which resembles already a very large area for potential exploration activities. Thus, *Bühler* does not rely on single specific technologies or products, but on know-how about processes for the goal of processing food.

Focusing on outcomes, applications, and functions may enable the firm to realize the greater value of their products. Thus, it might make sense to focus on and build up competencies with respect to functions and applications and therefore to consider the benefit for the customer rather than focusing on established technologies which might have contributed to the firm's past success. Prahalad and Hamel (1994) argue that managers need to escape a product-centric view of their firm and examine the capabilities that the products are build on. In a similar light, Henderson and Clark argue that the ability to produce more radical innovations are found in the knowledge about a product's architecture, which is why they call this type of innovation 'architectural innovation' (Henderson and Clark 1990). The notion of building on capabilities pertaining to know-how about products' architectures rather than final products or product designs bears the potential for developing more radical innovations. This relationship according to Henderson and Clark is depicted in figure 19:

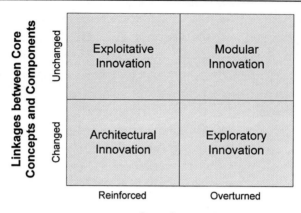

Source: Henderson and Clark (1990)

Figure 19: Relationship between product core concepts and core components

All case firms have a strong application orientation, which is based on the same concept as focusing on the architecture of their products. *Hilti* products are, apart from accessories, typically quite complex and involve many different technologies and components. As a natural consequence, it is of utmost importance to be proficient in the single technologies and their interplay to understand the outcome in an assembled product. This might be the reason for *Hilti* to focus on applications and thus also on the underlying value chain, which it is in full control of. *Gore* also strongly focuses on where and how its core technology can be applied, and how existing products can be improved by it. PTFE has many unique traits, which are, however, very versatile in their use. Applying these traits to meet specific outcomes is the overall *Gore* strategy. *Ciba* produces compounds which serve a specific goal, which is why they naturally focus on applications anyway. *Ciba* maintains tables where all compounds are listed with their exact chemical outcome and in what applications they are used or can potentially be used. Therefore, *Ciba* has maybe by the nature of its business a very clear picture of their 'products' architecture. Although *Bühler's* main business is planning and building entire mills and food processing plants, they also maintain deep know-how in the single components of the entire 'product'. Apart from the food process know-how, this involves material know-how for the rollers as well as nanotechnology for improved food processing in their extruders. Furthermore, *Bühler* is in control of all these elements within the entire process, implying a deep architectural know-how pertaining to all parts of the product's value chain.

The focus on applications and architectures rather than specific technology or product platforms is also visible in the formulation of the firms' respective innovation strategies. None of the case firms' strategies entails conditions to focus on specific technologies, products, or even industries. Instead, they focus on 'construction' in the case of *Hilti*, on 'protection and comfort' in the case of *Gore*, on 'food processing' in the case of *Bühler*, and on 'protection and stabilization' in the case of *Ciba*. This rather abstract formulation in corporate strategy leaves the organization enough leeway to explore new knowledge, and offers the opportunity to learn by identifying analogous solutions in other technological or industrial settings. In this regard, the CTO of *Hilti* stated that they are constantly looking for how "we can make ourselves superfluous" by identifying analogous technologies which might have the same outcome but with improved performance. In general terms, abstractness in contrast to concreteness potentially spurs creativity in exploration activities, as associations from entirely different domains to the original problem setting can be made (e.g. Holyoak and Thagard 1995; Hargadon and Sutton 1997; Majchrzak, Cooper et al. 2004).

Meta search
Abstract search terms
The case studies reveal that the firms engage in exploration activities based on search or innovation fields that are imposed by corporate innovation strategy. For example, *Bühler* has derived search fields in which the exploration for new ideas and business opportunities is conducted. *Hilti* has defined corporate innovation fields which are derived from the brand image of *Hilti* products. With respect to their terminology, these search fields are fairly abstract and are not confined to any technologies, industries or other limitations, which is logic consequence of the firms' application orientation. In the case of *Bühler*, the search field 'Life Science' with its sub-field 'Health & Nutrition' doesn't associate with any internally existing knowledge, technologies or capabilities, but leaves the search space fairly open. Since *Bühler* regularly scans these search fields for new technology and market developments, the people who actually engage in exploration may have a wide array for associating observed external developments with internal capabilities, and may thus be able to come up with new ideas or identify business opportunities. For *Gore* and *Hilti*, protection pertaining to their products plays a critical role. According to several interviewees, people have abstract terms like 'protection' in mind, both consciously and subconsciously, when they explore new domains. As a consequence, new information may be connected to existing demands in

the firm, which subsequently may lead to the combination of new pieces of knowledge (De Bono 1990; Holyoak and Thagard 1997; Fleming 2001).

Abstractness of a search term arguably allows the individual to associate many more things to this term. Therefore, individuals are more likely to come up with creative ideas or to identify business opportunities. The case studies showed that particularly upper managers were aware that - apart from pure product development activities - people had to be given some degree of freedom in their exploration activities, meaning that the search should not be too confined regarding specific technologies or markets. According to the CTO of *Hilti*, this approach has proved to be successful especially with people with a broad experience background from different industries, who were much more able to associate valuable external information with *Hilti*-internal demands.

Environmental scanning
The regular monitoring and scanning of technological developments and of competitors is a common activity in all case firms. As to this, researchers as well as practitioners have emphasized the importance of environmental scanning for firms operating in uncertain and changing business environments (Lenz and Engledow 1986). Firms which are able to identify and absorb information about their changing environment have the brightest prospects for long-term survival (Lenz and Engledow 1986; Teece, Pisano et al. 1997). Hambrick defines scanning to include both formal and informal search which can be either directed or undirected (Hambrick 1982). Environmental scanning can include the search for weak signals such as emerging technologies, markets, or general trends in the socio-economic environment.

The exploration of new domains which are close to the core business is accompanied by the firms' exploration activities which target a greater realm. The case studies show that trends in the business environment are scanned on a regular basis. *Bühler* engages in exploring mega trends which have an effect on the society, which is why they believe that it will have an impact on their conduct of business at some time as well. *Hilti* conducts regular workshops both internally and in collaboration with 'futurists', which entails the development of scenarios based on current and future possible trends. This is conducted both for specific applications and for finding out how future scenarios could impact *Hilti's* way of doing business, and where *Hilti* might possibly become active. At *Gore*, R&D people across the entire organization scan environmental developments and engage in scenario analyses.

5.3 Cross-case analysis

Developments in the business environment have an influence on the firm's strategy. However, the case firms distinguish between developments which occur in their immediate core business area, and developments which affect society in general and which must be interpreted with respect to the impact they have on future business. The case firms' scanning behavior seems to concur with studies which have shown that the search breadth often depends on where it is conducted in the hierarchy of the firm (Hambrick 1982). Thus, business-level strategies tend to lead to more narrow search within known sectors and familiar technologies, whereas corporate-level strategies tend to lead to much broader scanning activities aiming at the identification of weak signals in the firm's general business environment (Hambrick 1982). In fact, *Hilti's* scanning activities at the business area level or in the business units are typically focused on finding proximate solutions to existing problems. On corporate level in Corporate Research & Technology, scanning activities rather focus on mega trends and the development of scenarios which might have an impact on future business. Also *Bühler* has a two-fold approach to scanning environmental developments, where corporate R&D scans mega trends with impact on the whole society and where divisions and business units scan emerging technologies which might be useful for solving specific problems.

Depending on the corporate and business-level strategy, firms are more or less inclined to scan their competitive environment. The case firms clearly aspire to be the product and application leader in almost all of their respective markets. Therefore, they must engage in activities which will ensure that this corporate vision is met. To this end, they can be considered 'prospectors' in their respective markets. Miles and Snow (1978) have identified three types of strategies which have a direct impact on the firm's scanning activities. *Defenders* are organizations that offer a stable set of products or services and compete primarily on the basis of price, quality, and delivery. *Prospectors* try to pioneer in the development of new products or services and compete primarily by stimulating and meeting new market opportunities. Finally, *analyzers* represent an intermediate type which make fewer and slower product and market changes than prospectors, and which are less committed to stability and efficiency than defenders. Because of the different strategies, prospector firms typically devote themselves to entrepreneurial tasks such as identifying and selecting new markets, while defenders primarily focus on tasks that will improve their efficiency for the current competitive domain (Miles and Snow 1978; Pfeffer and Salancik 2003). The case studies reveal that the firm strategies correspond with prospector strategies, which is why they probably engage in extensive scanning activities across the entire organization to defend and strengthen their position.

Capability orientation
Leveraging capabilities
A common pattern across all case firms is their attempt to base activities in new domains on existing competencies. This becomes particularly apparent in the cases of *Ciba* and *Gore* whose explicit exploration strategy is to search in areas adjacent to the core. From the perspective of the new domains to be explored, it can be argued that existing competencies of a firm are underutilized, and that the range where they can be potentially applied is much larger. The ability to extract additional value from underutilized resources has been referred to as 'leveraging capability' (Danneels 2007). Leveraging entails drawing on existing competencies while using it as a basis to build new competencies. As firms learn, they are able to apply capabilities learned in one situation to another to serve a different market or opportunity. With respect to technological competence leveraging, this has been defined as a "combination of the exploitation of an existing technological competence and the exploration of competencies to serve new customers" (Danneels 2007).

The process of technology leveraging firstly involves the identification of a competence which is distinct from the product in which it is embodied. Thus, competencies are not bound to a specific single product, but are transferable to other products or applications (Wernerfelt 1984; Prahalad and Hamel 1990; Danneels 2002). Secondly, in order to make use of leveraging, complementary market-related assets are needed to access new markets (Tripsas 1997; Gambardella and Torrisi 1998; Thomke and Kuemmerle 2002). Danneels (2007) refers to the first step as 'de-linking', which involves 'viewing the technology in its own right, as distinct from its embodiment in products.' The second step then entails 're-linking', involving the application of a technology to a new product that addresses new customers (see figure 20).

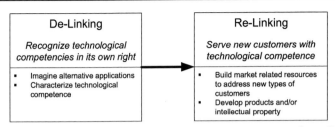

Source: Danneels (2007)

Figure 20: Concept of technological competence leveraging

De-linking entails abstraction from the product in which the competence is embedded and the identification of this competence as unique and product-spanning. "Decoupling the linkage between the technology and the product involves stepping back from the current product, and identifying what technological competencies are embedded in it" (Danneels 2007). This also involves a characterization of the technology, as the functionalities of the technology have to be understood before they can be linked with benefits in different market applications. Prahalad and Hamel (1994) argue that managers need to escape a product-centric view of their firm and examine the capabilities that the products are build on in order to leverage competencies. In a similar light, Teece (1986) distinguishes between core and complementary assets, or, in terms of this thesis, core and complementary resources and capabilities. Core resources are considered as knowledge that is fundamentally required to create a product or a service. Examples for such core resources include core technological knowledge and knowledge of customer needs (Helfat and Lieberman 2002). Complementary resources and capabilities are those subsequently required to profit from core knowledge, such as finance, marketing, or sales. Furthermore, Teece distinguished between specialized and generalized resources and capabilities. Specialized firm resources and capabilities are specific to particular circumstances and therefore also only useful in a limited range of applications. Generalized resources and capabilities, in contrast, can be applied more broadly and include general organizational capabilities (Helfat and Lieberman 2002).

As a consequence, technological competencies, which consist of a bundle of technological resources, can be used or refined to serve multiple purposes. In fact, several researchers found that technologies are often not fully utilized (Thomke and Kuemmerle 2002), and that "the productive potential of a firm's technological competencies may extend beyond the boundaries set by its product-market strategy at any time" (Burgelman 1994). In this sense, one technology can have application potential in many markets and also underlie many products (Hargadon and Sutton 1997; Patel and Pavitt 1997). Patel and Pavitt (1997) furthermore found that large firms have a broader range of technologies than products. This indicates that firms tend to have much more application potential of their technologies than can be actually utilized in existing product platforms.

According to the interviewees, the firms' exploration approach is based on a clear picture of their core business and core competencies. Prahalad and Hamel (1990) define core competencies as "the collective learning in the organization, especially how to coordinate diverse production skills and integrate multiple streams of technologies." Based on the picture about the core business, exploration is conducted in areas which are adjacent to the core business such as learning new knowledge about new (geographic) markets. While *Ciba*'s strategy is to apply its core competencies in areas which are 'beyond the core', *Gore* has even defined the steps for exploration in adjacent areas. In fact, all firms state that they will not engage in markets or products where they would have virtually no experience at all. Therefore, the case firms' exploration activities are typically conducted in areas where they have prior knowledge or experience. In fact, interview partners from all case firms and across all hierarchical levels state that the exploration of random pieces of knowledge entails too much uncertainty regarding the potential value of the new knowledge. This is in line with research which has shown that firms tend to enter markets where they have prior knowledge and related resources and competencies (Helfat and Lieberman 2002).

For *Hilti* and *Bühler*, the exploration scope is particularly large as both firms control the entire value chain from research and development over manufacturing to sales. For both cases, process know-how and thus architectural know-how is a core competence. Therefore, their capability to reconfigure existing product architectures and their know-how pertaining to the application of specific components within the end-product bears great potential to leverage existing capabilities beyond current products and markets. Although *Ciba* and *Gore* cover only parts of the value chain, they also leverage their capabilities. *Ciba* engages in exploration by leveraging its technological capabilities to domains and applications where protection and stabilization play a critical role. For example, *Ciba* explored and ultimately entered the home and personal care market when they realized that protection on a chemical basis was also needed in skin protection such as sun blockers. *Gore's* core technology PTFE is extremely versatile, which is why it is found in virtually every industry, and which lends support to the assumption that the potential of PTFE is still not yet completely exploited.

Table 11 provides an overview of the case firms' leverage potential pertaining to their competencies and capabilities.

	Ciba	Gore	Hilti	Bühler
Core competencies	▪ know-how with respect to chemical compounds and manufacturing processes	▪ know-how with respect to technologies	▪ know-how with respect to technologies and manufacturing processes	▪ know-how with respect to technologies and manufacturing processes
Leverage potential	▪ medium	▪ high	▪ high	▪ high
Core capabilities	▪ application of compound know-how to new domains	▪ application of core technology to new domains	▪ application of technological, process, and application know-how to new domains	▪ application of technological and process know-how to new domains
Leverage potential	▪ high	▪ high	▪ high	▪ high

Table 11: Overview of sample firms' leverage potential

Matching capabilities

The leveraging of capabilities beyond the core business requires adaptation efforts to fit the requirements of the new domain. Thus, merely the potential for capability leverage is not sufficient for commercial impact, but firms must also build complementary market-related assets where the leverage potential can be exploited (Teece 1986; Tripsas 1997; Gambardella and Torrisi 1998). While capability leverage is an inherent element of the exploration process based on existing core business and competencies, capability match may be considered as a fundamental subsequent requirement in this same process. However, capability match as a crucial part in the exploration process becomes more transparent as all case firms engage in environmental scanning which might influence current business in such a way that existing capabilities may in fact have to be matched and adapted to exogenous developments.

The case studies reveal that scanning and scenario analyses are conducted to see how future developments might influence current business. *Gore* and *Hilti* experiment with new materials and develop prototypes to see how new products might meet the demands of future developments. For example, *Hilti* conducts scenario analyses about how future construction sites might look like in 30 years from now. In one scenario, instead of people, there will be only robots working, which has many implications on how future products are operated and handled and which requirements pertaining to environmental influences such as dirt and heat they might have to fulfill. *Gore*, for example, experiments with PTFE-membranes which are used in the medical industry, both for protection of surgeons as well as implants such as artificial arteries and coronary vascular walls.

In order to meet the requirements of such new applications, firms must adapt their existing competencies while they acquire new knowledge at the same time. In the course of exploration activities, a technical and organizational feasibility study is typically conducted to see if and how existing competencies can be adapted to the new domain. For example, after initial exploration efforts, *Gore* develops a 'one-pager' where future business potential is roughly assessed and *Hilti* estimates in its 'trait studies' both future business potential and how existing capabilities might need to be adapted to be successful in the potential new domain. In early stages of exploration, experiments are conducted and prototypes are possibly developed. While in these stages typically no financial calculations pertaining to business potential and potential revenues are required, this is different in later stages where with advancing developments more accurate calculations are demanded. This is true for all case firms, where the exploration phase typically ends with a business plan containing all relevant information about the market, the technology, investments to be made, and if and how the organization is able to reach this goal. A typical element of preliminary assessments in the exploration process is how and why the firm fits in the new market. Thus, for example in the case of *Hilti* and *Bühler*, it must be explained how the new business opportunity fits with corporate innovation strategy and what the estimated efforts are to match lacking competencies. All firms also engage in alliances or other types of cooperation in case competence gaps are too big. This typically depends on how far the adjacency is away from the core, as adjacencies also have certain band widths.

In summary, the case firms try to stretch and match their competencies to environmental developments which at some point in the future will probably have an impact on how business is done. This is most apparent in the cases of *Gore*, *Hilti* and *Bühler* who actively scan mega trends and conduct scenario analyses to see how the future might develop. As capability matching with external developments which the firms cannot control is different from adjacency moves which are within the strategy and control of the firm, the case firms engage in alliances when internal competence development is too difficult. Figure 21 illustrates the process of stretching and matching capabilities in the process of exploration depending on if exploration is conducted based on an 'inside-out' or 'outside-in' perspective. Inside-out exploration refers to the firm's search activities based on internal capabilities to be stretched to new external domains to form new business opportunities. Outside-in exploration, in contrast, refers to the firm's general scanning of external developments to identify new business opportunities and to see if internal capabilities can be adapted.

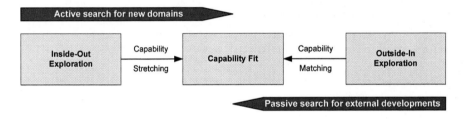

Figure 21: Capability stretching and matching within exploration

The findings show that exploration in the case firms is conducted in two ways. The first approach is induced by corporate innovation strategy and can thus be considered endogenous, that is, new domains which are adjacent to the core business and which are based on existing core competencies are explored. The second approach, which runs parallel to exploring adjacencies, is induced by external developments in the firm's business environment. Here, emerging trends and mega trends are scanned on a regular basis and firms also conduct scenario analyses to see how the future might develop. By this exogenously induced exploration, firms try to forecast future requirements on their existing competencies. As a result of this, existing competencies are stretched to future requirements, which leads to matching existing and future competencies for sustained firm competitiveness.

Summary
The efficacy of exploration activities in the case firms depends on their overall innovation strategy and on their approach how these strategies are actually implemented. The focus on unexploited opportunities which are located around the

existing core business serves as starting point for exploration activities. By expanding core activities and thus by stretching existing capabilities to new frontiers, the firms build on existing knowledge while simultaneously stretching and renewing them. Thus, it can be argued that the firms have found effective ways to combine both exploratory and exploitative activities in a beneficial way. With respect to literature on ambidextrous organizations, this lends new insights and extends this literature stream.

Furthermore, the case firms' exploration strategy and implementation may be argued to be fairly effective as search efforts take place within strategic boundaries but beyond the limitations of specific technologies or markets. This is achieved by using abstract search or innovation fields which are derived from the overall innovation strategy. This approach ensures that search activities will likely yield beneficial outcomes as they cohere to strategic parameters. Thus, abstractness within strategic boundaries allows the firms to leverage their existing capabilities to new domains and adapt them to external developments.

The results provide insights into the strategic importance of exploration and into how exploration strategies are designed. All sample companies view the activity of exploration as very critical for firm success and therefore invest dedicated resources in exploration activities. The case studies reveal that a link to existing business and competencies is ensured when engaging in exploration. Thus, exploration is not conducted in random areas, but in areas which are adjacent to the existing core business. This becomes evident in the way the firms search for new business opportunities in domains which are adjacent to the core and in the way they position themselves in the value chain. However, the distinction between exploration and exploitation within and adjacent to the core business is often a matter of degrees, which shows that both activities form a continuum.

These insights extend existing literature on exploration in several ways. First, from an organizational learning perspective, notions about 'undirected search' as a concept found in practice is moderated. Although in reality there may exist firms whose dominant search strategy is to engage in random search for any type of new knowledge, be it within or outside of the core business, the cases show that these successful firms do not engage in undirected or random but directed search based on higher-level strategies. Therefore, the concept of undirected search might have to be reconsidered with respect to its fit with business reality.

5.3.3. Elements impacting exploration efficiency

Respondents from management level from all case firms agree that exploration can only have successful outcomes when the firm provides an environment which is protected from the necessities arising in daily business. Therefore, all case firms provide dedicated resources for exploration activities, and furthermore separate exploration activities from exploitation activities. Insights from the case studies suggest that this increases the efficiency of exploration as people can fully concentrate on their tasks without being involved in, for example, mere product development activities. Furthermore, as it is the individual who actually engages in exploration, cognitive abilities and personal traits seem to influence the degree to which new ideas can be created and new business opportunities identified. These variables are further analyzed ion the following sections.

Dedicated resources

The cases reveal that all firms do strategic investments in exploration activities and thus enable exploration to happen in the first place. *Ciba* invests 25% of the group-wide R&D budget in beyond-the-core activities. This percentage is constant over the years, and the CTO who is responsible for all major exploration activities has freedom as to how exactly this money is spent. Exploration activities at NGP are not subject for detailed scrutiny until a concept is worked out which is presentable to the management board. Thus, *Ciba* actually grants freedom for the pursuit of exploration activities, and proves this by significant up-front investments. The CTO of *Ciba* states that by this, management wants to signal the importance of innovation, and furthermore spur people's interest in exploration activities. *Gore*, already by their innovation culture, constantly engages in exploring new business opportunities and technologies which support their core technology PTFE. All employees are encouraged to use their dabble time for exploring aspects which are new to *Gore*, as long as such activities are reconfirmed and assessed in their impact on the firm with fellow employees. At *Hilti*, about 4% of annual turnover is invested in R&D of which about 10% is invested in activities which are exclusively reserved for exploration activities. This clear commitment is a result from corporate strategy to be the global market leader in professional construction tools. *Bühler* also invests about 1% of group-wide annual turnover in exploration activities. Just as is the case with *Hilti*, this financial commitment results from corporate strategy and the claim to be the global market leader and expert in the food processing industry. Furthermore, the CTO annually reviews divisional strategies and actively gets involved in strategy formulation when there is a too strong emphasis on incremental innovation activities.

The allocation of dedicated resources is arguably a very critical precondition for exploration to be effective. Studies have found that the firm's exploratory efforts with respect to the targeted identification of highly new knowledge is likely to require considerable slack resources (Ahuja and Lampert 2001). Also, it is argued that the creation of new competencies requires deliberate efforts by management to invest or reallocate resources to the production of new competencies (Dorroh, Gulledge et al. 1994).

The case studies show that corporate management is willing to invest dedicated resources into exploration activities. With the exception of *Gore*, this is accomplished by allocating a large fraction of 10-25% of the annual R&D budget for these activities. The fact that the firms do this with a fixed budget might be due to the insight that otherwise there would be too much emphasis on exploitative projects and activities. As a consequence, firms are splitting the R&D budget for exploratory and exploitative activities, with the much larger amount being invested in exploitation activities.

To some degree, this sheds a new light on discussions on exploration and exploitation. The insights gained from the case studies are somewhat contrary to the conventional view that there is a crowding-out effect between exploration and exploitation in favor of exploitative innovation activities (He and Wong 2004; Gupta, Smith et al. 2006). Although it is generally agreed across the firms that exploitative activities are typically much more common, and that, in fact, the majority of the R&D budget is invested in improving existing product-market combinations, firms circumvent the tension between exploration and exploitation by committing themselves to up-front financial investments. Furthermore, the case firms embrace uncertainty inherent in exploration activities and state that without doing this they would not be able to reap the benefits of any of such activities. Therefore, the firms emphasize more the chances and opportunities in which exploration activities might result than focusing on the risks and cost of potential exploration failure. Thus, up-front investments in exploration activities, which are enabled by strategic directives, avoid crowding-out effects between exploration and exploitation activities. Crowding-out effects then only describe the case where both activities compete for the same scarce resources, which would naturally take place in the conventional NPD process. However, the case firms avoid this situation by committing themselves up-front to strategic investments in exploration activities.

Organizational separation

Except for the case of *Gore*, the case studies reveal that the firms clearly separate exploration from exploitation activities. The case firms maintain distinct organizational units which exclusively engage in exploration activities. *Ciba* maintains a unit New Growth Platform which on corporate level which directly reports to the CTO. NGP recruits people from throughout the entire organization who are sponsored by NGP for the time the exploration activity is running. *Gore* maintains NBD units on corporate and divisional level, whose task is to explore new markets and identify new business opportunities. NBD closely collaborates with R&D to ensure the fit between potential business opportunities and existing technological competencies. *Hilti* engages in exploration exclusively on corporate level in the unit Corporate Research & Technology. CR&T employs people who are fully dedicated to exploring their respective area of expertise such as mechanics, physics, or materials. In parallel, *Hilti* conducts trait studies which explore specific industries in detail to see if there is future business potential. *Bühler's* conducts exploration both on corporate and divisional level, and also separates exploration from exploitation activities by implementing people or groups within the divisions who exclusively engage in exploration.

Ciba finances and grows exploration activities exclusively in NGP typically for several years until the knowledge is turned into a sound business model and where the continued project would be self-sustaining. When this situation is reached, *Ciba* initiates internal start-ups which exclusively try to commercialize the intended innovation in a first step. In a second step, the 'venture' is integrated into existing business within one of the divisions or spun out to create distinct external units. At *Bühler*, new organizational units are created within corporate R&D in which the continued exploration of the new knowledge is pursued. Corporate R&D serves as an incubator for these activities and also finances all exploration activities. Similar to *Ciba*, *Bühler* flexibly either reintegrates the new venture into existing business or continues to operate the new venture as a separate new organizational unit, as was the case with nanotechnology. *Gore* and *Hilti* do not build separate organizational units for their exploration activities, but conduct exploration activities in corporate R&D (*Hilti*) or in self-operating teams (*Gore*). However, they both show common patterns again regarding the reintegration of exploratory inventions into existing business or spin-offs.

Thus, the case firms are quite flexible in their organizational structure to create and dissolve units which engage in exploration. Furthermore, they show common approaches how to commercialize the new innovation, that is, either by creating internal start-ups, by integrating them into existing business, or by spinning them out to self-operating external units. In summary, the case firms can be considered fairly flexible in their organizational structure which allows for efficient exploration. Thus, organizational flexibility can be argued to be a vital precondition for exploration activities to be successful. Table 12 provides an overview of locus of new knowledge exploration and exploitation across the sample firms.

	Ciba	*Gore*	*Hilti*	*Bühler*
Locus of new knowledge exploration	▪ New Growth Platforms distinct unit within corporate research	▪ New Business Development units and R&D	▪ Corporate Research & Technology	▪ Corporate Technology and new units within Corporate Technology
Locus of new knowledge exploitation	▪ Internal start-ups, existing business, or spin-offs	▪ Existing business	▪ Existing business or spin-offs	▪ Internal start-ups or existing business

Table 12: Locus of knowledge exploration in sample firms

Literature on ambidexterity argues that exploration needs to be separated from exploitation activities as both are very different in their character (Duncan 1976; Tushman and Anderson 1986; O'Reilly III and Tushman 2004). The cases reveal that the firms separate exploration from exploitation activities to ensure that exploration can be conducted effectively by providing a secured atmosphere in an organizational unit which typically operates on corporate level. Thus, the findings from the case studies mostly support this literature. However, as the case of *Gore* shows, a distinct organizational separation between the two activities can be avoided if other structures such as a general environment conducive to exploration is provided.

Cognitive capabilities of the individual
Although the case studies reveal that exploration is a fairly strategic activity, exploration is ultimately conducted by people. To a large extent, exploration requires the individual's ability to absorb relevant knowledge in the environment as well as the

5.3 Cross-case analysis

ability to see relationships between external developments and internal competencies, and, at last, to recognize business opportunities. Therefore, the individuals' backgrounds and particularly their cognitive abilities are critical when exploring new knowledge. From an individual perspective, an entrepreneurially minded can identify and exploit new opportunities because he possesses cognitive abilities that enable him to perceive a different meaning to ambiguous situations (Alvarez and Barney 2002). Interview partners from all case firms state that they try to involve people in exploration activities who stand out by having both broad and deep industry, application, and/or technological know-how. For example, on the one hand, exploration at *Bühler* is conducted by senior people who have a profound knowledge of the firm as well as of the industry they are competing in. On the other hand, corporate R&D serves as a 'flow-heater' for young people who just received their university degree and who explore new domains from their specific knowledge background. Although they do not have deep firm or industry insights, they closely collaborate with senior people and thus are able to explore new business potential by combining their knowledge. *Hilti's* exploration activities are conducted by people who have a deep firm and technology know-how. In addition, they employ their own sales people to conduct industry-specific trait studies, because the sales people have a distinct intuition for customer needs. At *Gore*, people typically take the initiative who are driven by the desire to change things and who like to explore new things. Therefore, *Gore* possibly does not need to establish any further separated organizational units apart from NBD which would engage in exploration. Rather, those people who are willing to explore actually do it and find fellow colleagues who are equally willing to contribute.

Furthermore, the abstract formulation of corporate innovation strategies, as is to different degrees done by all case firms, may be another facilitator for individual creativity at exploration to become successful. On a rather strategic and less problemistic level, abstractness in the formulation of strategies allows for creative thinking and finding 'solutions' which are related to the original problem setting. This kind of creative thinking requires cognitive abilities of the individual as well as experiences the individual person has made in the past. Cognitive abilities enable the identification of analogies to the original problem setting based on past experiences (Gick and Holyoak 1980; Reeves and Weisberg 1993). The role and importance of analogies in problem solving has also been widely discussed by creativity researchers (Prince 1970; Boden 1990; Rickards 1990; Csikszentmihalyi 1996), and analogies are a central mechanism in many creativity techniques (Gordon 1969; De Bono 1990;

Ceserani and Greatwood 1995). In fact, "divergence and lack of shared experiences are critical for developing new ideas" (Majchrzak, Cooper et al. 2004). From cognitive psychology perspective, analogical thinking entails the transfer of knowledge from one domain that usually already exists in memory to the domain to be explained (Gick and Holyoak 1983; Vosniadou and Ortony 1989). Management scholars have argued that the use of analogies typically includes the transfer of knowledge (Majchrzak, Cooper et al. 2004), where knowledge acquired in one situation is applied to another (Argote and Ingram 2000). This aspect is illustrated in figure 22 as adapted from Gassmann and Zeschky (2008).

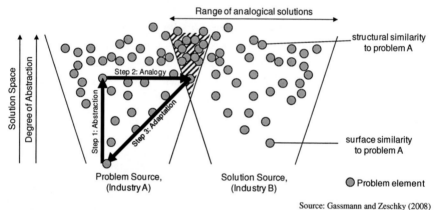

Source: Gassmann and Zeschky (2008)

Figure 22: Concept of abstraction and analogy in exploration

Personal traits of the individual

When asked why and how he came into position of the CTO at *Hilti*, he answered "probably because I am somewhat strange in my thinking, and because I have a broad technology and industry experience". The CTO of *Bühler* probably came into position because of his distinct willingness to change things and because of his ambition to position the firm in the long run by constantly developing entirely new products and not just incremental improvements. When *Ciba* established its New Growth Platform, its design and strategic layout was put in the hands of people who had been involved in exploration activities and formulating exploration strategies for a long time, and who showed a distinct will to change things for the better. In fact, when NGP was not implemented yet, these people were somewhat frustrated with the way business was done at *Ciba*, and they realized that moving beyond incremental improvements was a critical factor for staying competitive. As mentioned earlier, exploration at *Gore* is typically conducted by people who have an entrepreneurial mindset, and they are able to motivate and convince fellow colleagues to participate in an exploratory project. This 'self-selection' is to a large amount possible because of the strategic and cultural conditions, which are achieved by setting challenging objectives pertaining to the value an opportunity adds to the existing business (McGrath and MacMillan 2000). However, exploration at *Gore* is foremost done because of people who are driven by their willingness to innovate.

The cases of *Ciba* and *Bühler* show that people are in charge of formulating exploration strategies or engage in exploration activities who show a distinct intrinsic motivation for change. At *Gore* and *Hilti*, people are willing to spend their own time beyond what is already granted and invest resources into exploration activities despite knowing that there might be no outcome. Furthermore, as becomes most clearly in the case of *Gore*, they also have the ability and motivation to convince others about the necessity to go beyond daily business, and they are able to either allocate respective resources or make them available. People with such a mindset search for opportunities in uncertain business environments and subsequently determine the capabilities needed to successfully exploit them (McGrath and MacMillan 2000; Covin and Slevin 2002).

Summary
Insights from the case studies show that exploration activities are successful when both organizational and individual competencies are in place. From an organizational perspective, strategic up-front investments in exploration activities ensure that exploration is allowed for in the first place. Furthermore, the case studies show for three of the four cases that exploration activities are separated from exploitation activities by means of separated organizational units which exclusively engage in exploration activities. By this, the firms try to ensure that exploration can be conducted efficiently as it is not affected by daily business which typically focuses in exploitation activities.
On the individual level, people who actually engage in the search for new knowledge, technologies, and business opportunities show abilities to absorb relevant information in the external environment which they can bring within the business context of the firm. Therefore, from firm perspective, exploration seems to be particularly successful if individuals are actually able to relate external events to internal capabilities. Furthermore, the findings show that absorbing relevant knowledge and recognizing business opportunities is typically accompanied by fairly flexible organizational structures. Exploration activities are conducted within corporate R&D which serves as

an incubator, and the outcome of these activities are integrated into existing business or spun out into internal or external organizational units when activities have reached a certain point.

5.4. Summary of the conceptual model

The refinement of the conceptual framework emerges from the findings of the cross-case analysis. Various strategic approaches and organizational determinants effect how exploration is actually conducted in the firm. Exploration is seen as a critical means to develop more radical innovations and to secure the long-term competitiveness of the firm. Thus, exploration is a quite strategic issue which is enabled and supported from corporate level.

The alignment of innovation and search strategies have an important impact on the firm's exploration propensity and efficacy. While an overarching innovation strategy influences the intensity and direction of exploration activities, performance feedbacks from search influence the firm's innovation strategy. The search strategy with a focus on core business, on capabilities, and on applications rather than product or technology platforms are critical preconditions for increasing exploration efficacy and efficiency in terms of economically viable outcomes. Furthermore, organizational assets such as dedicated financial resources combined with respective organizational structures and cognitive abilities of the individual are vital preconditions on the micro-level for exploration to function.

Figure 23 summarizes the findings of the cross-case analysis pertaining to cause and effect relationships and completes the conceptual framework to the final conceptual model.

5.4 Summary of the conceptual model

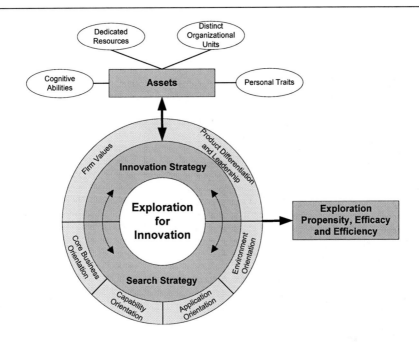

Figure 23: Summary of the conceptual model

The conceptual model is the result from analyzing and reflecting the case data on existing literature and theory on exploration. The insights gained from this analysis, and more specifically the conceptual model's constructs and relationships are in the following chapter further sharpened. Thus, the next chapter derives testable hypotheses which are based on this conceptual model. Through this approach, existing literature on exploration is further extended.

6. Theoretical implications

In this chapter, the conceptual model and its relationships are further sharpened. In chapter 6.1, organizational learning literature pertaining to exploration is moderated by discussing how firms engage in what can be called 'directed exploration'. In chapter 6.2, the theory of absorptive capacity as the theoretical base for this research is introduced. Using this theoretical perspective, the subsequent chapters derive research hypotheses on exploration for innovation, thereby extending existing literature on exploration.

6.1. Directed exploration in organizational learning

The combined development of a constant stream of incremental innovations as well as of rather radical innovations is a hallmark of successful firms. The case study analysis in the previous chapters shows that firms have developed successful exploration approaches which share many strategic commonalities but which are idiosyncratic in their detail. Insights from the case analysis show that firms' exploration approaches depart from the common image of exploration the way it is mostly described by organizational learning literature. (March 1991; He and Wong 2004; Holmqvist 2004) Thus, notions of organizational learning about exploring entirely new and/or random knowledge is not replicated by the data, which implies that the conventional understanding of what exploration for new knowledge entails may need to be moderated. If the common assertion is true that for firms to be successful they need to engage in both exploration and exploitation, then the firms investigated in this research fit this postulate. This is, without exception, because the firms in this research have since long been leaders in most of their markets with respect to technological innovations and market share and still continue to be. Therefore, they can be argued to have found effective ways to successfully engage in exploration and exploitation.

The firms' exploration approach is based on fairly clear strategies which influence the organization and execution of exploration activities. Firms seek and learn new knowledge based on their existing core business and on existing competencies which can be subsumed as their prior knowledge. From another perspective, the firms do not explore random pieces of knowledge, and the development of rather exploratory innovation does – from their point of view – neither typically nor necessarily depend on the exploration and subsequent exploitation of entirely new knowledge. Rather, the successful development of exploratory innovations follows the logic that new knowledge is combined with existing knowledge by means of a structural link between old and new knowledge. This implies that existing knowledge is both necessary and beneficial for exploring new knowledge for subsequent development of exploratory innovation. The difference between exploitative and exploratory innovations is thus merely a function of the distance of the new knowledge from existing knowledge. The case analysis shows that firms have found viable approaches how the distance of knowledge to be explored can be kept such that uncertainty inherent in the new knowledge remains controllable.

Based on insights from the case analysis, it can be argued that firms do not engage in blind search but in what can be called 'directed exploration' for new knowledge. While most literature on exploration is fairly vague on what exploration actually entails apart from it being concerned with learning new knowledge, this research shows that firms have strategies as to what kind of new knowledge is learned and as to how this is achieved. Therefore, insights from this research extend existing literature on exploration by contributing to the practical understanding of exploration and, in particular, by showing that firms engage only in exploration activities and search in areas which yield the potential for commercially viable knowledge. Thus, firms engage in directed exploration based on fairly clear strategies and not, as most literature on exploration might imply, in random search for new knowledge.

6.2. Theoretical base for exploration for innovation

The prior remarks imply that for exploration for new knowledge to be successful, firms require existing knowledge to which the new knowledge can be related. Therefore, although exploration can generally be conducted in any search direction, meaningful information can only be extracted and absorbed if the new knowledge can be put in a business context, and thus if it can be related to existing knowledge. The case firms consider exploration activities only successful when their outcome yields knowledge which can be successfully used for innovation. Furthermore, the firms engage in exploration based on existing knowledge, which suggests that relevant information stemming from exploration activities can only be absorbed based on that existing knowledge. The firm's ability to absorb relevant information from the environment has been termed as the firm's 'absorptive capability' which has first been introduced by Wesley Cohen and Daniel Levinthal (1989; 1990). Absorptive capacity refers to one of the firm's fundamental learning processes: its ability to identify, assimilate, and exploit knowledge from the environment. The theory of absorptive capacity might allow to transfer and utilize some of the theory's insights to explain the firms' exploration approach and success. Using insights from this theory yields the possibility to derive managerial implications as to how to effectively engage in exploration. Therefore, the following chapter briefly introduces the theory of absorptive capacity. The subsequent chapters then use insights from this theory to derive research hypotheses pertaining to firms' exploration approach.

6.2.1. The absorptive capacity of firms

Cohen and Levinthal (1990) define absorptive capacity as the firm's ability 'to recognize the value of new, external information, assimilate it, and apply it to commercial ends.' The theory of absorptive capacity originates from research on the competitive advantage of firms and has been used to analyze diverse and complex organizational phenomena (Zahra and George 2002). Absorptive capacity has received wide acknowledgement in scholarly literature due to its overlapping with other popular areas of organizational research such as organizational learning, strategic alliances, knowledge management, and the resource-based view of the firm (Lane, Koka et al. 2006).

Cohen and Levinthal (1990) argue that the ability to evaluate and utilize outside knowledge is largely a function of the level of prior related knowledge. Prior knowledge can have many attributes and can range from basic skills or a shared language to the most recent scientific or technological developments. As such, it is actually the firm's or an individual's prior knowledge which confers the ability to recognize and assimilate the value of new information. Absorptive capacity is strongly based on insights from cognitive and behavioral sciences which argue that, on the individual level, accumulated prior knowledge increases the ability to acquire new knowledge and, therefore, to learn. Because learning is cumulative, learning performance is greatest when the object of learning is related to what is already known. Furthermore, prior knowledge facilitates the recall and use of the new knowledge, because an increased amount of objects, patterns, and constructs in the memory enables easier acquisition of new information about these constructs. The cognitive pattern underlying this is that learning happens by establishing linkages with pre-existing concepts, which has been called 'associative learning' (Holyoak and Thagard 1997).

The degree to which absorptive capacity might lead to the identification of more radical knowledge depends on the distance of the new knowledge to existing knowledge. For effective knowledge absorption and the development of more radical new ideas, Cohen and Levinthal (1990) argue that the existing knowledge must to some extent be very closely related to the new knowledge, and that some fraction of that knowledge must be fairly diverse, although still related, to permit effective, creative utilization of the new knowledge. Knowledge diversity in the organization also plays a critical role in the question what and what not can be absorbed (Kogut and Zander 1992). In a setting in which there is uncertainty about the knowledge domains from which potentially useful information may emerge, a diverse background provides a more robust basis for learning because it increases the prospect that incoming information will relate to what is already known.

Absorptive capacity at the level of the firm ultimately depends on the absorptive capacities of the individual members (Cohen and Levinthal 1990). However, as absorptive capacity is defined to entail the ability to exploit newly acquired knowledge to commercial ends, not only individual but also organizational aspects affect overall absorptive capacity. Thus, apart from the organization's interface with the external environment, intra-organizational transfer of the knowledge is as important as the acquisition itself. With respect to the organizational process of absorbing external knowledge, Zahra and George (2002) extended the original model developed by Cohen and Levinthal and define absorptive capacity as a set of organizational routines and processes by which firms acquire, assimilate, transform, and exploit knowledge. They argue that these four capabilities play different but complementary roles in explaining how firms' absorptive capacity can influence innovation performance (see figure 24).

6.2 Theoretical base for exploration for innovation

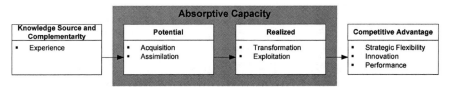

Source: Zahra and George (2002)

Figure 24: Potential and realized absorptive capacity

Zahra and George (2002) split absorptive capacity into 'potential' and 'realized' absorptive capacity, where potential absorptive capacity refers to the firm's capability to value and acquire external knowledge, while realized absorptive capacity refers to the transformation and exploitation of the newly acquired knowledge. They argue that potential and realized absorptive capacity coexist at all times and that each in isolation fulfills a necessary but insufficient condition to improve firm performance. For example, firms cannot possibly exploit knowledge without first acquiring it, similarly, without having the transformation and exploitation capabilities, the acquisition and assimilation of new knowledge is nearly meaningless. As a consequence, a high potential absorptive capacity does not necessarily lead to enhanced performance.

In this model, diverse external knowledge is a key antecedent for absorptive capacity. External knowledge can emerge from diverse sources such as acquisitions, contractual agreements, and other interorganizational relationships such as R&D consortia, alliances, or joint ventures (Zahra and George 2002). Also, the breadth and depth of knowledge exposure influences a firm's propensity to explore new and related knowledge. Therefore, knowledge diversity influences acquisition and assimilation capabilities of the firm. Furthermore, and in line with Cohen and Levinthal, Zahra and George argue that past experience influences the development of future acquisition capabilities by directing knowledge search areas. They define experience to be mainly the result of environmental scanning, benchmarking, interactions with customers, and alliances with other firms, while some experience is also gained from learning-by-doing.

The firm's potential absorptive capacity consists of the acquisition and assimilation of new knowledge. The acquisition of new knowledge is argued to be influenced by the firms' search intensity, search speed, and search direction in acquiring new knowledge. Assimilation of the new knowledge refers to the firm's routines and processes that allow it to analyze, process, interpret, and understand the information obtained from the external sources. In contrast, the firm's realized absorptive capacity consists of the transformation and exploitation of the previously acquired and assimilated knowledge. The transformation of knowledge resembles the firm's capability to develop and refine the routines that facilitate combining existing and newly acquired knowledge. Zahra and George (2002) argue that the ability to 'recognize two apparently incongruous sets of information and then combine them to arrive at a new schema represents a transformation capability'. This ability is furthermore argued to shape the formation of an entrepreneurial mindset which in turn facilitates the recognition of opportunities and alters the way the firm sees itself and its competitive landscape. The exploitation of new knowledge, finally, refers to the firm's capability to refine, extend, and leverage existing competencies or create new ones by incorporating acquired and transformed knowledge into its operations. However, also within absorptive capacity theory, the way new knowledge is acquired and assimilated is not clear. Listing the sources of new knowledge is not sufficient for explaining how knowledge assimilation actually works. Therefore, the search for new knowledge (i.e. the acquisition) remains again a black box in absorptive capacity literature.

Firms which have the capability to acquire, assimilate, transform, and exploit external knowledge may achieve higher competitive advantage than firms which lack one or more of these capabilities. One source of firms' difference in intraindustry performance lies in the difference in firms' utilization of organizational resources and capabilities (Barney 1991; Teece, Pisano et al. 1997). Thus, valuable, rare, inimitable, and non-substitutable resources can give the firm a competitive advantage (Barney 1991). A firm's capability to effectively create, manage, and exploit external knowledge is one such critical capability. Therefore, absorptive capacity as a bundle of knowledge-based capabilities can be a source of competitive advantage (Zahra and George 2002).

The distinction between potential and realized absorptive capacity, and more particularly, the distinction of the absorptive capacity process in a chain of successive capabilities as depicted in figure 24 allows a more proper analysis of the single factors within this process. The absorptive capacity model developed by Zahra and George offers a valuable framework to explain the case firms' exploration behavior. In particular, insights from the cases show that potential absorptive capacity pertaining to the acquisition and assimilation of new knowledge is of critical importance. The firms allow exploration to happen in the first place and try to improve environmental conditions so that organizational routines with respect to the exploitation of the new knowledge can take effect. Although the transformation and exploitation of external knowledge are critical stages in the absorptive capacity process, towards the background and research aim of this study, potential absorptive capacity pertaining to the question how firms engage in exploration (and not in exploitation as a subsequent stage) is considered and discussed in the following.

6.2.2. Firms' exploration approach and absorptive capacity

The cases show that experience and prior knowledge in terms of existing business and capabilities are the most critical factors in firms' exploration strategy and efficacy. Apart from firms' engagement in activities such as environmental scanning, customer and alliance activities, the firms employ existing capabilities, and therefore prior knowledge, as guiding principles to explore new knowledge domains. Thus, an inherent part of the firms' exploration strategy is to ensure a high congruence between existing knowledge and the knowledge to be explored. Although the new knowledge cannot be understood in the beginning, knowledge congruence implies that there are structural similarities between existing and new knowledge (Holyoak and Thagard 1997; Dahl and Moreau 2002) such as, for example, different technologies with similar effects or new geographical markets which are close to an existing market. As such, the knowledge to be explored is related to the existing knowledge but diverse enough to yield potential to be creatively combined for innovation (Cohen and Levinthal 1990). As a consequence, firms are likely to absorb this type of related yet diverse knowledge much better than entirely new knowledge which does not show any linkages to prior knowledge or experience.

In the case of *Ciba* and *Gore*, exploration activities are conducted around the core business and based on existing technological and organizational capabilities. *Hilti* engages in exploration activities which are within previously defined innovation fields originating from corporate strategy. *Ciba*, *Hilti* and *Bühler* engage in exploration activities along the value chain. The exploration strategies pursued by the case firms show a strong link between existing knowledge and knowledge domains to be explored. Therefore, the case firms can be argued to have a high absorptive capacity in the domains which they explore and a low absorptive capacity in areas outside of their defined innovation fields and beyond their capabilities. This also implies that the firm's potential absorptive capacity is not only a function of its R&D intensity and knowledge diversity (Cohen and Levinthal 1990; Kogut and Zander 1992), but that it is also a function of the firm's exploration strategy. This relationship is illustrated in figure 25, where potential absorptive capacity consisting of knowledge acquisition and assimilation is detailed and ultimately replaced by the knowledge exploration model as developed in the conceptual model in figure 23. In contrast to the model by Zahra and George, the knowledge sources are neither already existent (such as, for example, R&D consortia), nor is it clear that new knowledge will be found in such sources, but they must be actively searched for. Prior experience based on existing capabilities stemming from the core business, as well as a focus on applications and developments in the external environment serve as a guideline for the direction of search for new knowledge, possibly long before any R&D consortia, for example, might be established. Therefore, the acquisition of new knowledge is not in any form granted, but is based on an active search and sense-making of external knowledge. As a consequence, a firm's potential absorptive capacity largely depends on the firm's innovation and search strategy, and therefore, on *how* firms explore for new knowledge (see figure 25).

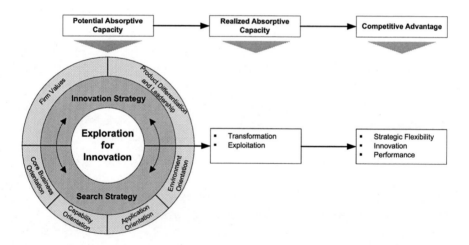

Figure 25: Relationship between firms' absorptive capacity and exploration

In the following chapters, the constructs and relationships pertaining to firms' exploration approach which emerged during the case analysis are further sharpened using the theory of absorptive capacity. Based on the conceptual model, literature and theory on exploration with respect to the question how firms engage in exploration is extended by deducting research hypothesis. In analogy to the cross-case analysis, the first chapter (6.3) responds to insights gained pertaining to the firms' propensity to engage in exploration. The next chapter (6.4) considers the question how firms ensure that their exploration efforts yield a high likelihood for beneficial outcomes of their exploration activities. Finally, the last chapter (6.5) concerns the question how firms allow for an efficient exploration.

6.3. Hypotheses on firms' exploration propensity

Firm values
The case analysis shows that firms' fundamental values pertaining to how they believe they should compete in the market influences their attitude and approach towards exploration. For example, *Hilti* has 'traditionally' been the leader in its respective markets, which is a result of the company founder's belief that innovation and technological leadership are what shall distinguish *Hilti* from competitors and how competitive advantage shall be achieved. Also *Ciba* and *Bühler* believe that they must go beyond a minimum threshold of investments in exploration activities to maintain their future competitiveness. In fact, when *Ciba* was suffering from declining market shares after the year 2000, management decided to invest even more in exploration to regain lost market shares and to position itself as an innovation leader.

Ciba, Hilti, and *Bühler* invest fixed fractions ranging between 15-25% of annual R&D budget in pure exploration activities. This is done disregarding current competitive performance. Therefore, the case firms will always invest in exploration and not overly question these investments. In fact, these firms believe that exploration is a good and beneficial activity per se, which has already turned into a company culture. The firms' willingness to engage in exploration becomes not only evident in the balance sheet, but also by statements of interviewees. For example, the CTO of *Ciba* states: "we want to ensure a minimum amount of investments in the development of radical innovations, even though we can never be sure if this has a positive outcome. But if we do not do it and only play safe, we will soon be out of business". The CTO of *Hilti* states that "to think crazy and try out seemingly absurd things is my job, this is what I am getting paid for". Thus, the case studies support the assumption that firm values and fundamental beliefs about the positive effect of exploration activities will have a positive effect on the firm's propensity to engage in exploration. Hypothesis 1 summarizes this finding:

> **Hypothesis 1**
>
> *Firms' fundamental values and beliefs pertaining to innovation is positively correlated to their exploration propensity.*

Product strategy

The type of product strategy that a firm pursues influences both its exploration propensity and the direction in which new knowledge is searched. At the extreme, firms will engage more in exploration when the product strategy is to be product leader, and engage comparably less in exploration when they pursue a follower strategy. In the case of *Gore* and *Hilti*, the corporate innovation strategy is to be product leader in most of its product categories. *Ciba* has a clear strategy in which chemical compounds and product platforms they want to be market leader, and in which areas they pursue a position which places them as number two or three in the market with respect to market share. As a consequence, they engage in increased exploration activities in areas where they aim to be leader and less in others. In the case of *Gore*, a member of the core technology group stated: "we do not explore in technological areas where we know others are already active, or where we have the feeling that we will not be able to reach product leadership". Thus, the firms are aware that in order to achieve product leadership they constantly have to engage in exploration activities to sustain this claim. This relationship is summarized in hypothesis 2:

> **Hypothesis 2**
>
> *Firms' overall product strategy has an impact on their exploration propensity. The more firms target product leadership, the more they will engage in exploration activities.*

Firms' product strategy also has an impact on the exploration scope and exploration direction. As the case of *Hilti* shows, they try to be in control of the entire value chain in order to be able to react immediately to exogenous developments and to ensure that the best product and manufacturing technologies are applied. Thus, *Hilti* is not willing to outsource critical elements of the value chain but rather likes to be in control. Through this, they are able to influence all important parts of the value chain which have an impact on the product architecture and quality. Although *Gore* and *Bühler* may not be in control of the entire value chain, *Bühler* covers the most critical and value adding part of their value chain, while *Gore* controls everything that has to do with applying their core technology. As a consequence of controlling major parts of the value chain, the firms are able to explore in several directions. For example, *Hilti* is able to explore new product technologies as well as process technologies. This is different for *Gore* which is not in control of the manufacturing process of its value chain. However, except for *Ciba*, all firms maintain close contact with the final customer at the end of the value chain, which also allows for the exploration of new markets and customer segments. In the case of *Ciba*, they are dependent on intermediaries which integrate *Ciba's* products (i.e. the chemical compounds) into their products, which in turn may be only modules or systems of an even more complex product.

As a consequence of product strategy, firms may strive to control larger parts of their value chains to both generate more value as well as to be in control of critical parts of the value chain for increased quality assurance and exploration possibilities. This insight leads to the following hypotheses:

Hypothesis 3a

The extent to which firms are in control of their value chain impacts their exploration scope. The larger the firms' control over the value chain, the larger are their exploration scope and propensity.

Hypothesis 3b

The extent to which firms are in control of their value chain impacts their exploration direction. The larger the firms' control over the value chain, the more they will explore up-stream and/or downstream the value chain.

6.4. Hypotheses on firms' exploration efficacy

Impact of core business

The case studies show that exploration from the perspective of the firm is not conducted to solve specific problems. Problem solving in terms of technological exploitation is considered daily business and targets at product development and the improvement of existing product platforms. Therefore, exploration from firm perspective rather focuses on the identification of new business opportunities which may involve new market and technology knowledge. However, as argued in chapter 6.1, the firms in this research do not engage in random exploration activities, but they explore in directions where they have reasonable belief that they will find valuable knowledge for subsequent innovation. For example, while *Hilti* and *Bühler* strongly engage in exploration along the value chain, *Ciba* and *Gore* have explicit approaches how they explore around their core business. For example, *Gore* engages only in one exploratory step around the core at a time. Interviewees across all case firms stated that they do not blindly engage in exploration but always cohere to strategic corporate imperatives when searching for new knowledge and new business opportunities. Therefore, the following hypothesis emerges:

> Hypothesis 4
>
> *Firms' core business has an impact on the direction where exploration is conducted. Firms mainly explore new domains which are in line with their corporate strategy and which strengthen and expand their core business.*

Impact of capabilities

Firms engage in directed exploration to avoid unacceptably high uncertainty. All firms stated explicitly that they do not explore domains to which they have no related knowledge or capabilities. Thus, firms ensure that future business and therefore the exploration of new domains have a relationship to existing business. In this regard, existing business, and existing capabilities in particular, have a major impact on the direction of exploration activities. As the case studies show, firms try to leverage their existing capabilities to new domains to tap unexploited market potential, and they use these capabilities as a starting point for exploration. As the CTO of *Ciba* states: "we try to ask ourselves what we are able to do instead of what we are supposed to do". The exploration of new domains for new business opportunities based on existing capabilities is fairly evident also in the case of *Bühler*, which systematically explores its value chain to see where they can offer their extensive know-how in food-processing. As a consequence, they offer consulting services both in their core business (i.e. equipment) as well as in non-food applications which require extensive process know-how.

Capabilities play a critical role in exploration because they are not limited to specific products. Rather, they represent individual or organizational abilities to achieve a special result disregarding the fact how this is achieved (Danneels 2007). As such, firm capabilities with respect to products are 'holistic' and concern the firm's ability to act on relationships rather than products. Thus, a capability can potentially be applied to many different situations, while the product which is assembled on certain capabilities can often be used only in a specific situation. Therefore, capabilities have a broader application range than the products which the firm produces. By the same token, firms' focus on capabilities rather than products or technologies may increase their absorptive capacity. This is because capabilities are rather abstract and tacit compared to final products and technologies which are clearly defined in their way of operation and which thus are fairly explicit. As a consequence, an individual might be better able to identify more and/or improved relationships between existing and new knowledge. Based on these insights, the following hypothesis emerges.

> Hypothesis 5
>
> *Firms' existing capabilities have an impact on the exploration efficacy. The more related required capabilities in unfamiliar domains are to existing capabilities, the more effective are subsequent exploration activities pertaining to commercial outcome.*

Impact of application orientation

In a similar light to the effect that existing capabilities have on the efficacy of exploration activities, firms' focus on applications rather than product or technology platforms have an impact on the outcome of technology exploration activities. *Gore* and *Hilti* clearly focus on the application chain of products and on outcomes of products. This enables them to deflect their attention away from final products or specific markets to customer benefits and thus to what really makes the company different from competition. The CTO of *Hilti* states that the firm does not only focus on products or platforms but also on entire applications and how the effect that the customer wants to achieve can be improved disregarding any underlying technologies. As a consequence, *Hilti* would be willing to cannibalize existing technologies which may have served them well in the past and in which *Hilti* may have accumulated extensive know-how. *Gore* also focuses on customer benefit and thus on the effect that their products have when used by the customer. Although all their final products are based on their core technology, *Gore* focuses on how the technology can serve specific products best.

Especially in the case of *Gore* and *Hilti*, the difference between outcomes and effects on the one hand and products that lead to these outcomes and effects on the other hand becomes apparent. Thus, products can be considered merely as the tool through which a certain outcome is achieved. This makes clear that the product per se does not matter apart from design and brand image aspects for some industrial goods. In fact, the product becomes worthless if it doesn't serve the customer's desired outcome. Therefore, firms which focus on outcomes and thus on applications rather than products are more likely to explore new technologies which may serve or contribute to the same outcome than firms which try to defend existing products and their underlying architecture. Furthermore, firms which operate outcome-oriented are more likely to explore new technologies which might cannibalize their existing knowledge base. Therefore, the following hypotheses emerge:

Hypothesis 6

The degree to which firms focus on applications, effects, and outcomes has an impact on the efficacy of their exploration activities. The more firms focus on applications, effects, and outcomes rather than products, the more valuable knowledge they will find at exploration.

Hypothesis 7

The degree to which firms focus on applications, effects, and outcomes has an impact on their propensity to give up existing know-how. The more firms focus on applications, effects, and outcomes rather than products, the more likely they are to cannibalize existing know-how which might have served them well in the past.

6.5. Hypotheses on firms' exploration efficiency

Dedicated resources and organizational separation

A common pattern across all case studies is that firms provide dedicated resources to exploration activities. While *Ciba*, *Hilti*, and *Bühler* all invest a specific and constant ratio of their annual corporate R&D budget in exploration activities, *Gore* decides on a project basis how much is invested in exploration. However, all firms have in common distinct organizational units such as new business development units or distinct groups within corporate research and development whose explicit task is to explore new markets and business opportunities. According to several interviewees from corporate management, dedicated resources ensure that people who actually engage in exploration can fully focus on these activities without being distracted by urging issues of daily business and project requirements.

The case insights suggest that dedicated resources increase the efficiency of exploration activities. Just as the interviewees state, the general mechanism may be that people who actually engage in search activities are not involved in any other activities which concern the daily business of the firm. Thus, dedicated exploration resources have a protecting effect from exploitative activities, and they allow full concentration on exploration activities which inherently require more freedom, take longer time, and may not fit with current ways of business conduct. Therefore, the following hypothesis emerges:

> Hypothesis 8
>
> *Dedicated resources for exploration activities have an impact on the efficiency of these activities. Firms' increased provision of dedicated exploration resources is positively related to increased learning effects with respect to information quantity and quality.*

In the same light as the provision of dedicated resources, the organizational separation of exploration and exploitation seems beneficial for outcomes of exploration activities. As illustrated, all case firms pursue some type of separation. Organizational separation of both activities rely on the same basic mechanism as dedicated exploration resources: separated exploration units provide a protected environment which is conducive for the efficiency of search activities. Several interview respondents have repeatedly emphasized that exploration activities and the people who actually engage in the search need freedom to arrive at results at all. According to their experience, combining both activities in existing processes and organizational structures typically leads to conflicts, because people who are supposed to engage in exploration are permanently asked to assist in urgent project matters emerging from daily business. As the R&D leader of the fabrics division of *Gore* states: "product development requires more of a finisher type of person, and in the fuzzy front end we require more of a starter type of person. It's rather the exception that we find both types in one person". Because of these insights, the following hypothesis is formulated:

> Hypothesis 9
>
> *The firm's organizational structure pertaining to exploration activities has an impact on their exploration efficiency. Organizational separation of exploration activities from exploitation activities is positively related to increased learning effects with respect to information quantity and quality.*

Cognitive capabilities and personal traits of the individual

Although providing resources and creating an environment conducive for exploration is necessary to allow for exploration to happen in the first place, it is ultimately people who actually operatively engage in exploration activities. In this light, cognitive capabilities of the individual are critical because it is he who interprets new information and ultimately identifies new business opportunities (Keane 1987; Holyoak and Thagard 1997; Shane 2000). Researchers have argued that people differ with respect to their capabilities to grasp and process information and make sense of these information to form new ideas and recognize new business opportunities (Shane 2000). The ability to recognize opportunities also depends on the prior experience and knowledge that an individual has accumulated. Therefore, *Hilti* and *Bühler*, for example, try to engage people in exploration activities who have broad industry experience. In addition, *Bühler* in particular involves people in their exploration activities who do not have a long firm or industry background, but who bring in new knowledge which they might be able to connect to existing business.

Prior experience and knowledge increase the base from which individuals can retrieve existing information and to which they can relate new and ambiguous information. From cognitive psychology perspective, analogical thinking entails the transfer of knowledge from one domain that usually already exists in memory to the domain to be explained (Gick and Holyoak 1983; Vosniadou and Ortony 1989). The process of remapping information stored in memory to new settings is directly related to individual's ability to think in analogies (Gordon 1969; De Bono 1990; Ceserani and Greatwood 1995). As a consequence, people are better able to establish analogies between old experiences and new domains the broader their experience background is. With respect to the cognitive abilities of the individual in the process of exploration, the following hypothesis emerges:

6.4 Hypotheses on firms' exploration efficacy

> **Hypothesis 10**
>
> *The individual's cognitive abilities have an impact on the efficiency of exploration activities which he engages in. The amount of his experience background is positively related to the identification of new ideas and new business opportunities.*

With respect to the individual, personal traits impact his tendency to engage in exploration and how efficient exploration activities are pertaining to the identification of new business opportunities and the development of new ideas based on newly learned knowledge. According to interviewees across all case firms some individuals are more prone to identify new business opportunities than others. According to the interviewees and in line with existing research, people who have an intrinsic motivation to improve the way how things are done are more likely to arrive at beneficial outcomes from exploration activities. This is because people who have an 'entrepreneurial mindset' are more eager than others to engage in exploration and are motivated to identify new and valuable knowledge (McGrath and MacMillan 2000). The importance of such traits becomes apparent in the case of *Gore* which ensures already in the recruiting process that the potential new employee shows entrepreneurial characteristics. *Ciba* employs only people at the New Growth Platform permanently who both have a broad company experience and who show a distinct interest in exploration activities. Based on these insights, the following hypotheses are derived:

> **Hypothesis 11**
>
> *Personal traits of the individual have an impact on his tendency to engage in exploration activities. An individual's openness towards change is positively related to his willingness to engage in exploration activities.*

> **Hypothesis 12**
>
> *Personal traits of the individual have an impact on the efficiency of his exploration activities. An individual's openness towards change is positively related to his intensity of engaging in exploration activities.*

6.6. Summary of hypotheses

Table 13 summarizes the hypotheses derived from insights from the cross-case analysis.

Variable	No.	Hypothesis
Exploration propensity	H1	Firms' fundamental values and beliefs pertaining to innovation is positively correlated to their exploration propensity.
	H2	Firms' overall product strategy has an impact on their exploration propensity. The more firms target product leadership, the more exploration they will engage in exploration activities.
	H3a	The extent to which firms are in control of their value chain impacts their exploration scope. The larger the firms' control over the value chain, the larger are their exploration scope and propensity.
	H3b	The extent to which firms are in control of their value chain impacts their exploration direction. The larger the firms' control over the value chain, the more they will explore up-stream and/or downstream the value chain.
Exploration efficacy	H4	Firms' core business has an impact on the direction where exploration is conducted. Firms mainly explore new domains which are in line with their corporate strategy and which strengthen and expand their core business.
	H5	Firms' existing capabilities have an impact on the exploration efficacy. The more related required capabilities in unfamiliar domains are to existing capabilities, the more effective are subsequent exploration activities pertaining to commercial outcome.
	H6	The degree to which firms focus on applications, effects, and outcomes has an impact on the efficacy of their exploration activities. The more firms focus on applications rather than products, the more valuable knowledge they will find at exploration.
	H7	The degree to which firms focus on applications, effects, and outcomes has an impact on their propensity to give up existing know-how. The more firms focus on applications rather than products, the more likely they are to cannibalize existing know-how which might have served them well in the past.
Exploration efficiency	H8	Dedicated resources for exploration activities have an impact on the efficiency of these activities. Firms' increased provision of dedicated exploration resources is positively related to increased learning effects with respect to information quantity and quality.
	H9	The organizational structure pertaining to exploration activities has an impact on exploration efficiency. Organizational separation of exploration activities from exploitation activities is positively related to increased learning effects with respect to information quantity and quality.
	H10	The individual's cognitive abilities have an impact on the efficiency of exploration activities which he engages in. The amount of his experience background is positively related to the identification of new ideas and new business opportunities.
	H11	Personal traits of the individual have an impact on his tendency to engage in exploration activities. An individual's openness towards change is positively related to his willingness to engage in exploration activities.
	H12	Personal traits of the individual have an impact on the efficiency of his exploration activities. An individual's openness towards change is positively related to his intensity of engaging in exploration activities.

Table 13: Overview of hypotheses

7. Managerial implications

Based on the cross-case analysis, on the conceptual model, and on the hypotheses, this chapter derives managerial implications for exploration for innovation at the level of the firm. In analogy to the structure used in the cross-case analysis, this chapter first discusses managerial implications pertaining to the propensity to engage in exploration. Then, implications pertaining to the firm's exploration efficacy and efficiency are discussed.

7.1. Design parameters for increased exploration propensity

7.1.1. Living firm values

Exploration for innovation may be a desirable activity in general for most firms across diverse industries. However, exploration does not automatically happen in every organization and is a strategic activity that must be enabled and fostered to come to effect. Therefore, firms must do more than merely provide the necessary resources to engage in exploration. The cases show that successful exploration for innovation is tightly connected to the firm's overall mindset regarding the value of innovation both for the image and the competitive advantage of the firm. A positive upper management attitude which values the organization's attempts to permanently improve products and processes certainly has an effect on the overall organization's mindset with respect to innovation.

As the cases show, fundamental aspects such as firm values and beliefs have enabled the firms to emerge as market and innovation leaders for decades and more. Hypothesis 1 implies that firms whose fundamental beliefs highly value innovation are more inclined to engage in exploration activities which aim beyond the development of mere incremental innovations. However, fundamental values and beliefs are not easily implemented in a short period of time, but are the result of constant and year-long demonstration by means of executives living these values. Hypothesis 1 therefore implies that managers must demonstrate and communicate their convictions to the organization, underline this by acting accordingly, and thus serve as a role model by living these values. Only if this is continued over a long time span, and in particular, if this is successfully continued even in times when exploratory behavior seems inappropriate, firm values will permeate the organization and lead to increased exploration propensity. Such behavior is particularly appropriate for firms which aspire to be leaders in their markets. In contrast, firms which do not pursue a leadership strategy may have to live other values which, for example, focus more on exploitation of existing capabilities.

7.1.2. Defining a challenging product strategy

The cases show that the firms pursue fairly clear strategies for most of their products. The firms' product strategies define how they want to compete in the respective product-market, that is, if they want to be product leader or if they rather pursue a follower strategy. The goal to be product leader must have corresponding effects on the formulation and execution of the respective product (or even) innovation strategy. Firms which aim to be product leader for a specific product cannot afford to passively react to external developments but need to shape the competitive setting themselves. Therefore, apart from conventional environmental scanning activities to identify new technologies and other developments, product leading firms must actively explore the environment and create new business opportunities. While firms with a follower strategy scan the environment and adapt to new opportunities, leader firms must create those opportunities and make others adapt to them.

The definition of a proper product strategy must be in line with existing capabilities and other potentially confining parameters such as, for example, a super-ordinate corporate strategy. In particular, proper product strategies cannot be proclaimed and executed in an instant, but are the result of a sound analysis if, among other, such a strategy makes sense at all and if it can be realized based on existing capabilities. For example, *Ciba* and *Gore* have clear strategies for where they want to be product leader, and for where they 'only' want to be among the top three or five players. As hypothesis 2 implies, the product strategy must consequently have an impact on how intensely exploration with respect to the specific product is conducted. Thus, in areas where product leadership is targeted, exploration must be engaged more aggressively than in areas where the firm pursues a follower strategy.

As a consequence, management must ensure in which areas and to what extent exploration is conducted. While it may be sufficient to regularly scan external developments in the case of follower strategies, leadership firms must actively create new business opportunities by exploring new technologies, new markets, and by trying to create new business models around existing and/or new product-market combinations. Leadership firms must define a challenging product strategy because this allows for broader and more creative exploration activities in the organization. Product leadership is a clear yet abstract goal at the same time: it is clear because the organization knows what final goal to achieve, but it is abstract because this goal does not prescribe the way how it is achieved. As a consequence, the organization is given multiple pathways to engage in any kind of exploration which aim at meeting these goals.

In general, abstractness in the formulation of otherwise concrete goals has the potential to lead to the (unintended) stretching of organizational competencies. To some degree, it might be natural that exploration for innovation involves renewing or adapting existing competencies. However, the extent to how much this happens also depends on how strategic goals are formulated. Abstractness in strategic goal formulation fosters the individual's creativity pertaining to the broadness of his exploration efforts. It influences how the organization perceives and operationalizes such strategies, as the cognitive abilities of individuals serve as a 'filter' for interpreting information. Abstracting from specific problem situations and searching for solutions which then are readapted to the original problem situation is a common creativity technique for finding new solutions (De Bono 1990). The concept of this becomes particularly clear in the case of *Hilti*, whose brand image is based on two terms which are completely detached from any products or applications: outperform and outlast. As a consequence, all innovation activities aim at reaching better levels to these ends, regardless any underlying technologies. The strong focus on product leadership, as is also the case with *Gore*, does therefore not limit the scope of exploration activities, quite in contrast, organizational efforts are aligned towards better outcomes of the product goals.

Abstract goal formulation probably even fosters motivation within the organization as well as a sense of self-actualization because people are allowed to pursue their own approaches. Thus, for people in the organization who are in charge of exploring new domains, corporate managers should provide concrete corporate goals which leave, however, enough space for the individual to unfold his exploration creativity.

7.2. Design parameters for increased exploration efficacy

7.2.1. Stretching existing capabilities

Firms must ensure that exploration activities entail a minimum expectation value with respect to exploration success. Even if management provides dedicated resources for exploration activities, and even if those people responsible for exploration are granted their necessary freedom in their activities, the meaning of exploration will be questioned if there is no outcome which can be turned into innovation.

Past research in the context of firm diversification has shown a curvilinear relationship between the distance of the new to the existing business and the performance of the new business (Ahuja and Lampert 2001; Miller 2003). Exploration in domains which are too distant from existing business and capabilities may be prone to failure, suggesting a curvilinear relationship as well. This assumption is supported by statements from all case firms, in that exploration beyond the firm's capabilities is often followed by project failure. As a consequence, the firms ensure that exploration activities maintain a structural link to existing business and capabilities, implying that potential new business and innovations are required to involve to some extent existing capabilities. Therefore, as hypothesis 4 implies, management needs to design exploration strategies which include how and where exploration is conducted. As the cases of *Ciba* and *Gore* show, they have implemented exploration strategies which entail where and how far around the core business exploration is conducted. Through this, the efficacy of exploration activities is increased, because people will not explore domains which are outside of the boundaries as defined in the strategy, and which would therefore be of no value to the firm. Furthermore, as capabilities describe the firm's ability to reconfigure resource bundles to serve different purposes, firms must carefully analyze how their core capabilities might be able to serve more than merely their core business. The concept of stretching existing capabilities then involves the exploration of domains where these capabilities are also required, either directly or in an abstract and thus similar sense. In a second step, firms must analyze and decide if the new domain to which existing capabilities could be stretched fits the previously defined innovation strategy. Through this approach, exploration activities in terms of finding new knowledge for generating innovation or new business will be more effective (see hypothesis 5) because the organization is to some degree familiar with the new domain because both existing and new domains are based on the same capability (i.e. there is a structural fit), and because the new domain will be tested for fit with existing strategies.

These remarks imply that firms' exploration scope is confined by their innovation strategy, existing capabilities, and by developments in the business environment. While existing capabilities may be the most constraining factor, an innovation strategy can and must be formulated such that existing capabilities can be stretched to new domains. External developments such as socio-economic mega trends (e.g. health, energy, mobility, etc.) are the most 'opening' factor, to which firms must try to adapt their capabilities, however, within the limits of strategy. Thus, the exploration space is a function of two endogenous factors, i.e. strategy and capabilities, and one exogenous factor, i.e. developments in the environment which cannot be really controlled by the firm. Therefore, an increase of exploration space by an emerging trend in the business environment (such as the emergence of a new technology in another industry) can still be constrained by a strategy which sets limits to the new space or by limited capabilities which cannot be stretched to these external developments.

Thus, the potential exploration space is constrained by strategic postures and existing capabilities as firm-endogenous factors and therefore results in what can be called the factual exploration space. A firm can actively extend or limit the exploration space at any point by increasing its organizational capabilities or by expanding its corporate strategy to consider, for example, entirely different industries.

7.2.2. Focusing on applications, effects, and outcomes

A concept quite similar to formulating somewhat abstract strategies is thinking in applications, effects, and outcomes rather than in concrete products when engaging in technology exploration. While organizational capabilities may refer to the firm's ability to achieve a certain strategic result, technological capabilities may refer to the firm's ability to a achieve a certain product-related result. Therefore, from a more problemistic and thus from a more product development perspective, the scope of exploration activities with respect to new technology knowledge is increased when considering that different technologies might result in the same effect (such as e.g. Otto and Diesel technology in engines). For example, *Ciba* considers the effects that their compounds create, *Gore* considers the outcome of applying their PTFE membranes in different applications, *Hilti* ponders on how to best make a hole, and *Bühler* investigates how better health can be attained by their food processing know-how. These questions are detached from any specific product or technology platforms or even markets and customers, but focus on the best possible outcome.

The abstract consideration of rather concrete problems prior to active engagement in exploration increases chances that new yet structurally related knowledge is found (see hypothesis 6). People who engage in exploration for new knowledge benefit from abstracting from the underlying problem. Abstracting concrete problems opens up the solution space in a first step, where, in the second step, new knowledge which is structurally similar to the original problem can be searched and found. Finally, in the last step, the abstract solution can be transferred and adapted to the original problem. Thus, abstraction from concrete problems generally increases the space in which exploration can be conducted, and increases exploration efficacy because the new knowledge which is explored will have some similarities with the original problem setting, thus decreasing the uncertainty of the new knowledge. Table 14 briefly summarizes the implications that focusing on applications and effects/outcomes has on the exploration scope and efficacy.

Focus	*Implication*
Focus on applications	▪ Allows to identify underlying and accompanying functions of the product
	▪ Allows to focus on true customer benefit
Focus on effects/outcomes	▪ Allows to consider entire product architecture
	▪ Allows to consider alternative approaches which result in the same effect

Table 14: Implications of focusing on applications, effects, and outcomes

7.2.3. Exploring along the value chain

The value chain of a product from product development, manufacturing, to sales involves many different parties such as suppliers, manufacturers, and customers. Also, the more complex a product is, the more complex value chains can become. However, value chains, and particularly complex ones, offer a broad scope of exploration potential. Firms which cover a large part or all of the value chain are naturally able to engage in much more exploration with respect to overall possible search areas. Thus, for example, firms covering the entire value chain can potentially engage in vertical exploration by exploring new technologies (e.g. materials, chemicals, systems, etc.), explore new manufacturing technologies (e.g. such as high-speed manufacturing technologies, rapid prototyping technologies, etc.), and explore new markets such as new geographies or customer segments (see figure 26). In contrast, firms which cover only a small part of the value chain are more likely to engage in horizontal exploration pertaining to their respective core business such as for example research and development. In a sense, horizontal exploration resembles the search for new knowledge and technologies which aim at improving existing solutions.

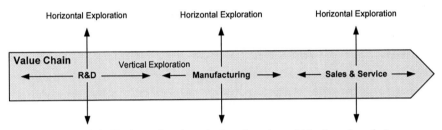

Figure 26: Horizontal and vertical exploration within the value chain

As a consequence, firms who might want to increase their vertical exploration scope might want to expand into up- or downstream value chain activities. *Hilti* covers the entire value chain from research and development over manufacturing to controlling the sales channels and are therefore also in direct contact with the final customer. Thus, their exploration activities are quite broad, and they even maintain a distinct organizational unit which exclusively engages in exploring manufacturing technologies. *Ciba* products (i.e. their chemical compounds), for example, typically pass many more intermediaries before their products as part of larger systems reach the final customer. Therefore, compared to *Hilti*, *Ciba's* exploration space extends 'only' to R&D and manufacturing while they are limited in exploring new sales channels.

An increased exploration scope by covering larger parts of the value chain leads not only to more exploration within the single stages of the value chain, but also offers increased exploration of entirely new business models. While a new technology might change the structure and design of a specific product and thus offers new commercial opportunities, an existing product might be manufactured with a new manufacturing technology and therefore be manufactured in regions previously untapped, leading to entering a new market. Thus, new business models can be created by the fact that a firm covers specific parts of the value chain and is able to reconfigure it, or by recombining an exploratory innovation with parts of the value chain. Therefore, firms must consider if they want and are able to expand their activities into other parts of the value chain, and adjust their corporate innovation strategy accordingly.

7.3. Design parameters for increased exploration efficiency

7.3.1. Designing an exploration organization

Dedicated resources

Exploration is often crowded out by, in the short run, more important activities which aim at meeting urgencies from daily business. Therefore, firms must ensure that exploration can be conducted on a regular and undisturbed basis, both in order for exploration to be effective and to be efficient. People who engage in exploration activities but are frequently distracted by other tasks have difficulties to finish exploratory projects, thus limiting quality and quantity of exploration activities.

As discussed earlier, management must not only communicate their beliefs pertaining to the necessity of exploration but they must also act accordingly. Therefore, management must provide dedicated resources for exploration to enable the search for new knowledge in the first place (see hypothesis 8). As the case studies show, most firms invest a fixed fraction of about 10-25% of the annual R&D budget into exploration activities. Dedicated resources help the organization to keep up a minimum amount of exploration activities, which would otherwise be crowded out by more urging tasks. Furthermore, by ensuring a constant amount of exploration in times of even more constrained budgets, firms are more likely to enjoy the benefits of exploration more frequently than firms which engage only in exploration in times of more relaxed budgets. As hypothesis 8 implies, the consequence of dedicated exploration resources is an increased exploration efficiency. This is because people who conduct exploration will not be disturbed by other tasks, because the provided budget gives them the necessary freedom to pursue their exploratory projects. Again, in contrast, the consequence of one budget for both exploratory and exploitative activities would be that either exploration is crowded out in the first place or that people have difficulties to focus on their exploration activities because they are frequently distracted.

7.3 Design parameters for increased exploration efficiency

Separating exploration from exploitation activities

In the same light as the implication pertaining to the provision of dedicated resources, firms must not only provide the necessary resources but also install organizational mechanisms which ensure that the resources are utilized in an optimal way. As the cases show, firms have separated exploration from exploitation activities by means of an organizational separation, which consequently also leads to different processes between the two activities. This is why such dedicated units often are directly supervised by corporate management which are able to grant a corresponding budget for this type of activity. Therefore, the organizational design of exploration is again a fairly strategic task, and needs to be initiated and supervised by corporate management.

Organizational separation of exploration and exploitation allows full concentration on either one of the activities. Organizational separation can be achieved by establishing a fully dedicated unit with people who engage exclusively in exploration activities and which is directly supervised by upper management. As the cases of *Ciba* and *Gore* show, another successful way of organizational separation is by establishing a separated exploration unit which recruits itself on a case-by-case basis from people throughout the entire organization which is sponsored by the budget of the exploration unit during the time the exploration activity is on-going. Furthermore, the combination of both approaches, i.e. an exploration unit which is fully dedicated and which is enriched by people who join in for the time of their exploration activity yields the highest potential for exploration to be successful.

For most product developing firms, some degree of exploration pertaining to the search for new technological knowledge is rather common. However, firms must also establish structures which pursue the exploration of new non-technological knowledge. As the case studies show, firms separate technology from market and/or new business opportunity exploration. While exploration pertaining to new technologies is usually conducted within R&D, exploration pertaining to new markets and business opportunities is conducted in separated organizational units such as, for example, new business development units. Firms which separate technology from other types of exploration must, however, ensure that people have a sufficiently large technical background in order for them to recognize new business opportunities.

7.3.2. Fostering broad and deep knowledge structures

As the case studies show and as has been argued in literature, cognitive abilities of the individual are important when engaging in exploration. People with distinct abilities to recognize relationships in seemingly disparate pieces of knowledge are therefore better able to recognize business opportunities. As a consequence, these people have an impact on the efficiency of exploration activities, because they will recognize valuable knowledge faster than other people (see hypothesis 10). This implies that management must ensure that such people are responsible for and involved in the design of exploration strategies and especially in the conduct of exploration. As broad and deep knowledge and experience are crucial for the identification of new business opportunities, exploration units must be staffed with a combination of people who have such backgrounds. Thus, firms must ensure that these characteristics are present either in a single person, or are distributed across a group of people. Furthermore, firms might have to check for these characteristics already during the recruiting process in case they want to employ new people for exploration activities.

In the same light as the implication above, personal traits of the individual are important for the efficiency of exploration activities. People who have an intrinsic motivation to change things for the better tend to be naturally interested in exploring new knowledge. Therefore, these people might be more efficient at exploration than people who are assigned this task without actually being personally interested in such activities. As an interview respondent from *Gore* stated, there are different types of people with respect to their quality of starting or finishing projects. Thus, for exploration activities and initiating new projects, firms need people who can raise new questions and think divergently, while in product development, firms rather need people who implement and finish things and who think more convergent.

7.4. Summary

In general, firms' corporate strategy has a tremendous impact on the scope, depth, and effectiveness of exploration activities. Strategic directives determine the scope of exploration by defining what belongs to the core business and what is outside of the core business. Subsequently, this helps defining the location and the type of adjacencies to the core. In a first step, this may require an in-depth analysis of the firm's core capabilities and the activities and products where these capabilities are applied.

Furthermore, strategic directives determine what parts of the value chain of the firm's product palette are covered, and therefore furthermore determine the scope of exploration activities. However, all strategies may only be effective to the degree that top management actively supports these strategies and provide a role model in implementing them. Therefore, living firm values which foster innovation and leadership are crucial antecedents of successful exploration. Because this behavior will eventually permeate the entire organization and become firm culture, the overall propensity to engage in exploration will ultimately increase.

Another crucial task of top management and R&D leaders is defining a challenging strategy which will stretch existing competencies and thus create new business potential. Challenging strategies with respect to growth and innovation entail that existing competencies, technologies, and products are permanently questioned and that they are subject for renewal or even substitution in order to reach the goals of the strategy. A challenging strategy must focus on outcomes instead of prescribing specific ways and be abstract in a sense that it leaves the individuals enough leeway to pursue different ways of reaching strategic goals. This also includes that some strategic boundaries are given pertaining to what and what not belongs to the firm's core business, but that freedom is given pertaining to the direction of exploration and to the question how strategic goals are achieved. Exploration of adjacent core-areas implies that existing core competencies are stretched to the adjacencies, which ensures a link between existing and future competencies. As a consequence, uncertainty in exploring new domains is effectively limited. Over time, exploration is enabled beyond the core business which addresses what the organization is capable of doing rather than adapting to externally imposed developments. In summary, top management must enable exploration which is conducted within the scope of a corporate strategy or vision, but which is beyond current core business.

Finally, for exploration to be efficiently conducted, it is important to have the right people in place. Despite being a generic statement, firms have the chance to select and engage people in exploration activities who are because of their background and personality more inclined to search for new and valuable knowledge and business opportunities. People with an intrinsic motivation to promote the firm's competitive advantage will make an increased effort to make sense of the information obtained while exploring new knowledge and therefore come up with increased new ideas and business opportunities. In support of such people, firms must prevent exploration activities from being influenced by the requirements of daily business. Therefore, exploration should be conducted in separated organizational units, ensuring full dedication.

The overall managerial implications are illustrated in figure 27.

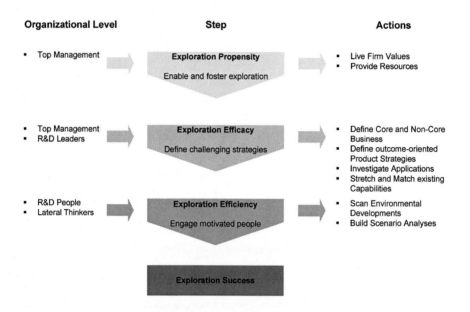

Figure 27: Summary of managerial implications

8. Conclusion

Based on the analysis and discussions of the previous chapters, this chapter summarizes the key findings of this research and highlights the central implications for management theory and practice.

8.1. Implications for management theory

The implications for management theory pertain to the insights gained from the case-study analysis and the conceptual model as well as hypotheses derived from them. While the first part illustrates the contributions to management research, the second part offers pathways for future research opportunities.

8.1.1. Summary and contributions to research

Clarifying the concept of exploration

This study contributes to theory and literature pertaining to several management fields such as entrepreneurship, organizational learning, and technology and innovation management by investigating and clarifying the concept of exploration for innovation. Organizational learning literature, in particular, has treated the concept of exploration for new knowledge with the goal of subsequent innovation as a fairly abstract phenomenon. Although exploration is acknowledged to be vital for the long-term survival of the firm, most literature has only reconfirmed this statement, without analyzing what exploration means, what activities it entails, and how firms actually manage to conduct exploration. Moreover, several management literature streams argue that firms must achieve a balance between exploration and exploitation activities. However, it is difficult to debate how a balance might be achieved if there is no insight on what exploration and exploitation actually mean in business reality, and how firms cope with the challenges inherent in both activities. This research addresses this blank spot by investigating how firms successfully engage in exploration with the goal of innovation.

To clarify the concept of exploration, this study understands and investigates exploration towards the background of developing innovation which is more than incremental in nature. Consequently, literature on entrepreneurship and technological innovation is considered which is concerned with the identification and subsequent exploitation of new business opportunities and with the search for new ideas and the subsequent development of new products respectively. Findings from the cases show that exploration is neither vague nor impossible to implement. In fact, this study illustrates how firms engage in exploration and how the challenges inherent in exploration are tackled. The practical consideration of exploration in entrepreneurship and technological innovation literature and the respective insights gained by in-depth analysis of four firms therefore extends understanding of exploration and may serve as a base for future research on the construct.

Because of the reflection of exploration on entrepreneurship, technological innovation, and organizational learning literature, this study also contributes to the integration of these literature streams. As a consequence, insights from the single streams are mutually transferred and help explain not only the construct of exploration itself, but also how and why firms search for new ideas, new problems, or new business opportunities. Thus, this study sets forth one of the first attempts to integrate several research streams to clarify the overarching construct of exploration for innovation.

Development of a reference framework and hypotheses
The development of the reference framework pertaining to exploration at the level of the firm entails relationships which explain the firm's exploration propensity, efficacy, and efficiency. As such, it serves as a framework for improved investigation of cause and effect relationships. Based on this, this study reveals that exploration is not an activity which has a predictable or even quantifiable outcome, but that it is a strategic activity which – if pursued correctly – increases the likelihood for outcomes which contribute to the competitiveness of the firm. The relationships in the reference framework reveal that exploration must be enabled on corporate level in the first place before it can have any effect at all. Furthermore, it reveals that strategies must be in place to ensure efficacy of subsequent exploration activities. Finally, it suggests that specific people are more fit to engage in exploration than others. Thus, the reference framework contributes to the understanding of exploration in that exploration is a multi-facetted phenomenon to whose success several different organizational hierarchies contribute. This implies that exploration is not an activity which can be conducted

8.1 Implications for management theory

detached from other organizational activities, but that it needs to be carefully planned, and that important antecedents for exploration may take a long time to be implemented.

The reference framework comprises three sets of hypothesized relationships. The first set pertains to relationships between a firm's belief in firm values and product strategy and its propensity to engage in exploration.

- One general assumption of this study is that exploration cannot be executed per prior order, but that the amount and success of exploration activities ultimately depend on if management believes in the benefits of it. Therefore, only if management believes in the benefits of innovation and acts on this respectively will the organization engage more intensely in exploration.
- A firm's product strategy strongly influences how much the firm will and must engage in exploration. While product leadership strategies require more sophisticated exploration activities, firms with a follower strategy need to invest less in exploration. In the same light, product leadership strategies require more exploration in the value chain of the respective product to ensure firm-specific quality standards.

The second set of hypotheses speculates that the relationship between exploration activities and their subsequent efficacy is moderated by the way how firms design their exploration strategies.

- With respect to new business and innovation, firms do not explore domains which are entirely detached from existing business. Rather, they employ strategies which posit to explore domains which have a structural link to existing business and existing capabilities. This approach promises to minimize uncertainty inherent in exploration activities. Hence, hypotheses are proposed which suggest that firms will learn knowledge conducive to the subsequent development of ideas pertaining to new business and innovation if they explore domains which show a structural link to existing business and capabilities.
- Focusing on applications, effects, and outcomes influences exploration efficacy because this approach deflects the individual's attention away from currently existing solutions. As a consequence, exploration activities can be conducted detached from existing firm constraints but still lead to learning knowledge which serves the same goal. Therefore, hypotheses are generated which suggest that more valuable knowledge will be found when considering specific problems abstractly.

The third set of hypotheses suggests that organizational characteristics in form of dedicated resources and separated organizational structures increase the efficiency of exploration activities. Furthermore, this set suggests that the personal background and traits of an individual influence the quality and quantity of new knowledge resulting from exploration.

- Since it is generally difficult to perform several tasks at the same time, organizational separation with respect to exploration and exploitation activities increases both activities simultaneously. Thus, hypotheses suggest that when dedicated resources are in place and when people are able to perform exploration activities dedicatedly, the quality and quantity of learned new knowledge will increase.
- People with broad experience in many areas and a deep understanding of existing firm problems are more likely to sense relationships between two seemingly disparate pieces of knowledge. Thus, their cognitive abilities allow them to realize more and faster valuable relationships during the course of exploration. Similarly, the open-mindedness of an individual as well as a personal interest in new and unknown matters positively influences exploration efficiency. This is because intrinsic motivation will lead to more enthusiasm and perseverance in exploration activities. Therefore, hypotheses are formulated which suggest a positive correlation between individual traits and exploration efficiency.

Extending understanding of firms' absorptive capacity
This study tries to explain the success of firms' exploration activities by applying the theory of absorptive capacity. In its origin, this theory argues that firms will be better able to absorb development outside of the organization if they increase their R&D expenditures (Cohen and Levinthal 1990). Through this, the organization will attain a broader knowledge level which enables them to assess better external developments. The firm's absorptive capacity is defined as its ability to recognize the value of new knowledge, assimilate it, and apply it to commercial ends. Although several scholars have discussed and extended the theory of absorptive capacity, the process of knowledge recognition and assimilation has been remarkably neglected. Instead, this process is treated as black-box and has been termed, for example, knowledge acquisition (Zahra and George 2002). However, this theory does not consider how new knowledge is actually acquired, that is, recognized in its value and assimilated.

This study responds to this shortcoming by digging into the black-box of knowledge acquisition. The value of new knowledge can only be recognized in the process of exploration, and much depends on the cognitive abilities of the individual while engaging in exploration. As a consequence, exploration is an inherent part of the absorptive capacity process and delineates the concept of knowledge acquisition. As illustrated in figure 25, the value of new knowledge depends on the overall strategic goals of the firm. This implies that 'value' of new knowledge is a relational concept which is judged against super-ordinate goals such as corporate strategies.

8.1.2. Directions for further research

During the course of this research, several new and interesting research questions have emerged. Thus, while the main research questions of this research have been answered, their value could be even more enriched by considering the following future research paths.

- The topic of exploration has been elaborated in several literature streams in a fairly abstract manner. However, there is considerable difference in the understanding, which is why there are many different definitions of exploration. Although this research has provided insights in what exploration for new knowledge means in the context of globally leading firms, management literature still has to create a clearer picture about the understanding and concept of exploration. Therefore, from a terminology perspective, a more uniform definition and understanding of exploration across several management fields would help facilitate future research.
- Because this study is one of the first to investigate the concept of exploration in the context of business reality, first insights reveal basic relationships. Therefore, the reference framework developed in this study illustrates broad relationships between exploration propensity, efficacy, and efficiency. Thus, there is a need for further research which delineates the findings from this study. For example, it would be valuable for practitioners to understand even better the process of strategy formulation and its effect on exploration efficacy. Similarly, it would be interesting to better understand the relationship between the single variables depicted in this thesis (such as, for example, focus on applications and outcomes) and subsequent exploration success.
- Exploration is not a single activity but involves many protagonists and different actions. Even a firm culture conducive to exploration and brilliant exploration

strategies may still not result in exploration success because much can go wrong in the course of, for example, strategy formulation and market introduction. Therefore, it is difficult to define measures that accurately reflect 'exploration success'. Further research might investigate what measures could be applied to better understand cause-and-effect relationships.
- This research has focused on firms which are global leaders in their respective markets. As such, insights from the case sample support statements in several literature streams that mostly cash-rich and large companies with slack resources are able to engage in exploration. However, there is reason to believe that also smaller companies with rather strict budget constraints are able to successfully engage in exploration. In fact, particularly small firms are associated with intense exploration activities which might result in radical innovations that may change the rules of established industries. Thus, investigating how smaller firms engage in exploration would be valuable and further extend the findings of this study.

8.2. Implications for management practice

This section first summarizes central statements and recommendations which are provided throughout this research. The summary is followed by illustrating potential future research directions and trends emerging in the field of management.

8.2.1. Central statements and recommendations

This research illustrates how successful firms, which are global market leaders in their respective markets, engage in exploration for new knowledge. Exploration activities in these firms are conducted according to clear strategic parameters, which originate at corporate level. Thus, exploration is a very strategic activity and serves as the basis for the long-term competitiveness of the firm. In terms of product innovation, exploration is a means to develop innovations which go beyond mere incremental improvements of existing products and platforms. Therefore, this research might lend some insights into the question how more radical innovations might be developed in a more systematic way.

The insights gained in this study show how firms engage in exploration which is not initiated based on a concrete problem. As such, it is important to point out that the recommendations provided here refer to situations where firms go beyond conventional innovation activities to sustain the short-term survival of the firm (such as continuous improvements for existing products and technologies). Exploration, in that sense, refers to activities which are aimed at finding new knowledge and business opportunities which lead –from the perspective of the firm – to more radical innovations, and which are therefore not initiated by a specific or urgent problem in the organization. The firms illustrated in this study are aware that their exploration activities might not always result in a commercially viable outcome, however, they are willing to invest into these activities and have established ways how the odds of exploration success can be increased. The managerial recommendations provided in the following sections refer to this situation.

The managerial recommendations provided in this section are based on insights derived from the cross-case analysis as well as the hypotheses how to improve exploration success. In general, the process of how to engage in exploration is immensely valuable to corporate management, innovation managers, and R&D professionals. In this spirit, this study shows that there are ways how firms can explore new knowledge with a certain probability that this new knowledge will ultimately be of commercial value. Put differently, there are ways to find the right problems and to search effectively for new ideas and business opportunities. This research reveals that successful exploration of new knowledge for innovation is influenced by three parameters: the firm's propensity to engage in exploration in the first place, its strategies of how and where to effectively explore for new knowledge, and the deployment of dedicated organizational structures and of people with a background conducive to exploration to increase the efficiency of exploration activities.

Recommendations to improve exploration propensity, efficacy, and efficiency
For exploration to have an effect at all, firms must enable it in the first place and actively encourage the organization to pursue activities which go beyond mere incremental improvement activities. This is a mandatory precondition for subsequent exploration activities to have an impact at all. Therefore, the following recommendations are provided:
- *Provide role-model for exploration activities.* The intensity of how exploration is engaged in the organization largely depends on how top management perceives and communicates the benefits of innovation. Fellow employees will engage less enthusiastically and aggressively in exploration if their bosses do not seem

convinced of the benefits of exploration themselves. Thus, management must live their convictions and provide the necessary resources for exploration activities. Through this, a signal is sent throughout the entire organization which communicates the value of exploration and innovation.
- *Define challenging product strategies.* The propensity and intensity of exploration activities are increased when firms pursue a product leadership strategy in contrast to product follower strategies. Therefore, in a first step, management must determine for which products they strive to be product leader. In a second step, they must actively foster exploration for the products where they pursue leadership strategies. Through this, the overall exploration propensity will be ultimately increased.

Exploration activities can only be effective when they are enabled and fostered. As the case analysis reveals, firms have found ways how to ensure that their exploration activities are effective. Based on these insights, the following recommendations are provided.
- *Define core competencies and core business.* The case firms are all well aware of their core competencies and have designed strategies which reinforce and leverage these competencies. Thus, it is paramount for firms to have a very clear picture of their core business and core competencies as well as to know what is beyond their core business. In a first step, this might require the extensive analysis of technological and organizational competencies. For exploration to be effective, management must make the competencies and core business transparent throughout the entire organization, as the knowledge of this serves as a guideline for all exploration activities. Furthermore, corporate strategy must be formulated such that it leaves the organization enough freedom to explore entirely new domains which may stretch the competencies of the firm.
- *Stretch existing competencies to new domains.* Exploring knowledge in domains which are entirely detached from current business and competencies is unlikely to lead to commercially viable impact. Therefore, firms must establish routines which ensure a link between existing competencies and future product-market combinations. This can be done, as is the case with *Ciba* and *Gore*, by defining guidelines about how many steps away from the core business exploration can be conducted to still yield potential for subsequent commercial impact. Furthermore, the cases have shown that it is beneficial to explore one new dimension at a time. The exploration of new technologies for new markets is an

extremely risky endeavor and is more prone to failure. However, exploring one new dimension of the core business at a time seems to be a promising approach.
- *Focus on outcomes instead of products.* Focusing on products, technology platforms, or industries may limit the organization in its ability to absorb crucial knowledge and developments. For example, a drilling machine might most commonly be used on construction sites, however, holes need to be made in many other circumstances and contexts outside of construction. The same is true for PTFE membranes, which are not only beneficial for skin comfort, but whose lightweight and chemical character has a versatile application range. Therefore, in order to foster creativity in exploration, the product strategy must entail an outcome focus rather than an industry or product focus.
- *Derive abstract exploration fields from concrete strategic goals.* Exploration activities can be beneficially conducted throughout the entire organization. In order to enable and foster this, an concrete strategic goals must be delineated into abstract sub-fields, in which subsequent exploration can be conducted. This is particularly beneficial for business units and product lines which are typically problem-driven and have less resources to engage in exploration. However, by providing guidelines in terms of innovation fields which might yield potential to find valuable knowledge, exploration can be more effective.

Finally, if exploration is conducted according to strategic imperatives, and if exploration activities are therefore likely to yield beneficial outcomes, the operational search activities can be increased by considering the following recommendations.
- *Separate exploration from exploitation activities.* Exploration activities entail the search for new knowledge outside the current business. Therefore, it is important that exploration activities are conducted without the bias of daily business and requirements in terms of responding to permanent short-term project requirements. Furthermore, people engaging in exploration activities must be granted sufficient resources to be effective, which includes a clear commitment by upper management.
- *Employ people with broad experience and deep knowledge.* Exploration is ultimately conducted by individuals. Furthermore, it requires creativity to make sense of the new knowledge and to recognize the value of new knowledge for existing business. Therefore, people with broad experience and a deep knowledge and understanding of the demands of current and future business are destined to engage in exploration activities. Management must therefore ensure

to actively recruit and foster people who have an intrinsic motivation to change things for the better, who have a broad experience and knowledge background, and who are able to think.

In summary, the most important parameter for exploration to be successful are the firm's efforts to allow for and foster exploration in the first place. A firm which does not appreciate exploration efforts in the organization is likely to ignore such efforts and to crowd them out in favor of exploitation activities. This given, the firm's biggest lever then to influence exploration success is probably its ability to craft effective exploration strategies. As this research reveals, firms are well advised if they align their exploration strategy such that current and future business are linked by employing and stretching existing competencies. Exploration, in that sense, implies the active search for domains which show a structural link to existing business. It also implies that scanning activities must be performed such that the new knowledge is checked for – more or less abstract – structural links to existing business or capabilities. Any exploration activities must therefore entail the check if and how existing capabilities can cover potential new business. This ensures a certain familiarity with the knowledge of the new domain and therefore reduces uncertainty effectively, as the firm can much better assess risks and benefits. It also contributes to the recognition of more valuable new knowledge which might subsequently lead to the creation of new ideas and to tapping new business opportunities. Therefore, capability-based exploration is a more systematic approach to the development of more than incremental innovations.

8.2.2. Future directions and trends

This research reveals several insights which offer new research opportunities on the subject of exploration and the search for new knowledge. Based on the concepts provided throughout this study, the following comments represent future directions and trends which could be elaborated to gain even deeper insights about the cause-and-effect relationships of exploration within the context of innovation.
- What emerged during the course of the case investigations is that the firms do engage in exploration pertaining to different types of knowledge. This knowledge includes new technologies, new markets and customers, increased portions of the value chain, and new business opportunities in general. Especially with respect to new business opportunities, firms are exploring how internally existing knowledge such as competencies can be leveraged to entirely

new domains. Therefore, it is interesting to investigate in more detail how firms are searching for the right problems, and what 'class' of knowledge they seek (e.g. technological knowledge or crafting new business models around existing technologies). This would also be in contrast to daily business such as maintenance of existing product and technology platforms. As the cases show, monitoring trends in society and the natural environment and subsequent adaptation of existing competencies to these trends or scenarios seems a promising approach. However, further research is needed which investigates the process of analyzing, interpreting, and adapting existing organizational competencies to these future trends. Furthermore, it would be very valuable for management practice to investigate the organizational set up of these processes.

- The cases have revealed the importance of the characteristics of the people who are in charge of exploration activities. This is true for both upper management which defines strategic directions as well as the individual who actually engages in exploratory search. Both management and R&D people must be able to think in abstract ways to recognize opportunities which link external developments with internal competencies. Furthermore, R&D people must be able to recognize patterns and relationships between different functions that serve the same outcome. Therefore, the success of exploration strongly depends on the individual. For future research and for management, it would be interesting to investigate how such people can systematically be developed in an organization.

- Exploration as depicted in this research is strongly related to corporate vision and corporate strategy. In all firms, innovation is the main lever for growth, prosperity and long-term competitiveness. Therefore, it would be worthwhile to investigate the relationship between an overarching corporate strategy and innovation strategy. Interesting paths would be to gain more insights about how innovation is encapsulated in corporate strategy, and how, in fact, corporate goals limit or foster exploration activities in the organization. Deeper understanding about relationships between different hierarchical levels of strategy would be valuable for strategy formulation when increase of exploratory innovations is targeted.

In summary, this research addresses several areas which are important for management practice across different industries and technologies. Literature on organizational learning, strategic management, organization design, technological innovation, and knowledge management is still limited regarding insights about exploration. In particular, future research might gain more insights about the effects of strategy on subsequent exploration success. The findings in this study provide first insights into this area and thus serve as guideline for the management of exploration. Furthermore, this study serves as a starting point for further research into this highly relevant topic, which is the basis for every firm's future competitiveness.

References

Abernathy, W. J. and K. B. Clark (1985). "Innovation: Mapping the winds of creative destruction." *Research Policy* 14(1): 3.

Afuah, A. (2002). "Mapping technological capabilities into product markets and competitive advantage: The case of cholesterol drugs." *Strategic Management Journal* 23(2): 171.

Ahuja, G. and C. M. Lampert (2001). "Entrepreneurship in the large corporation: a longitudinal study of how established firms create breakthrough inventions." *Strategic Management Journal* 22(6-7): 521-543.

Almeida, P., A. Phene and R. Grant (2003). Innovation and Knowledge Management: Scanning, Sourcing, and Integration. The Blackwell Handbook of Organizational Learning and Knowledge Management. M. Easterby-Smith and M. Lyles. Malden, Blackwell Publishing.

Alvarez, S. A. and J. Barney (2002). Resource-based theory and the entrepreneurial firm. Strategic entrepreneurship: Creating a new mindset. M. A. Hitt, R. D. Ireland, S. M. Camp and D. L. Sexton. Oxford, Blackwell Publishing.

Argote, L. (1999). Organizational learning: Creating, retaining and transferring knowledge. Boston, Kluwer Academic.

Argote, L. and P. Ingram (2000). "Knowledge Transfer: A Basis for Competitive Advantage in Firms." *Organizational Behavior and Human Decision Processes* 82(1): 150.

Argyris, C. (1999). On Organizational Learning. Oxford, Blackwell Publishing.

Baden-Fuller, C. and H. W. Volberda (1997). Strategic Renewal in Large Complex Organizations. Competence-Based Strategic Management. A. Heene and R. Sanchez. Chichester, Wiley & Sons.

Barney, J. (1991). "Firm Resources and Sustained Competitive Advantage." *Journal of Management* 17(1): 99-120.

Benner, M. J. and M. Tushman (2002). "Process Management and Technological Innovation: A Longitudinal Study of the Photography and Paint Industries." *Administrative Science Quarterly* 47(4): 676.

Benner, M. J. and M. L. Tushman (2003). "Exploitation, Exploration, and Process Management: the Productivity Dilemma revisited." *Academy of Management Review* 28(2): 238.

Boden, M. A. (1990). The creative mind. Myths & Mechanisms. London, Weidenfeld and Nicholson.

Brown, S. L. and K. M. Eisenhardt (1995). "Product Development: Past Research, Present Findings, and Future Directions." *The Academy of Management Review* 20(2): 343.

Burgelman, R. A. (1983). "Corporate entrepreneurship and strategic management: Insights from a process study." *Management Science* 29(12): 1349-1364.

Burgelman, R. A. (1991). "Intraorganizational ecology of strategy making and organizational adaptation: Theory and field research." *Organization Science* 2(3): 239.

Burgelman, R. A. (1994). "Fading Memories: A Process Theory of Strategic Business Exit in Dynamic Environments." *Administrative Science Quarterly* 39(1): 24-56.

Burgelman, R. A. (2002). "Strategy as Vector and the Inertia of Coevolutionary Lock-in." *Administrative Science Quarterly* 47(2): 325.

Burns, T. and G. M. Stalker (2001). The Management of Innovation. Oxford, Oxford University Press.

Casson, M. (1995). Entrepreneurship and Business Culture. Aldershot/UK, Brookfield/US, Edward Elgar.

Ceserani, J. and P. Greatwood (1995). Innovation & Creativity. London, Kogan Page.

Chandy, R. K. and G. J. Tellis (1998). "Organizing for Radical Product Innovation: The Overlooked Role of Willingness to Cannibalize." *Journal of Marketing Research (JMR)* 35(4): 474.

References

Cheng, Y.-T. and A. H. van de Ven (1996). "Learning the Innovation Journey: Order out of Chaos?" *Organization Science* 7(6): 593.

Christensen, C. M. (1997). The innovator's dilemma: when new technologies cause great firms to fail. Boston (Mass.), Harvard Business School Press.

Christensen, C. M. and J. L. Bower (1996). "Customer power, strategic investment, and the failure of leading firms." *Strategic Management Journal* 17(3): 197-218.

Christensen, C. M., M. W. Johnson and D. K. Rigby (2002). "Foundations for Growth." *MIT Sloan Management Review* 43(3): 22-31.

Cohen, W. M. and D. A. Levinthal (1989). "Innovation and learning: The two faces of R&D." *Economic Journal* 99(397): 569-596.

Cohen, W. M. and D. A. Levinthal (1990). "Absorptive Capacity: A New Perspective on Learning and Innovation." *Administrative Science Quarterly* 35(1): 128.

Colarelli O'Connor, G. and P. R. Mark (2001). "Opportunity recognition and breakthrough innovation in large established firms." *California Management Review* 43(2): 95.

Conant, J. S., M. P. Mokwa and P. R. Varadarajan (1990). "Strategic types, distinctive marketing competencies and organizational performance: A multiple measures-based study." *Strategic Management Journal* 11(5): 365-383.

Cooper, R. G. (1990). "Stage-gate systems: A new tool for managing new products." *Business Horizons* 33(3): 44.

Cooper, R. G. (1994). "Third-Generation New Product Processes." *Journal of Product Innovation Management* 11(1): 3-14.

Cooper, R. G. (1999). "From Experience: The Invisible Success Factors in Product Innovation." *Journal of Product Innovation Management* 16(2): 115.

Cooper, R. G., S. J. Edgett and E. J. Kleinschmidt (1998). "Best practices for managing R&D portfolios." *Research Technology Management* 41(4): 20-33.

Cooper, R. G. and E. J. Kleinschmidt (1986). "An Investigation into the new product process: Steps, deficiencies, and impact." *Journal of Product Innovation Management* 3(2): 71-85.

Cooper, R. G. and E. J. Kleinschmidt (1987). "New products: What separates winners from losers?" *Journal of Product Innovation Management* 4(3): 169-184.

Covin, J. G. and D. Slevin (2002). The entrepreneurial imperatives of strategic leadership. Strategic entrepreneurship: creating an entrepreneurial mindset. M. A. Hitt, R. D. Ireland, S. M. Camp and D. L. Sexton. Oxford, Blackwell Publishing.

Covin, J. O. and M. P. Miles (1999). "Corporate Entrepreneurship and the Pursuit of Competitive Advantage." *Entrepreneurship: Theory & Practice* 23(3): 47-63.

Crossan, M. M. and I. Bedrow (2003). "Organizational Learning and Strategic Renewal." *Strategic Management Journal* 24(11): 1087.

Csikszentmihalyi, M. (1996). Creativity. Flow and the Psychology of Discovery and Invention. New York, HarperCollins.

Cyert, R. and J. G. March (1992). A behavioral theory of the firm. Cambridge, Massachusetts, Blackwell Publishers.

D'Aveni, R. A. (1994). Hypercompetition: Managing the Dynamics of Strategic Maneuvering. New York, Free Press.

D'Iribarne, P. (1996). "The usefulness of an ethnographic approach to the international comparison of organizations." *International Studies of Management & Organization* 26(4): 30-47.

Dahl, D. W. and P. Moreau (2002). "The Influence and Value of Analogical Thinking During New Product Ideation." *Journal of Marketing Research (JMR)* 39(1): 47.

Daily, C. M., P. P. McDougall, J. G. Covin and D. R. Dalton (2002). "Governance and Strategic Leadership in Entrepreneurial Firms." *Journal of Management* 28(3): 387-412.

Danneels, E. (2002). "The Dynamics of Product Innovation and Firm Competences." *Strategic Management Journal* 23(12): 1095.

Danneels, E. (2007). "The process of technological competence leveraging." *Strategic Management Journal* 28(5): 511-533.

De Bono, E. (1990). Lateral Thinking for Management. London, Penguin Books Ltd.

Dess, G. G., R. D. Ireland, S. A. Zahra, S. W. Floyd, J. J. Janney and P. J. Lane (2003). "Emerging Issues in Corporate Entrepreneurship." *Journal of Management* 29(3): 351-378.

Dillon, J. T. (1992). Problem-Finding and Solving. Source book for creative problem solving. S. J. Parnes. Buffalo/New York, Creative Education Foundation Press.

Dorroh, J. R., T. R. Gulledge and N. K. Womer (1994). "Investment in Knowledge: A Generalization of Learning by Experience." *Management Science* 40(8): 947-958.

Dosi, G., R. Nelson and S. Winter (2000). Introduction: The nature and dynamics of organizational capabilities. The nature and dynamics of organizational capabilities. G. Dosi, R. Nelson and S. Winter. New York, Oxford University Press.

Dougherty, D. and C. Hardy (1996). "Sustained product innovation in large, mature organizations: Overcoming innovation-to-organization problems." *Academy of Management Journal* 39(5): 1120-1153.

Dougherty, D. and T. Heller (1994). "The Illegitimacy of Successful Product Innovation in Established Firms." *Organization Science* 5(2): 200-218.

Drucker, P. F. (2007). Innovation and Entrepreneurship. London, Butterworth-Heinemann.

Duncan, R. B. (1976). The ambidextrous organization: Designing dual structures for innovation. The Management of Organization. R. H. Kilmann, L. R. Pondy and D. Slevin. New York, North-Hollan.

Eckhardt, J. T. and S. A. Shane (2003). "Opportunities and Entrepreneurship." *Journal of Management* 29(3): 333-349.

Eisenhardt, K. M. (1989). "Building theories from case study research." *Academy of Management Review* 14(4): 532-550.

Eisenhardt, K. M. (1989). "Making Fast Strategic Decisions in High-Velocity Environments." *The Academy of Management Journal* 32(3): 543.

Eisenhardt, K. M. and M. E. Graebner (2007). "Theory building from cases: opportunities and challenges." *Academy of Management Journal* 50(1): 25.

Ettlie, J. E., W. P. Bridges and R. D. O'Keefe (1984). "Organization strategy and structural differences for radical versus incremental innovation." *Management Science* 30(6): 682.

Eversheim, W., W. Bochtler, Gräßling, R. ler and W. Kölscheid (1997). "Simultaneous engineering approach to an integrated design and process planning." *European Journal of Operational Research* 100(2): 327.

Fiet, J. O. (1996). "The Informational Basis of Entrepreneurial Discovery." *Small Business Economics* 8(6).

Finke, R. A. (1995). The creative cognition approach. Creative realism. S. M. Smith, T. B. Ward and R. A. Finke. Cambridge, MA, MIT Press: 303-326.

Fiol, C. M. and A. S. Huff (1992). "Maps for managers: Where are we? Where do we go from here?" *Journal of Management Studies* 29(3): 267-285.

Fiol, C. M. and M. A. Lyles (1985). "Organizational Learning." *The Academy of Management Review* 10(4): 803-813.

Fleming, L. (2001). "Recombinant Uncertainty in Technological Search." *Management Science* 47(1): 117.

Fleming, L. and O. Sorenson (2004). "Science as a map in technological search." *Strategic Management Journal* 25(8-9): 909-928.

Floyd, S. W. and P. J. Lane (2000). "Strategizing throughout the organization: Managing role conflict in strategic renewal." *Academy of Management Review* 25(1): 154.

Gaglio, C. M. and J. A. Katz (2001). "The Psychological Basis of Opportunity Identification: Entrepreneurial Alertness." *Small Business Economics* 16(2): 95-111.

Gagne, C. L. and E. J. Shoben (1997). "Influence of thematic relations on the comprehension of modifier-noun combinations." *Journal of Experimental Psychology: Learning, Memory, and Cognition* 23(1): 71.

Gambardella, A. and S. Torrisi (1998). "Does technological convergence imply convergence in markets? Evidence from the electronics industry." *Research Policy* 27(5): 445-463.

Garcia, R. and R. Calantone (2002). "A critical look at technological innovation typology and innovativeness terminology: a literature review." *Journal of Product Innovation Management* 19(2): 110.

Gassmann, O. and M. Zeschky (2008). "Opening up the Solution Space: The Role of Analogical Thinking for Breakthrough Product Innovation." *Creativity & Innovation Management* 17(2): 97-106.

Gavetti, G. and D. Levinthal (2000). "Looking Forward and Looking Backward: Cognitive and Experiential Search." *Administrative Science Quarterly* 45(1): 113.

Gavetti, G., D. A. Levinthal and J. W. Rivkin (2005). "Strategy making in novel and complex worlds: the power of analogy." *Strategic Management Journal* 26(8): 691.

Gentner, D. and M. J. Rattermann (1993). "The roles of similarity in transfer: Separating retrievability from inferential soundness." *Cognitive Psychology* 25(4): 524.

Geschka, H. (1992). Creativity techniques in product planning and development: a view from West Germany. Source book for creative problem solving. S. J. Parnes. Buffalo/New York, Creative Education Foundation Press: 282-298.

Geschka, H. (1996). "Creativity Techniques in Germany." *Creativity and Innovation Management* 5(2): 87-92.

Getzels, J. W. (1992). Problem-finding and inventiveness of solutions. Source book for creative problem solving. S. J. Parnes. Buffalo/New York, Creative Education Foundation Press.

Ghemawat, P. and J. E. R. I. Costa (1993). "The Organizational Tension between Static and Dynamic Efficiency." *Strategic Management Journal* 14: 59.

Gibson, C. B. and J. Birkinshaw (2004). "The Antecedents, Consequences, and Mediating Role Of Organizational Ambidexterity." *Academy of Management Journal* 47(2): 209.

Gick, M. L. and K. J. Holyoak (1980). "Analogical problem solving." *Cognitive Psychology* 12(3): 306.

Gick, M. L. and K. J. Holyoak (1983). "Schema Induction and Analogical Transfer." *Cognitive Psychology* 15: 1-38.

Gordon, W. J. J. (1969). Synectics - the Development of Creative Capacity. New York, Harper and Row.

Grant, R. M. (1991). The Resource-Based Theory of Competitive Advantage: Implications for Strategy Formulation. California Management Review, California Management Review. 33: 114.

Grant, R. M. (1996). "Toward a knowledge-based view of the firm." *Strategic Management Journal* 17: 109.

Grant, R. M. and C. Baden-Fuller (2004). "A Knowledge Accessing Theory of Strategic Alliances." *Journal of Management Studies* 41(1): 61-84.

Greve, H. R. (2003). Organizational learning from performance feedback: A behavioral perspective on innovation and change. Cambridge, Cambridge University Press.

Greve, H. R. (2007). "Exploration and exploitation in product innovation." *Industrial and Corporate Change*: 1-31.

Gupta, A. K., K. G. Smith and C. E. Shalley (2006). "The interplay between exploration and exploitation." *Academy of Management Journal* 49(4): 693.

Guth, W. D. and A. Ginsberg (1990). "Guest Editors' Introduction: Corporate Entrepreneurship." *Strategic Management Journal* 11: 5-15.

Hambrick, D. C. (1982). "Environmental Scanning and Organizational Strategy." *Strategic Management Journal* 3(2): 159-174.

Hamel, G. and A. Heene (1994). Competence based competition. Chichester, John Wiley.

Hamel, G. and C. K. Prahalad (1994). "Competing for the Future." *Harvard Business Review* 72(4): 122-128.

Hampton, J. A. (1998). "Conceptual combination: Conjunction and negation of natural concepts." *Memory & Cognition* 25(6): 888.

Hargadon, A. and R. I. Sutton (1997). "Technology Brokering and Innovation in a Product Development Firm." *Administrative Science Quarterly* 42(4): 716.

He, Z.-L. and P.-K. Wong (2004). "Exploration vs. Exploitation: An Empirical Test of the Ambidexterity Hypothesis." *Organization Science* 15(4): 481.

Helfat, C. E. and M. B. Lieberman (2002). "The birth of capabilities: market entry and the importance of pre-history." *Industrial & Corporate Change* 11(4): 725.

Henderson, R., J. Del Alamo, T. Becker, J. Lawton, P. Moran and S. Shapiro (1998). "The Perils of Excellence: Barriers to Effective Process Improvement in Product-Driven Firms." *Production and Operations Management Society* 7(1).

Henderson, R. M. and K. B. Clark (1990). "Architectural Innovation: The Reconfiguration of Existing Product Technologies and the Failure of Established Firms." *Administrative Science Quarterly* 35(1): 9.

Herriott, S. R., D. Levinthal and J. G. March (1985). "Learning from Experience in Organizations." *American Economic Review* 75(2): 298.

Herrmann, A., O. Gassmann and U. Eisert (2007). "An empirical study of the antecedents for radical product innovations and capabilities for transformation." *Journal of Engineering & Technology Management* 24(1/2): 92.

Hill, C. W. L. and F. T. Rothaermel (2003). "The performance of incumbent firms in the face of radical technological innovation." *Academy of Management Review* 28(2): 257.

Hitt, M. A., L. Biermant, K. Shimizu and R. Kochhar (2001). "Direct and moderating effects of human capital on strategy and performance in professional service firms: A resource-based perspective." *Academy of Management Journal* 44(1): 13.

Hitt, M. A., R. D. Ireland, S. M. Camp and D. L. Sexton (2001). "Strategic entrepreneurship: entrepreneurial strategies for wealth creation." *Strategic Management Journal* 22(6-7): 479-491.

Hoang, H. and H. Ener (2007). When and where do firms explore? Product development in an entrepreneurial context. INSEAD.

Holmqvist, M. (2004). "Experiential Learning Processes of Exploitation and Exploration Within and Between Organizations: An Empirical Study of Product Development." *Organization Science* 15(1): 70.

Holyoak, K. J. and P. Thagard (1995). Mental Leaps: Analogy in Creative Thought. Cambridge, MA, MIT Press.

Holyoak, K. J. and P. Thagard (1997). "The analogical mind." *American Psychologist* 52(1): 35.

Hrebiniak, L. G. and W. F. Joyce (1985). "Organizational Adaptation: Strategic Choice and Environmental Determinism." *Administrative Science Quarterly* 30(3): 336.

Huber, G. P. (1991). "Organizational Learning: The Contributing Processes and the Literatures." *Organization Science* 2(1): 88-115.

Huff, A. S. (1990). Mapping Strategic Thought. New York, Wiley.

Ireland, R. D., M. A. Hitt, S. M. Camp and D. L. Sexton (2001). "Integrating entrepreneurship and strategic management actions to create firm wealth." *Academy of Management Executive* 15(1): 49-63.

Ireland, R. D., M. A. Hitt and D. G. Sirmon (2003). "A Model of Strategic Entrepreneurship: The Construct and its Dimensions." *Journal of Management* 29(6): 963-989.

Ireland, R. D. and J. W. Webb (2007). "A cross-disciplinary exploration of entrepreneurship literature." *Journal of Management* 33(6): 891-927.

Jansen, J. J. P., F. A. J. Van Den Bosch and H. W. Volberda (2005). "Managing potential and realized absorptive capacity: How do organizational antecedents matter?" *Academy of Management Journal* 48(6): 999.

Jansen, J. J. P., F. A. J. Van Den Bosch and H. W. Volberda (2006). "Exploratory Innovation, Exploitative Innovation, and Performance: Effects of Organizational Antecedents and Environmental Moderators." *Management Science* 52(11): 1661-1674.

Jelinek, M. and C. B. Schoonhoven (1990). The Innovation Marathon: Lessons from High-Technology firms. Oxford, Blackwell.

Katila, R. and G. Ahuja (2002). "Something Old, Something New: A Longitudinal Study Of Search Behavior and New Product Introduction." *Academy of Management Journal* 45(6): 1183.

Keane, M. (1987). "On retrieving analogues when solving problems." *The Quarterly Journal of Experimental Psychology Section A* 39(1): 29 - 41.

Khurana, A. and S. R. Rosenthal (1997). "Integrating the Fuzzy Front End of New Product Development." *Sloan Management Review* 38(2): 103.

Kim, J. and D. Wilemon (2002). "Focusing the fuzzy front end in new product development." *R&D Management* 32(4): 269.

Kirzner, I. M. (1997). "Entrepreneurial Discovery and the Competitive Market Process: An Austrian Approach." *Journal of Economic Literature* 35(1): 60-85.

Kleinschmidt, E. J. and R. G. Cooper (1991). "The Impact of Product Innovativeness on Performance." *Journal of Product Innovation Management* 8(4): 240.

Kogut, B. and U. Zander (1992). "Knowledge of the firm, combinative capabilities, and the replication of technology." *Organization Science* 3(3): 383.

Kromrey, H. (1995). Empirische Sozialforschung: Modelle und Methoden der Datenerhebung und Datenauswertung. Opladen, Westdeutscher Verlag.

Lane, P. J., B. R. Koka and S. Pathak (2006). "The reification of absorptive capacity: a critical review and rejuvenation of the construct." *Academy of Management Review* 31(4): 833-863.

Lant, T. K. and S. J. Mezias (1990). "Managing Discontinuous Change: A Simulation Study of Organizational Learning and Entrepreneurship." *Strategic Management Journal* 11: 147-179.

Lavie, D. (2006). "Capability Reconfiguration: an analysis of incumbents responses to technological change." *Academy of Management Review* 31(1): 153.

Leifer, R., G. C. O'Connor and M. Rice (2001). "Implementing radical innovation in mature firms: The role of hubs." *Academy of Management Executive* 15(3): 102.

Lenz, R. T. and J. Engledow, L. (1986). "Environmental Analysis Units and Strategic Decision making: a Field Study of Selected 'Leading-edge' Corporations." *Strategic Management Journal (1986-1998)* 7(1): 69.

Leonard-Barton, D. (1992). "Core Capabilities and Core Rigidities: A Paradox in Managing New Product Development." *Strategic Management Journal* 13(5): 111-125.

Leonard, D. (1995). Wellsprings of knowledge: Building and sustaining the sources of innovation. Boston, Harvard Business School Press.

Levinthal, D. and J. G. March (1981). "A model of adaptive organizational search." *Journal of Economic Behavior & Organization* 2(4): 307-333.

Levinthal, D. A. and J. G. March (1993). "The Myopia of Learning." *Strategic Management Journal* 14(8): 95.

Levitt, B. and J. G. March (1988). "Organizational Learning." *Annual Review of Sociology* 14(1): 319-338.

Lewin, A. Y., C. P. Long and T. N. Carroll (1999). "The Coevolution of New Organizational Forms." *Organization Science* 10(5): 535.

Linde, H. J., D. M. Hall and G. H. Herr (1999). "Powerful and Structured Innovation using Contradictions for Gaining Orientation." *Journal of Engineering Design* 10(3): 205.

Lounamaa, P. H. and J. G. March (1987). "Adaptive coordination of a learning team." *Management Science* 33(1): 107.

Lumpkin, G. T. and G. G. Dess (1996). "Clarifying the Entrepreneurial Orientation Construct and Linking It to Performance." *The Academy of Management Review* 21(1): 135-172.

Lumpkin, G. T. and B. B. Lichtenstein (2005). "The Role of Organizational Learning in the Opportunity-Recognition Process." *Entrepreneurship: Theory & Practice* 29(4): 451-472.

Mahajan, V. and J. Wind (1992). "New product models: Practice, shortcomings and desired improvements." *Journal of Product Innovation Management* 9(2): 128-139.

References

Majchrzak, A., L. P. Cooper and O. E. Neece (2004). "Knowledge Reuse for Innovation." *Management Science* 50(2): 174.

March, J. G. (1991). "Exploration and Exploitation in Organizational Learning." *Organization Science* 2(1): 71.

Martin, X. and W. Mitchell (1998). "The influence of local search and performance heuristics." *Research Policy* 26(7/8): 753.

McCline, R. L., S. Bhat and P. Baj (2000). "Opportunity Recognition: An Exploratory Investigation of a Component of the Entrepreneurial Process in the Context of the Health Care Industry." *Entrepreneurship: Theory & Practice* 25(2): 81-94.

McGrath, R. G. (2001). "Exploratory Learning, Innovative Capacity and Managerial Oversight." *The Academy of Management Journal* 44(1): 118.

McGrath, R. G. and I. C. MacMillan (2000). The entrepreneurial mindset. Boston, Harvard Business School Press.

McGuinness, N. W. and H. A. Conway (1989). "Managing the search for new product concepts: A strategic approach." *R&D Management* 19(4): 297-308.

Meyer, G. D. and K. A. Heppard (2000). Entrepreneurial strategies. The dominant logic of entrepreneurship. Entrepreneurship as Strategy. Competing on the entrepreneurial edge. G. D. Meyer and K. A. Heppard. Thousand Oaks, Sage Publications.

Miles, M. B. and A. M. Hubermann (2005). Qualitative data analysis: An expanded sourcebook. Thousand Oaks, Sage Publications.

Miles, R. E. and C. C. Snow (1978). Organizational strategy, structure, and process. New York, McGraw-Hill.

Miller, D. (2003). "An asymmetry-based view of advantage: towards an attainable sustainability." *Strategic Management Journal* 24(10): 961-976.

Miner, A. S., P. Bassoff and C. Moorman (2001). "Organizational Improvisation and Learning: A Field Study." *Administrative Science Quarterly* 46(2): 304-337.

Mintzberg, H. (2005). Developing theory about the development of theory. Great Minds in Management: The Process of Theory Development. K. G. Smith and M. A. Hitt. Oxford, Oxford University Press.

Moenaert, R. K., A. De Meyer, W. E. Souder and D. Deschoolmeester (1995). "R&D-marketing communication during the fuzzy front-end." *IEEE Transactions on Engineering Management* 42(3): 243-258.

Montoya-Weiss, M. M. and R. Calantone (1994). "Determinants of New Product Performance: A Review and Meta-Analysis." *Journal of Product Innovation Management* 11(5): 397-417.

Morris, M. H. and D. F. Kuratko (2002). Corporate entrepreneurship. Mason, South-Western College Publishers.

Nelson, R. R. and S. G. Winter (1982). An evolutionary theory of economic change. Cambridge, Belknap Press of Harvard University Press.

Nerkar, A. (2003). "Old Is Gold? The Value of Temporal Exploration in the Creation of New Knowledge." *Management Science* 49(2): 211.

Nohria, N. and R. Gulati (1996). "Is slack good or bad for innovation?" *Academy of Management Journal* 39(5): 1245-1264.

O'Connor, G. C. and A. D. Ayers (2005). "Building a radical innovation competency." *Research Technology Management* 48(1): 23.

O'Reilly III, C. A. and M. L. Tushman (2004). "The Ambidextrous Organization." *Harvard Business Review* 82(4): 74.

OECD (2005). Science, technology and industry scoreboard. Paris.

Parnes, S. J. (1992). Creative problem solving and visionizing. Source book for creative problem solving. S. J. Parnes. Buffalo/New York, Creative Education Foundation Press: 133-153.

Patel, P. and K. Pavitt (1997). "The technological competencies of the world's largest firms: Complex and path-dependent, but not much variety." *Research Policy* 26(2): 141-156.

Pfeffer, J. and G. R. Salancik (2003). The external control of organizations: a resource dependence perspective. Stanford, Stanford University Press.

Prahalad, C. K. and G. Hamel (1990). "The Core Competence of the Corporation." *Harvard Business Review* 68(3): 79.

Prince, G. M. (1970). The Practice of Creativity. New York, Macmillan.

Punch, K. F. (2005). Introduction to social research: quantitative and qualitative approaches. London, Sage Publications.

Reeves, L. M. and R. W. Weisberg (1993). "Abstract versus concrete information as the basis for transfer in problem solving: Comment on Fong and Nisbett (1991)." *Journal of Experimental Psychology: General* 122(1): 125.

Reeves, L. M. and R. W. Weisberg (1994). "The role of content and abstract information in analogical transfer." *Psychological Bulletin* 115(3): 381

Reinganum, J. F. (1982). "Strategic search theory." *International Economic Review* 23(1).

Rice, M., D. Kelley, L. Peters and G. Colarelli O'Connor (2001). "Radical innovation: triggering initiation of opportunity recognition and evaluation." *R & D Management* 31(4): 409.

Rickards, T. (1990). Creativity and Problem Solving at Work. Hants, England, Gower Publishing Company Ltd.

Rickards, T. (1991). "Innovation and creativity: woods, trees, and pathways." *R&D Management* 21(2): 97-108.

Rickards, T. and G. Puccio (1992). Problem finding, idea finding and implementation. An exploratory model for investigating small-group problem-solving. Managing Organisations in 1992. Strategic responses. P. Barrar and C. L. Cooper. London/New York, Routledge.

Rivkin, J. W. and N. Siggelkow (2003). Balancing search and stability: Interdependencies among elements of organizational design. Management Sci. 49: 290.

Rosenkopf, L. and A. Nerkar (2001). "Beyond Local Search: Boundary-spanning, Exploration, and Impact in the Optical Disc Industry." *Strategic Management Journal* 22(4): 287.

Ross, B. H. (1989). "Distinguishing types of superficial similarities: Different effects on the access and use of earlier problems." *Journal of Experimental Psychology: Learning, Memory, and Cognition* 15(3): 456.

Sanchez, R., A. Heene and H. Thomas (1996). Towards the theory and practice of competence-based competition. Dynamics of competence-based competition: theory and practice in the new strategic management. R. Sanchez, A. Heene and H. Thomas. Oxford, Pergamon Press.

Sanchez, R. and H. Thomas (1996). Strategic Goals. Dynamics of competence-based competition: theory and practice in the new strategic management. R. Sanchez, A. Heene and H. Thomas. Oxford, Pergamon Press.

Schein, E. H. (1991). What is culture? Reframing organizational culture. P. J. Frost, L. F. Moore, M. Reis Louis, C. C. Lundberg and J. Martin. New York, Sage: 243-253.

Schoonhoven, C. B., K. M. Eisenhardt and K. Lyman (1990). "Speeding Products to Market: Waiting Time to First Product Introduction in New Firms." *Administrative Science Quarterly* 35(1): 177.

Schumpeter, J. (1934). The Theory of Economic Development. Cambridge, Harvard University Press.

Schumpeter, J. A. (1942). Capitalism, socialism and democracy. New York, Harper.

Shane, S. (2000). "Prior Knowledge and the Discovery of Entrepreneurial Opportunities." *Organization Science* 11(4): 448-469.

Shane, S. (2003). A general theory of entrepreneurship. The individual-opportunity nexus. Cheltenham/Northhampton, Edward Elgar.

Shane, S. and S. Venkataraman (2000). "The promise of entrepreneurship as a field of research." *Academy of Management. The Academy of Management Review* 25(1): 217.

Sharma, P. and J. J. Chrisman (1999). "Toward a Reconciliation of the Definitional Issues in the Field of Corporate Entrepreneurship." *Entrepreneurship: Theory & Practice* 23(3): 11-27.

Sheremata, W. A. (2000). "Centrifugal and centripetal forces in radical new product development under time pressure." *Academy of Management Review* 25(2): 389-408.

Sidhu, J. S., H. R. Commandeur and H. W. Volberda (2007). "The Multifaceted Nature of Exploration and Exploitation: Value of Supply, Demand, and Spatial Search for Innovation." *Organization Science* 18(1): 20.

Sidhu, J. S., H. W. Volberda and H. R. Commandeur (2004). "Exploring Exploration Orientation and its Determinants: Some Empirical Evidence." *Journal of Management Studies* 41(6): 913-932.

Simon, H. A. (1991). "Bounded rationality and organizational learning." *Organization Science* 2(1): 125-134.

Smith, C. G. and A. C. Cooper (1988). "Established companies diversifying into young industries: A comparison of firms with different levels of performance." *Strategic Management Journal* 9(2): 111-121.

Smith, K. G. and D. Di Gregorio (2002). Bisociation, discovery, and the role of entrepreneurial action. Strategic entrepreneurship: Creating a new mindset. M. A. Hitt, R. D. Ireland, S. M. Camp and D. L. Sexton. Oxford, Blackwell Publishing.

Smith, P. G. and D. G. Reinertsen (1998). Developing products in half of the time: New rules, new tools. New York, John Willey & Sons.

Solow, R. M. (1957). "Technical Change and the Aggregate Production Function." *The Review of Economics and Statistics* 39(3): 312-320.

Stevens, G. A. and J. Burley (2003). "Piloting the rocket of radical innovation." *Research Technology Management* 46(2): 16.

Stevenson, H. H. and J. C. Jarillo (1990). "A paradigm of entrepreneurship: entrepreneurial management." *Strategic Management Journal* 11(4): 17-27.

Stopford, J. (2001). "Should Strategy Makers Become Dream Weavers?" *Harvard Business Review* 79(1): 165-169.

Stopford, J. M. and C. W. F. Baden-Fuller (1994). "Creating Corporate Entrepreneurship." *Strategic Management Journal* 15(7): 521-536.

Stringer, R. (2000). "How To Manage Radical Innovation." *California Management Review* 42(4): 70.

Stuart, T. E. and J. M. Podolny (1996). "Local Search and the Evolution of Technological Capabilities." *Strategic Management Journal* 17: 21.

Subramaniam, M. and M. A. Youndt (2005). "The influence of intellectual capital on the types of innovative capabilities." *Academy of Management Journal* 48(3): 450.

Teece, D. J. (1986). "Profiting from technological innovation: Implications for integration, collaboration, licensing and public policy." *Research Policy* 15(6): 285-305.

Teece, D. J., G. Pisano and A. Shuen (1997). "Dynamic capabilities and strategic management." *Strategic Management Journal* 18(7): 509-533.

Thomke, S. and W. Kuemmerle (2002). "Asset accumulation, interdependence and technological change: evidence from pharmaceutical drug discovery." *Strategic Management Journal* 23(7): 619-635.

Tripsas, M. (1997). "Unraveling the process of creative destruction: complementary assets and incumbent survival in the typsetter industry." *Strategic Management Journal* 18(S1): 119-142.

Tushman, M. and D. Nadler (1986). "Organizing for Innovation." *California Management Review* 28(3): 74-92.

Tushman, M. L. and P. Anderson (1986). "Technological Discontinuities and Organizational Environments." *Administrative Science Quarterly* 31(3): 439.

Tushman, M. L. and C. A. O'Reilly III (1996). "Ambidextrous organizations: Managing evolutionary and revolutionary change." *California Management Review* 38(4): 8.

Tversky, A. and D. Kahneman (1986). "Rational Choice and the Framing of Decisions." *The Journal of Business* 59(4): S251-S278.

Utterback, J. M. (1994). "Radical innovation and corporate regeneration." *Research Technology Management* 37(4): 10.

Van de Ven, A. H. (2007). Engaged Scholarhsip: A Guide for Organizational and Social Research New York, Oxford University Press.

Venkataraman, S. (1997). The distinctive domain of entrepreneurship research: an editor's perspective. Advances in Entrepreneurship, Firm Emergence, and Growth. J. Katz and R. Brockhaus. Greenwich, JAI Press.

Veryzer Jr, R. W. (1998). "Discontinuous Innovation and the New Product Development Process." *Journal of Product Innovation Management* 15(4): 304.

Volberda, H. W. (1996). "Toward the Flexible Form: How to Remain Vital in Hypercompetitive Environments." *Organization Science* 7(4): 359.

von Hippel, E. (1986). "Lead Users: A Source of Novel Product Concepts." *Management Science* 32(7): 791.

Vosniadou, S. and A. Ortony (1989). Similarity and analogical reasoning: a synthesis. Similarity and analogical reasoning. S. Vosniadou and A. Ortony. Cambridge, Cambridge University Press: 1-17.

Voss, C., N. Tsikriktsis and M. Frohlich (2002). "Case research in operations management." *International Journal of Operations & Production Management* 22(2): 195-219.

Voss, G. B., D. Sirdeshmukh and Z. G. Voss (2008). "The effects of slack resources and environmental threat on product exploration and exploitation." *Academy of Management Journal* 51(1): 147-164.

Walsh, J. P. (1995). "Managerial and Organizational Cognition: Notes from a Trip Down Memory Lane." *Organization Science* 6(3): 280-321.

Ward, T. B. (1994). "Structured Imagination: the Role of Category Structure in Exemplar Generation." *Cognitive Psychology* 27(1): 1.

Ward, T. B., S. M. Smith and J. Vaid (1997). Conceptual structures and processes in creative thought. Creative thought: an investigation of conceptual structures and processes. T. B. Ward, S. M. Smith and J. Vaid. Washington, DC, American Psychological Association.

Weiss, E. (2004). "Functional market concept for planning technological innovations." *International Journal of Technology Management* 27(2/3): 320.

Wernerfelt, B. (1984). "A Resource-based View of the Firm." *Strategic Management Journal* 5(2): 171.

Winter, S. G. (2000). "The Satisficing Principle in Capability Learning." *Strategic Management Journal* 21(10/11): 981-996.

Winter, S. G. and G. Szulanski (2001). "Replication as Strategy." *Organization Science* 12(6): 730.

Yin, R. K. (2003). Case study research: Design and methods. Thousand Oaks, CA, Sage Publications.

Zahra, S. A. (1991). "Predictors and financial outcomes of corporate entrepreneurship: An exploratory study." *Journal of Business Venturing* 6(4): 259-285.

Zahra, S. A. and G. George (2002). "Absorptive Capacity: a review, reconceptualization, and extension." *Academy of Management Review* 27(2): 185.

Zollo, M. and S. G. Winter (2002). "Deliberate learning and the evolution of dynamic capabilities." *Organization Science* 13(3): 339-351.

Appendix

Interview-Guideline

Term Definition
- *Exploration*: Search for new knowledge and business opportunities both regarding technologies and markets with the aim of (radical) product innovation and new business development. This includes the search for new knowledge, which might not be of immediate benefit for innovation.
- *Exploratory activities*: Activities that aim at identifying new knowledge for innovation and business opportunities in the above sense. This includes e.g. experiments with new technologies.
- *Exploitation*: Use and refinement of existing technologies and markets which typically leads to the development of incremental innovations.
- *Entrepreneurship*: The organizational/individual behavior of identifying and exploiting new business opportunities

General Information
1. How would you describe the company's overall innovation strategy?
2. How would you characterize the company's competitive environment?
3. How would you describe your innovation strategy compared to your competitors?

Strategic Management of Resources
4. How would you describe the firm's commitment towards identifying new business opportunities and more radical innovations?
5. How do you balance activities that aim at improving and refining existing technologies and markets and activities that aim at identifying entirely new business opportunities?
6. How do (financial) resources reflect and support this strategy?
7. Does your firm provide extra resources that are exclusively used for exploratory activities? What do these resources look like and how are they employed?
8. Do you employ certain 'types' of people for the respective tasks? What distinguishes people who pursue exploration activities from those who pursue improvement activities?

9. How does prior experience influence the direction and success of your exploration activities?
10. How far do internal and external relationships between your employees and external organizations influence the direction and success of your exploration activities?

Entrepreneurial Alertness
11. Do you set objectives in such a way that they are challenging to achieve? How do you arrive at these objectives, and how do you formulate and communicate them?
12. What is the initial assessment criteria that makes you consider something a promising opportunity or search direction?
13. How does prior knowledge of existing or new markets affect your initial opportunity assessment?
14. Do you at all consider promising business opportunities which might not be immediately based on existing customer problems?
15. How would you describe the people in your firm who deal exclusively with exploring new business opportunities? How do they work? Are they more individualistic or do they involve everyone in the firm in identifying new opportunities?

Entrepreneurial Culture and Leadership
16. What is your attitude towards risk taking, failure tolerance and learning in general?
17. Is the importance of innovativeness in general and of new business opportunities in particular emphasized in the firm?

Exploration as Process
18. How do you search for entirely new business opportunities?
19. Where do you (as individual/firm) search for entirely new business opportunities and/or product innovation opportunities?
20. How do you decide which search direction might be most promising? What criteria are important to you when searching for new business opportunities?
21. How do you deal with risk regarding exploratory activities?
22. What activities does exploration for you include? Is there a specific process?

Prior Knowledge/Experience in Exploration

23. How do existing competencies influence the direction of your search for new business opportunities? Do you actively have in mind existing competences when exploring new directions?
24. What does the search process based on existing knowledge and competencies look like?
25. Do you explore opportunities where you have no existing competencies at all?
26. How do existing technologies inhibit or foster the search for new technologies?

Organizational Set-up for Exploration

27. Who and what organizational levels are involved in exploration and in the search and identification of new business opportunities?
28. Who decides in what directions exploratory activities are pursued?

List of interviews

Phase I: Investigation of exploration for innovation on a broad scale

Company	Name	Position	Place	Date
ABB	Dr. René Cotting	Group R&D and Technology	Phone Interview	May 22, 2007
Alcan	Dr. Ernst Lutz	Director Innovation & Future Options	Zurich	Nov 21, 2006
			Neuhausen	Jan 09, 2007
Bühler	Dr. Diethelm Boese	Head of Corporate Research & Technology	Uzwil	Jun 12, 2007
Bühler	Klaus-Jochen Lisner	Head of Corporate Technology	Uzwil	Jul 24, 2006
			Uzwil	Nov 28, 2006
BMW	Dr. Martin Stahl	Group Product Portfolio	Munich	Jul 10, 2007
Ciba	Dr. Dirk Simon	Global Head Technology Scouting & Evaluation Research & Technology Plastic Additives Segment	Basel	Nov 22, 2006
			Basel	Nov 22, 2006
Ciba	Dr. Andreas Valet	Head Research & Technology Plastic Additives Segment	Basel	Nov 22, 2006
Ciba	Dr. Martin Riediker	Chief Innovation Officer	St. Gallen	Sep 12, 2006
Georg Fischer	Dr. Olivier Carnal	Chief Technology Officer	St. Gallen	Nov 22, 2006
			Schaffhausen	May 23, 2007
Fischer	Alois Pieber	Leader Research & Development	Phone Interview	May 18, 2007
Hilti	Dr. Andreas Bong	Chief Technology Officer	Schaan	Oct 13, 2006
			Schaan	Dec 01, 2006
Hilti	Elke Baessler	Corporate Innovation Manager	Schaan	Oct 13, 2006
			Schaan	Mar 08, 2007
Leica Geosytems	Peter Frank	Business Process Manager	Heerbrugg	Jun 24, 2007
Lonza	PD Dr. Johann Brass	Coordinator Innovations R&D Microbial Biopharmaceuticals	Visp	Jul 11, 2007

Company	Name	Position	Place	Date
Lonza	Dr. Hans-Peter Meyer	Sales & Business Development, Technology Evaluations	St. Gallen	Dec 06, 2006
			Visp	Jan 25, 2008
Lonza	Dr. Stefan Borgas	Chief Executive Officer	Zurich	Jan 10, 2008
Lonza	Dr. Oleg Werbitzky	Head Peptides & Oligonucleotides Development Services	Visp	Jan 25, 2008
Schindler	Gert Silberhorn	Leader R&D - Technology Management	Ebikon	Nov 30, 2006
Schindler	Karl Weinberger	Chief Technology Officer	Ebikon	Nov 30, 2006
			Ebikon	Aug 29, 2007
Sevex	Dr. Wolfgang Assmann	Chief Executive Officer	Sevelen	Dec 01, 2006
			Sevelen	Jan 09, 2007
Sevex	Michael Tappe	Head of Product & Business Development	Sevelen	Dec 01, 2006
			Sevelen	Jan 09, 2007
Sevex	Axel Wagner	Business Development	Sevelen	Dec 01, 2006
SIG allCap	Dr. Roger Alther	Head of Basic R&D and Patents	Phone Interview	Jun 06, 2006
			Neuhausen	Jun 13, 2007
Reichle & DeMassari	Thomas Frei	Leader Innovations & Products	Wetzikon	Jun 29, 2007
Reichle & DeMassari	Dr. Giorgio Friedrich	CTO Innovations Fiber Optic	Wetzikon	Jun 29, 2007
Reichle & DeMassari	Matthias Gerber	CTO Innovations Copper	Wetzikon	Jun 29, 2007
W.L. *Gore* & Associates	Wolfgang Hohma	Leader Research & Development, Fabrics	St. Gallen	Aug 10, 2006
			Munich	Dec 04, 2006
W.L. *Gore* & Associates	Richard Leckenwalter	Leader New Business Development	Munich	Dec 04, 2006
ZF Friedrichshafen	Barbara Schmohl	Advanced Engineering Chassis, Corporate R&D	Friedrichshafen	Dec 12, 2006

Phase II: In-depth case studies

Company	Name	Position	Place	Date
Bühler	Dr. Diethelm Boese	Head of Corporate Research & Technology	Uzwil	Dec 08, 2008
			Phone Interview	Mar 05, 2009
Bühler	Klaus-Jochen Lisner	Head of Corporate Technology	Uzwil	Dec 08, 2008
			Phone Interview	Feb 26, 2009
Ciba	Dr. Dirk Simon	Global Head Technology Scouting & Evaluation Research & Technology Plastic Additives Segment	Basel	Feb 26, 2008
			Basel	Mar 11, 2008
Ciba	Dr. Andreas Valet	Head Research & Technology Plastic Additives Segment	Basel	Feb 26, 2008
Ciba	Dr. Martin Riediker	Chief Innovation Officer	Basel	Apr 02, 2008
Ciba	Dr. Werner Rutsch	Head Corporate Technology Office	Basel	Apr 02, 2008
Ciba	Dr. Andreas Hafner	Head Group Research Corporate Technology	St. Gallen	Apr 03, 2008
Ciba	Dr. Stephan Klotz	Head Operational Agenda Innovation Corporate Technology	Basel	Apr 02, 2008
Ciba	Dr. Thomas Stährfeldt	Head of Group Innovation Process Management	Basel	Feb 26, 2008
			Basel	Dec 11, 2008
Hilti	Dr. Andreas Bong	Chief Technology Officer	Schaan	Oct 11, 2007
			Schaan	Jan 30, 2008
			Schaan	Dec 16, 2008
Hilti	Elke Baessler	Corporate Innovation Manager	Schaan	Jan 15, 2008
Hilti	Dr. Reinhard Waibel	Head of Development Business Unit Measuring Systems	Schaan	Oct 18, 2007
Hilti	Dr. Adrian Kauf	Head of Applied Physics Corporate Research & Technology	Schaan	Oct 18, 2007

Company	Name	Position	Place	Date
Hilti	Dr. Walter Odoni	Head of Development Business Unit Direct Fastening	Schaan	Oct 22, 2007
Hilti	Dr. Horst-Dieter Mika	Head of Technology BA Fastening & Protection	Kaufering	Oct 26, 2007
Hilti	Josef Obermeier	Head of Technology BA Electronics & Drive	Kaufering	Oct 26, 2007
W.L. *Gore* & Associates	Wolfgang Hohma	Leader Research & Development Fabrics	Munich	Sep 30, 2007
			Newark	Nov 20, 2008
W.L. *Gore* & Associates	Benedikt Schlichting	New Business Development	Munich	Sep 30, 2007
			Munich	Dec 09, 2008
W.L. *Gore* & Associates	Richard Leckenwalter	Leader New Business Development	Munich	Sep 30, 2007
			Munich	Dec 09, 2008
W.L. *Gore* & Associates	Eleonore Steinbacher	Technology Leader Industrial Products Division	Munich	Sep 30, 2007
W.L. *Gore* & Associates	Dr. Heinrich Flik	Chairman of the Board	Munich	Sep 25, 2007
W.L. *Gore* & Associates	Bill Mortimer	Leader Core Technology Group	Newark	Nov 20, 2008